MW01493057

Kirtland, Ohio, from the northeast, August 7, 1907, by
George Edward Anderson. Courtesy LDS Church Archives.

# The First Mormon Temple

# The First Mormon Temple

## Design, Construction, and Historic Context of the Kirtland Temple

by

Elwin C. Robison

Brigham Young University Press
Provo, Utah

Library of Congress Cataloging-in-Publication Data

Robison, Elwin Clark, 1955–
The first Mormon temple : design, construction, and historic context of
    the Kirtland Temple / by Elwin Clark Robison.
        p.   cm.
    Includes bibliographical references and index.
    ISBN 0-8425-2333-2 (pbk.)
    1. Kirtland Temple. 2. Kirtland (Ohio)—Church history. 3. Reorga-
nized Church of Jesus Christ of Latter Day Saints—Ohio—Kirtland—
History. 4. Church of Jesus Christ of Latter-Day Saints—Ohio—
Kirtland—History. 5. Mormon Church—Ohio—Kirtland—History.
I. Title.
BX8677.K57R63  1997
246'.95893771334—dc21                                          97-21115
                                                                  CIP

Printed in the United States of America
10  9  8  7  6  5  4  3  2  1

*To all who labored and sacrificed to build,
conserve, and maintain the Kirtland Temple*

# Contents

# List of Illustrations

# Preface

This book had its beginning in 1986, when I first started serious study of the architecture of the Kirtland Temple. As a member of The Church of Jesus Christ of Latter-day Saints, I value the Kirtland Temple as an important religious symbol. Although my Mormon ancestors did not arrive in Kirtland until after the temple was completed, I—like others of my faith—feel its history is a part of my heritage.

My knowledge of the physical building fabric of the temple stems in part from an engineering study and from a historic structures report on the building I conducted for the Restoration Trail Foundation. These studies, which involved a survey and analysis of every structural member in the building, gave me great insight into the challenges the temple's builders faced. This book also depended upon the First Presidency of the Reorganized Church of Jesus Christ of Latter Day Saints, who kindly granted permission to photograph and study the building in detail.

I am indebted to a number of people for their assistance with this book. First and foremost, I would like to thank Priscilla Graham. As my coauthor for several papers on the Kirtland Temple (including "English Influence on the Architecture of the Kirtland Temple," presented at the Mormon History Association Annual Conference, July 1987, Oxford, England, and "Vernacular Building Tradition and the Mormon Temple in Kirtland, Ohio," presented at the Society of Architectural Historians Annual Meeting, April 1991, Cincinnati, Ohio) and as a reader of the manuscript, she has contributed significantly to this project. It was most disappointing when her health did not allow her full participation in the book project.

Next, I am grateful to Roger Launius and Karl Anderson for sharing their knowledge of Kirtland and the temple with me. The staff of the LDS Church Archives was most helpful, especially W. Randall Dixon and William B. Slaughter who were patient in meeting my requests. Likewise, the staff of the RLDS Church Archives was very helpful, and I would like to thank Ronald E. Romig for his input. Carl Engel of the Lake County Historical Society shared with me his list of *Painesville Telegraph* notices referencing the temple. Trevor Packer and others at BYU Studies deserve notice for their hours of careful research, source checking, and editing. The interpretive and maintenance staffs at the temple have given me invaluable assistance: Allen Walters shared much of his research with me, and Lachlan MacKay prevented me from making many errors in interpretation. His extraordinary assistance is testimony to his commitment to and respect for the building. The Kent State University School of Architecture and Environmental Design granted a one-semester sabbatical leave, and the Research and Development Office helped fund research travel and acquisition of photographs from archival collections.

Several institutions were helpful in granting permission to reproduce photographs and other images in this book: Library-Archives, Reorganized Church of Jesus Christ of Latter Day Saints, The Auditorium, Independence, Missouri; Church Archives, Historical Department, The Church of Jesus Christ of Latter-day Saints, Salt Lake City, Utah; Library of Congress; Utah State Historical Society Information Center; and Special Collections and Manuscripts, Harold B. Lee Library, Brigham Young University, Provo, Utah.

Many studies of early Mormon history subordinate historical inquiry to proving that Joseph Smith was either a saint or a scoundrel. Likewise, some discussions of the Kirtland Temple have a subtext attempting to show either how the temple was wrongfully wrested from the LDS Church or, conversely, how RLDS Church ownership has kept the temple out of the realm of secret ritual. In this study, my aim has been to let the Kirtland Temple tell its own story. However, I must state that I have a deeply rooted conviction of Joseph Smith's role as a prophet of God. Consequently, I make no claim to impartiality in this monograph. I can state only that what I have written reflects the facts as I know and understand them.

Elwin C. Robison
Kent, Ohio

# Introduction

Because the history of the Kirtland Temple involves several religious faiths, a brief outline of these groups will aid in understanding the context of this study. In 1820, Joseph Smith Jr., a farm boy in upstate New York, received a vision of God the Father and Jesus Christ in response to a prayer for guidance as to which church he should join. Told to join none of the existing churches, Joseph received other heavenly communications, which eventually led in 1830 to the organization of the Church of Christ in Fayette, New York. Joseph and his companions believed this to be a restoration of the church organization that existed in Jesus' time. Following Joseph's inspired direction, the Church's organization soon included Apostles, seventies, elders, and other offices mentioned in the New Testament. The initial name of the Church was changed by a conference of elders on May 3, 1834, to the Church of the Latter-day Saints,[1] the name that was originally painted on the facade of the Kirtland Temple. The two names were combined in 1838, when the Church was designated The Church of Jesus Christ of Latter-day Saints (D&C 115:4).

One of the Church's basic tenets is that Joseph Smith was a prophet who received instructions from God. During his brief life, Joseph introduced beliefs that were unique among Christian churches. One of these was the doctrine of sealing families for eternity, an ordinance that was conducted in a temple. This doctrine was not practiced until the 1840s, when the Church was headquartered in Nauvoo, Illinois, and so was not part of the initial history of the Kirtland Temple. However, the sealing of families and the related doctrine of plural marriage have affected interpretations of the Kirtland Temple's significance.

After the murder of Joseph Smith in 1844, the Quorum of the Twelve Apostles, under the leadership of Brigham Young, continued administration of the Church. Brigham organized the exodus to the Rocky Mountains and in 1847 was sustained as the second President of the Church. Headquartered in Salt Lake City, this organization retains the 1838 name, The Church of Jesus Christ of Latter-day Saints, and is referred to in the text as the LDS Church. With almost ten million members at the time of this writing, this is the largest of the churches concerned with the Kirtland Temple.

Although the majority of Church members followed Brigham Young to Utah, a significant number never accepted him as a successor to Joseph Smith, and several small groups formed, each with its own leader. During their period of immigration to and colonization of the West, The Church of Jesus Christ of Latter-day Saints had little to do with the Kirtland Temple. On the other hand, some of the groups that did not go to Utah congregated around places formerly settled by the Church, such as Kirtland, Ohio; Independence, Missouri; and Nauvoo, Illinois. In 1852, members of several smaller groups united as the "New Organization" of the Church; on April 6, 1860, at Amboy, Illinois, Joseph Smith Jr.'s son Joseph Smith III assumed leadership of what was then termed the Reorganized Church of Jesus Christ of Latter Day Saints. The RLDS Church rejects some of the doctrine taught by Joseph Smith Jr., especially that of the Nauvoo period. Currently headquartered in Independence, Missouri, the RLDS Church has approximately 250,000 members.

The RLDS Church gained legal ownership of the Kirtland Temple in 1880; since both the LDS and RLDS Churches stem from the religious group that constructed the building and since both organizations claim to be Christ's restored church on earth, little theological room is left for sharing. While the temple ownership issue was a source of friction in the nineteenth and early-twentieth centuries,[2] LDS and RLDS relations have evolved in a very different direction in the late-twentieth century. The sense of competition to prove each's legitimacy as the rightful heir to Joseph Smith's leadership has been replaced with increasing cooperation regarding preservation of the two churches' combined heritage. I hope this trend will continue.

Members of all branches of the Restoration have commonly been called "Mormons," or even "Mormonites." This term refers to their use of the Book of Mormon, which Joseph Smith translated from gold plates and which members of the Church believe to be a companion book of scripture to the Bible. Originally a term of derision, "Mormon" has been used so frequently that members of the LDS Church generally accept it without pejorative connotations, although the RLDS Church has distanced itself from the term in the past.[3] In contrast, members of both the LDS and RLDS branches of the Mormon community have always referred to themselves as "Saints," using the term in its New Testament context. I use it in this text because it is common to both groups in historic and contemporary usage.

This text also relies on the significant body of background information available on Joseph Smith and the church he restored. Beginning in the 1830s and continuing through the nineteenth century, the LDS Church went to great pains to document the often tragic events that marked its early history. Church members were encouraged to record their life histories. Several diaries and histories of early church leaders were published in an early periodical, the *Times and Seasons*. A large—but not comprehensive—portion of Joseph Smith's diaries, along with pieces of his correspondence and other papers, were published between 1842 and 1856 in Church periodicals. This documentary history of the Church was then edited and published by Church historian B. H. Roberts as a six-volume series in the early twentieth century. This history provides an invaluable guide to early Mormonism, although it should be noted that the editorial guidelines that were used occasionally distorted the sources.[4] Although some later reminiscences may confuse specific dates and times, their writers exhibit no confusion regarding obstacles they faced and their feelings about the events they lived through. In order to preserve these sources, I have retained their original spellings, though I have brought down raised letters and interlinear words.

Many documents used in this study make reference to revelations or other divine communications received by Joseph Smith and others. Other authors who have written about the temple have varied in their approach to these sources. For example, Laurel Andrew takes a rather skeptical view of Joseph Smith's divine communication, consistent with her underlying thesis that LDS temple architecture, along with the LDS temple ceremony, was derived from Masonic sources. On the other hand, Roger Launius emphasizes the Kirtland Temple's role in the spiritual lives of those who worshipped there, fully accepting its divine foundation.[5] This study likewise accepts the supernatural events surrounding the design and construction of the temple as reported by those who experienced them. Nevertheless, the building fabric of the Kirtland Temple does not prove or disprove the divinity of Joseph Smith's communications; in many ways, that determination is irrelevant to this study. What is important is that those who worked on the temple believed in Joseph Smith as a prophet of God and believed that in constructing this edifice they were following God's commandment. The building fabric of the Kirtland Temple is the record of this belief.

## Notes

[1] *History of the Church*, 2:62–63.

[2] For example, the establishment of the RLDS Utah mission must be viewed in this sense, notwithstanding the genuine concern individuals had for the spiritual welfare of their brothers and sisters (in terms of both brothers and sisters of the general human family and, in many cases, blood relations). In addition, the construction of the Auditorium in Independence, with its large domed hall and organ, can be understood in its competitive relationship to the Tabernacle in Salt Lake City.

[3] On the use of the term Mormon, see *History of the Church*, 2:254: "We thought no harm in advising the Latter-day Saints, or 'Mormons,' as they are reproachfully called." See also the short history written by Inez Smith, "approved by her father, Heman C. Smith, [RLDS] Church Historian," quoted by Upton, *History of the Western Reserve*, 1:128: "The Latter-Day Saints, erroneously called Mormons, a people whose history and doctrine have caused much comment in the historical world."

[4] Jessee, *Papers of Joseph Smith*, 1:xxxi–xxxii.

[5] Andrew, *Early Temples of the Mormons*; Launius, *Kirtland Temple*.

**1-1.** Southeast view, Kirtland Temple, ca. 1885.

# Chapter 1

# The Context of the Kirtland Temple

The Church of Christ, established by Joseph Smith in 1830, created a religious movement that has grown to almost ten million people. These individuals have created their own culture and traditions, which have in turn necessitated the creation of new architectural traditions. The House of the Lord in Kirtland, Ohio, more commonly referred to as the Kirtland Temple, is the first major permanent structure for worship built by the Mormons. It served as a direct pattern for the next five Mormon temples and strongly influenced numerous meetinghouses and tabernacles. Any study of Mormon building practices must start with the Kirtland Temple, and any study of the temple must begin with the circumstances surrounding its inception in the newly settled lands west of the Appalachian Mountains.

## The Western Reserve

In the early 1830s, northeastern Ohio was a natural destination for Americans seeking prosperity. Rocky soil and short growing seasons had pushed many New Englanders west in search of better farming opportunities. In the eighteenth century, the state of Connecticut claimed the northeastern portion of Ohio, making it a magnet for settlement. Political control of this so-called Western Reserve of Connecticut was relinquished for the right to profit from the sale of the land, and New England investors sold parcels primarily to other New Englanders seeking better farmland.

In addition to a gentler topography, richer soil, and milder climate, northeast Ohio had excellent transportation connections with major eastern markets. Lake Erie provided steamship transport to Buffalo, where items could be transferred to canal boats navigating the Erie Canal, open since 1825, and shipped to New York City and ports beyond.[1] Fairport Harbor, twelve miles to the north of Kirtland, was an especially important transportation node because high bluffs made it the last good anchorage until the

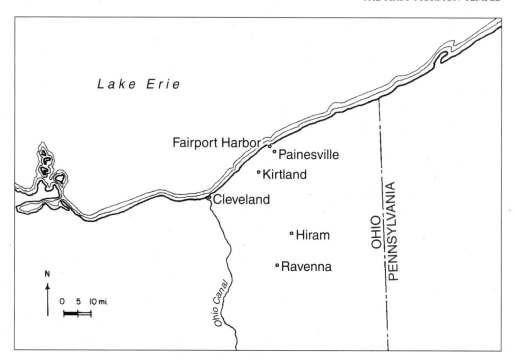

**1-2.** Map of the Kirtland area.

city of Cleveland, situated at the mouth of the Cuyahoga River. The Cuyahoga itself formed the first leg of the Ohio Canal, which after 1832 connected Lake Erie with the Ohio River and the entire Mississippi River system. Thus, Ohio farmers had the enviable position of having access to markets in both New York and New Orleans via inexpensive river transportation. Land speculators were not unaware of these natural advantages. By the 1830s, land prices in the Kirtland area were soaring, a fact that was to have a significant influence on the future of Mormonism and the Kirtland Temple.

## The Saints in Kirtland

The arrival of Mormonism in Kirtland and the construction of its first temple seem more a matter of chance than design. Joseph Smith's family left New England along with hundreds of other farm families after 1816, the disastrous "year without a summer," which saw snow in June and a crop-killing frost in July. Settling in the township of Farmington, which later became Manchester, New York, the Smith family purchased land on credit and commenced the arduous (and ultimately unsuccessful) task of making the payments. Here the teenaged Joseph Smith related to his family and fellow townspeople his reception of divine communications.

The ridicule one might expect from such a pronouncement became harassment after Joseph announced he possessed golden plates obtained from a heavenly messenger. The constant harrying by individuals and groups seeking to steal the plates forced him to move to his in-laws' house in Harmony, Pennsylvania, to continue his translating work. After the publication of the Book of Mormon and Joseph's return to New York, arrests on false charges of disorderly conduct drained both his time and money. Since Joseph's father had lost his farm the year before, there was little to keep the Smith family in upstate New York.

A Christian primitivist movement in Mentor, Ohio, just north of Kirtland, paved the way for Joseph Smith's move to the Western Reserve. This movement, led by the charismatic Sidney Rigdon, had been allied with the Campbellites, later known as the Disciples of Christ. News of the new religion that purported to restore Christ's ancient church struck a familiar chord with Rigdon and this congregation. In October–November 1830, about 130 members of Rigdon's group in Kirtland were converted to the church Joseph headed. In December, Rigdon himself traveled to New York to meet with Joseph and stayed with the Smith family for a few weeks. Later that month, Joseph Smith received a revelation commanding him to move, along with his followers, to Ohio (D&C 37:1, 3).

Ohio was never intended as a permanent settling place for the Saints.[2] The missionaries who had converted Sidney Rigdon were actually on their way further west to Missouri to proselyte among Native Americans. Joseph Smith and close associates followed this initial contact with the extreme western frontier with a journey to Independence, Missouri, in July 1831. A revelation received during this visit designated Jackson County, Missouri, as the land "appointed and consecrated for the gathering of the saints" (see D&C 57:1–4). Church leaders dedicated a site for a temple, and Joseph was instructed to purchase land for future settlement. Accordingly, a group of Saints settled at Independence and founded what they believed would be the New Jerusalem and City of Zion.

This ambitious beginning, however, was soon thwarted. One problem was the slow development of the United Firm, the communitarian economic organization of the early Saints who pooled their resources and then received back individual "stewardships" proportionate to each family's needs. As converts without personal resources moved to Independence and applied for entrance into the communitarian organization, community resources were stretched. Later prospective emigrants to Missouri had to obtain certificates from local leaders, who could then regulate both numbers and economic resources of applicants. Thus, growth of the Church in the Missouri area slowed during 1831 and 1832, and construction of the intended temple was postponed.

Another serious impediment to developing the City of Zion in Independence was opposition by established Missourians. Most Missourians were southerners who firmly believed in slavery, while the majority of Mormons were northerners who opposed slavery. Given the combination of the United Firm (which provided direct competition with established Missourian businesses) and the threat of a sizable antislavery voting bloc, the Missourians perceived the new immigrants as a challenge to their way of life. This, together with the Mormons' active solicitation of converts, created a volatile situation that began to spark in April 1833, when Missourians met to discuss the "Mormon Problem." By the end of July, the situation had deteriorated until mob violence ruled the area. Mormon settlers were expelled from Jackson County by November of that year.

As a result of all these factors, the temple in Independence, for which plans and specifications were sent to Missouri on June 25, 1833, was never built. Any hope of building a temple on the lot dedicated by Joseph Smith (seen as a precursor of the Second Coming of Christ and the establishment of a New Jerusalem) would have to wait until the Saints could establish themselves once again in Independence.

While persecutions raged in Missouri, Kirtland remained the primary center of the Church. Economic control of the United Firm was in Kirtland, and Church growth continued there when it waned in Missouri. Most significantly, Joseph Smith himself resided in Kirtland. These social and political conditions combined to make Kirtland the location of the first temple built by the Mormons.

## The Builders of the Kirtland Temple

Kirtland's population of newly settled converts influenced the construction of the temple. Most of the temple's builders were self-reliant craftsmen used to making do with materials at hand. No trained architect was involved with its design, and experienced builders were summoned only after plans for the structure had been completed. The few skilled joiners and masons in the group relied on the same architectural pattern books and vernacular aesthetics used by other craftsmen along the frontier. However, the temple's unusual arrangement of two main congregational spaces required nonstandard solutions in lighting and circulation. These nonstandard regions of the building tell us a great deal about the skill level of the artisans who built it.

The challenges and struggles faced by these workers are recorded in a large number of diaries and letters, which provide thorough documentation unusual for most frontier American structures. These sources about the

Kirtland Temple aid in our understanding the social dynamics of the early Mormon community. For example, events surrounding the establishment of the new religion required some of the designers and supervising craftsmen to leave the building site. Consequently, the Kirtland Temple displays several different building traditions and the mark of various builders. The magnitude of the project taxed the community both economically and technologically, and a high degree of personal sacrifice and group organization was required to complete it. A study of the temple's physical building fabric indicates how some of these obstacles were overcome, namely, what was purchased, what had to be made by hand, what had to be substituted, and what individual members of the Church contributed. Yet the motivation of the workers was not merely professional pride, but was primarily the belief that the Saints were literally building a house where God could dwell with them. Their efforts, recorded in the fabric of this building, represent the very best they could produce.

*Notes*

[1]See "Tolls Reduced," *Painesville Telegraph*, March 29, 1833, 3.

[2]In a revelation given September 11, 1831, the Lord stated, "For I, the Lord, will to retain a strong hold in the land of Kirtland, for the space of five years, in the which I will not overthrow the wicked, that thereby I may save some" (D&C 64:21).

2-1. Southwest view, Kirtland Temple, about 1880. Note how its height compares to that of the two-story building on the left.

# Chapter 2

# The Design of the Temple, 1832–1833

A special building for the Church in Kirtland was first mentioned in a revelation Joseph Smith received on December 27, 1832. This revelation called upon the Saints to "establish a house, even a house of prayer, a house of fasting, a house of faith, a house of learning, a house of glory, a house of order, a house of God" (D&C 88:119). This general outline of the temple's function—prayer, fasting, faith, and learning—could be applied to a house of worship of almost any religious denomination, but later details made it clear that the Kirtland Temple and the Independence Temple, whose construction was being planned at the same time, were not to be simple meetinghouses. Joseph Smith recorded on June 1, 1833, that in the temple the Lord would "endow those whom I [God] have chosen with power from on high," and he further recorded, "Let the house be built, not after the manner of the world . . . [rather] let it be built after the manner which I shall show unto three of you" (D&C 95:8, 13–14).

Part of what distinguished the temple's design from the "manner of the world" was the temple's two main spaces, one over the other, often referred to as the lower court and the upper court. The lower court was to function like a common Christian church sanctuary for preaching, administering the sacrament (communion), praying, and fasting. However, the upper hall was to be dedicated for the School of the Prophets, whose purpose was to give Church leaders both secular and religious instruction.[1] The temple's dual function as a place for worship and education is part of what sets the Kirtland Temple apart from other contemporary religious structures.

Also unlike its contemporaries, the Kirtland Temple was intended to continue the tradition of the Old Testament temples. The use of the term "house" parallels biblical references to the temple of Solomon (see 1 Chr. 28:10; 29:16). The term "court," referring to the main rooms of the Kirtland Temple, evokes the image of the courtyard of Solomon's temple (see 2 Chr. 4:9). This terminology reflects the Mormons' belief that they were restoring the ancient Christian organization of the Church.

## "The Building Appeared within Viewing Distance"

On June 3 or 4, 1833,[2] the Lord kept his promise to reveal to three Church members the manner in which the temple should be built. Joseph Smith, Sidney Rigdon, and Frederick G. Williams—the Presidency of the Church and the "three" mentioned in Doctrine and Covenants 95—received a vision in which they viewed plans for the temple, carefully observing its structure and design. Frederick G. Williams later described this experience to workers at the temple:

> Carpenter Rolph said, "Doctor [Williams], what do you think of the house"? [Williams] answered, "It looks to me like the pattern precisely." He then related the following: "Joseph [Smith] received the word of the Lord for him to take his two counselors, Williams and Rigdon, and come before the Lord, and He would show them the plan or model of the house to be built. We went upon our knees, called on the Lord, and the building appeared within viewing distance, I being the first to discover it. Then we all viewed it together. After we had taken a good look at the exterior, the building seemed to come right over us, and the makeup of the Hall seemed to coincide with that I there saw to a minutiae."[3]

One of the main challenges workers faced in building the Kirtland Temple was devising ways to create a building that conformed with what was seen in this vision. Though outside the limits of mainstream American architectural practice, this vision became the most important criterion against which temple design decisions were judged.

Some twentieth-century followers of Joseph Smith interpret Williams's statement that the completed temple coincided with his vision "to a minutiae" to mean that every element of the building was divinely inspired and carries symbolic meaning. For example, brochures distributed at the Kirtland Temple Historic Center in the 1980s gave theological significance to guilloche moldings in the column capitals.[4] However, analysis clearly shows that molding details were worked out by individual craftsmen using commonly available carpentry manuals and were not laid out in the plans developed by Joseph Smith, Sidney Rigdon, and Frederick G. Williams. This discrepancy does not invalidate Williams's assertion. My experience is that, when first walking through the temple, even individuals with architectural training will assume the two main rooms are identical, not noticing the numerous differences in detail. Similarly, though Williams perceived the vision and the built temple as corresponding perfectly, he probably overlooked minor differences craftsmen had introduced. The Presidency of the Church defined major elements of the Kirtland Temple design, but individual builders worked out structural and ornamental details to the best of their abilities.

## Independence Temple Drawings

Although the Presidency's vision specifically addressed the Kirtland Temple, the design received in the vision was also applied to plans for the never-built Independence Temple. The Kirtland Temple and the Independence Temple plans are remarkably similar in window layout, floor plan, and interior details. The entries in Joseph Smith's journal describing the plans for the Independence Temple and the entries describing the revelation concerning the Kirtland Temple occur within days of each other. Plans for the Independence Temple were mailed to Edward Partridge in Missouri on June 25, 1833, just three weeks after the vision of the Kirtland Temple was received.[5] Given their close correlation in scale and layout, the Independence drawings clearly represent the plan received by Joseph Smith, Sidney Rigdon, and Frederick G. Williams for the Kirtland Temple.

However, unlike the ample documentation of the Independence Temple design, no record of drawings for the Kirtland Temple exists. Since Joseph Smith, Sidney Rigdon, and Frederick G. Williams were in residence in Kirtland and available to explain details of the plan to builders, perhaps formal drawings were considered unnecessary. It is entirely possible the Kirtland Temple was built using only some written notes and perhaps a sketch taken from the Independence drawings, supplemented by verbal instructions. On the other hand, drawings often were worn out and tattered by constant reference during construction and were simply thrown away upon completion of the building. Since the Independence Temple was never built, its drawings were not worn out during the building process and hence have survived, while Kirtland Temple plans may have been used and discarded. Also, any plans and specifications for the Kirtland structure would not have had to be mailed and therefore were never logged in the daybook. Given the Kirtland Temple's awkward structural details, any drawings prepared for it must have been no more sophisticated than the crude drawings sent to Independence.

Two different sets of temple drawings were prepared and sent to Independence. The first drawing set consists of an unsigned sheet showing a plan and specifications on the recto (front) and front and side elevations with written specifications on the verso (back) (figs. 2-2, 2-4, 2-6). The second drawing set, signed by Frederick G. Williams, was sent to Independence a little later and was identified as a revised plan.[6] The second shows two bays added to the building, stretching it out by about twenty feet. Internal arrangements and the building height were kept the same (figs. 2-3, 2-5, 2-7, 2-8).

The crudeness of both sets of drawings clearly shows that none of the men involved with the design of the Independence and Kirtland Temples had architectural training. Joseph Smith had little formal schooling of any kind, although he probably learned about simple building practices by helping construct the family's frame house in Manchester.[7] Sidney Rigdon was a former

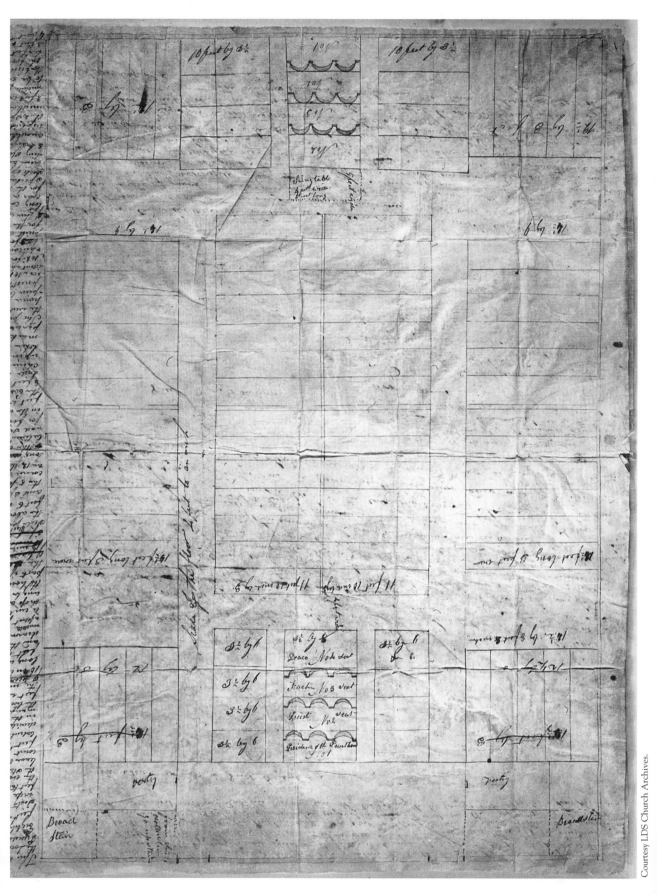

**2-2.** Plan for the interior of the Independence Temple, detail from the recto page of the first, unsigned set of plans.

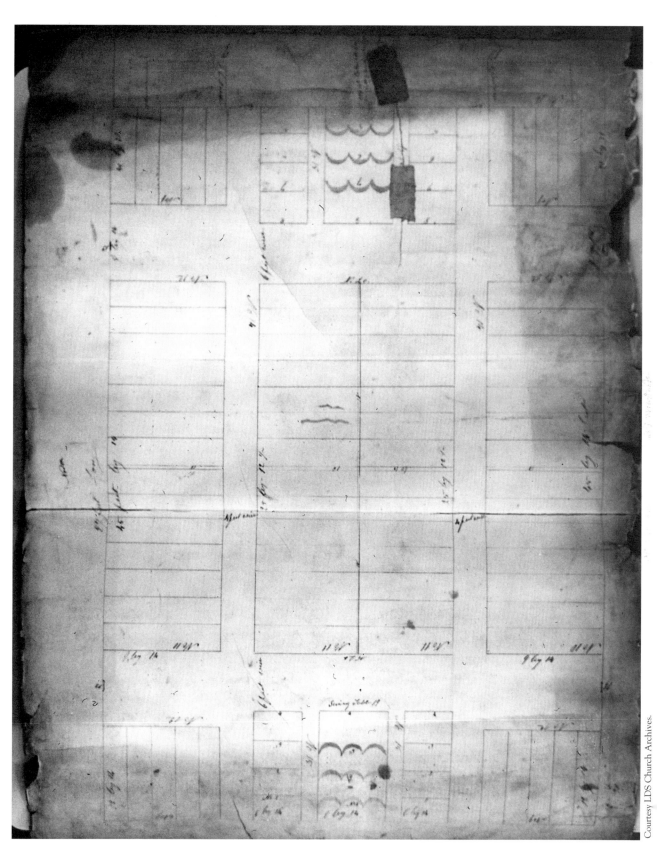

**2-3.** Plan for the interior of the Independence Temple, from the set signed by Frederick G. Williams. Although the plans called for a building twenty feet longer than the one in the earlier, unsigned plan, the proportions of both plans are nearly identical— both plans have fourteen rows of pews in the center section, and the relative sizes of the pulpits are virtually the same. Apparently, the difference in size between the two plans was to be communicated by written notes and not by the drawing.

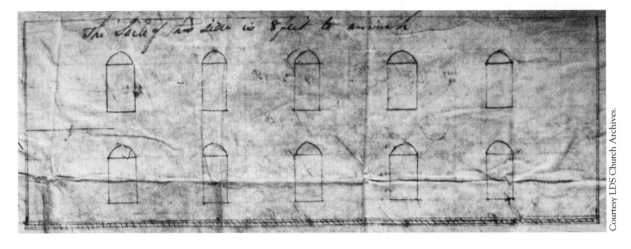

**2-4.** Side elevation of the Independence Temple, detail from the unsigned set of plans.

**2-5.** Side elevation of the Independence Temple, detail from the set signed by Frederick G. Williams. This version of the Independence Temple design is ninety-seven feet long with nine sets of windows on each side, whereas the earlier version was twenty feet shorter and had only five sets of windows on each side.

Campbellite preacher and likewise lacked formal training in building. Frederick G. Williams, the draftsman of the second set of drawings (and likely author of the first set, too), was a physician. Whether Williams's authorship of the drawings was due to superior building expertise or simply to his possession of the required pens and watercolors is not evident, but since the level of skill displayed in all the drawings is not high, Williams's building experience could not have been significantly greater than that of his colleagues in the presidency.[8]

The windows in Williams's west elevation drawing (fig. 2-8) were drawn at the wrong height, as can be seen by the pinpricks that show through from the opposite side of the sheet. Instead of redrawing the sheet, Williams

**2-6.** Front elevation of the Independence Temple, detail from the unsigned set of plans.

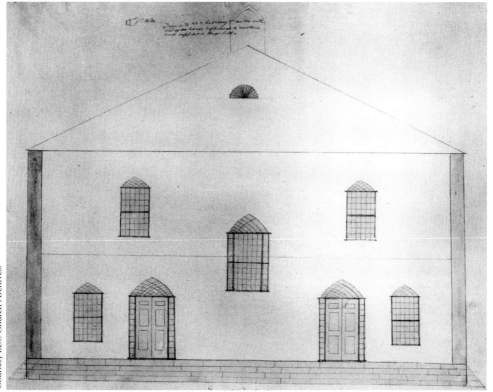

**2-7.** Front (east) elevation of the Independence Temple, detail from the set signed by Frederick G. Williams. On the original plans, walls, foundations, and windows are denoted by a watercolor wash. The horizontal line drawn through the center window of the front elevation does not refer to an exterior architectural feature but simply denotes the location of the interior floor level. Note the erasure of sloping foundation walls.

merely corrected the mistake with a written note.[9] Williams also gives the width of the plan as sixty-one feet, leaving a three-foot-thick wall around the fifty-five-foot-wide interior specified in the revelation. This tremendously thick wall was reduced to approximately two feet when the Kirtland Temple was built, almost certainly under the advice of an experienced builder who recognized that such a thick wall was unnecessary.

More revealing of the inexperience of the temple's designers is the omission of space allotted for the elliptical barrel vaults, the arched ceiling to run the length of each story. Written specifications for the Independence Temple describe the vaults, but neither the scaled drawings nor the height measurements listed in the specifications take them into account. The specifications, written on the first, unsigned set of drawings and logged in Joseph Smith's papers, state:

> Make your house fourteen feet high between the floors. There will not be a gallery [balcony] but a chamber; each story will be fourteen feet high, arched overhead with an elliptic arch. . . . The entire height of the house is to be twenty-eight feet, each story being fourteen feet; make the wall a sufficient thickness for a house of this size.[10]

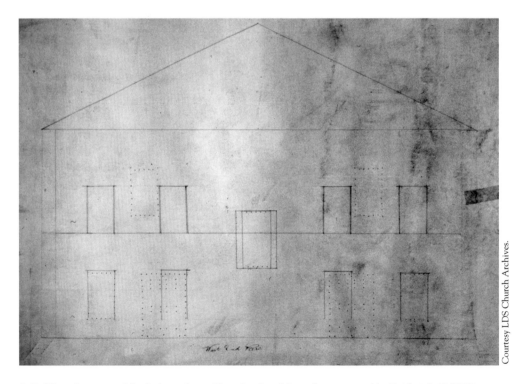

2-8. West elevation of the Independence Temple, detail from the set signed by Frederick G. Williams. The pinpricks visible in the drawing relate to the east elevation drawn on the reverse side of the sheet. The prick marks clearly show that the windows on the upper floor of the west elevation are set too low, placed on the level of the floor instead of about two and a half feet above the floor. This error was noticed and corrected in the written specifications accompanying the drawing. (The pinpricks have been enhanced to make them more visible.)

Courtesy LDS Church Archives.

Photo by author.

**2-9.** East facade, Kirtland Temple.

The fourteen-foot stories described here leave no room for the second-floor girders and joists or for the elliptical arch set into the ceiling of the lower floor. As a result, the actual height of the Kirtland Temple is about forty-five feet to the eaves of the roof rather than the specified twenty-eight feet. A comparison between the Kirtland Temple as built and the elevation drawing for the Independence Temple (figs. 2-7, 2-9) shows that if an additional twelve feet are added to the height of the Independence Temple drawing (four feet for the elliptical vaults, one foot for the floor structure, one foot for the working space above the vaults, times two for the upper and lower rooms) the proportion of width to height of the Independence and Kirtland Temples is very similar.

Williams corrected one of his errors by erasing the steeply sloping foundation that was originally drawn on the east elevation (fig. 2-7). Contemporaneous builders sometimes extended thicker foundation walls above-ground, creating a projection called a water table. But such projections were always on the order of a few inches instead of a few feet as in this case, and the foundation walls were almost always perpendicular to the ground.

Ironically, such an unusual foundation would have corrected a current weakness in the temple structure. Foundations should spread the weight of a building over a large enough area so that the structure does not settle unevenly into the soil. Unfortunately, the foundation walls of the Kirtland Temple were never sufficiently wide, and the building has suffered from differential settlement, resulting in some cracking of the outside walls. But before crediting Williams with structural insight, note that the excessive, three-foot-thick walls he drew on the elevation would have been heavy enough to negate some of the positive effect of the wider foundations—to say nothing of the additional labor and expense incurred in quarrying and transporting the stone for the thicker walls.

While the crudeness of both sets of drawings suggests an inexperienced hand, the author(s) did attempt to introduce some sophistication. The unsigned set of plans (figs. 2-2, 2-4, 2-6) consists of scaled drawings (eight feet to an inch) that have light, penciled trace lines used to lay out the building outline. Since no compass prick points are visible on the paper surface, a template was apparently used to draw the arches of the Gothic windows.[11] The revised set of drawings, signed by Williams (figs. 2-3, 2-5, 2-7, 2-8), uses similar drawing techniques but also accurately defines the number of glass panes in the windows and uses a watercolor wash to denote the wall thickness.

## The Style of the Temple: Drawing on Common Forms

The specifications for the Independence Temple drawings go into considerable detail on seating arrangements and pulpits, but the specifications for style (and materials) are limited. The only stylistic elements drawn on the exterior are the "Gothic tops" on the windows and doors. The bell tower or steeple, the most prominent element on the structure, was merely mentioned on the drawings: "There is to be a bellcony [sic] on the east end of the house sufficient to contain and support a large bell."[12] However, as in most building specifications of the day, many items were left unmentioned, not because they were unimportant, but because everyone involved understood what was desired. For example, the phrases "in the best workmanlike manner" and specifications for materials "of the best kind" clearly communicated the intention of the plan. This contrasts with late-twentieth-century architectural designs, which require prodigious quantities of drawings and specifications (many of which are produced for lawyers rather than contractors).

The Kirtland Temple as it now stands is a mixture of Georgian, Federal, Greek Revival, and Gothic elements. Although the dominant roof pediment and tower make it primarily Greek Revival in style, the temple has the tall, boxy proportions of an enlarged Federal house, not a classical Greek temple. The relatively thin moldings surrounding the windows also point to a Federal heritage, which was somewhat out of date in the mid-1830s. On the other hand, the quoins (stone blocks that articulate the corners) on the exterior and the carved ornament in the interior of the ground floor are primarily Georgian in derivation (fig. 2-10).

Such an eclectic approach to design was not unusual in the 1830s. Gothic windows like the ones at Kirtland are occasionally seen on contemporaneous

**2-10.** Exterior view of the west and south sides of the Kirtland Temple. The exterior combines Georgian, Federal, Gothic, and Greek Revival elements. Eclecticism was not unusual in Ohio at that time. Photographed by Carl F. Waite, April 1934.

Western Reserve churches. The Presbyterian Church in Kinsman, Ohio (about 1832) (fig. 2-11), for example, has Gothic windows on a building form that closely copies Asher Benjamin's design for the Old West Church in Boston. The Congregational Church in Atwater, Ohio (1837–41) (fig. 2-12), displays Gothic windows on an otherwise Greek Revival structure. Scholars have suggested Joseph Smith derived Gothic windows from buildings he saw during his trips to New York or Boston.[13] But the common use of Gothic windows on non-Gothic-style churches in the early nineteenth-century Western Reserve makes reliance on East Coast urban examples both unnecessary and unlikely.[14] Gothic windows were placed on churches in the United States and Canada because they were a cultural symbol for a church in the same way that small cupolas were the cultural symbol of a town hall or

Photo by author.

**2-11.** Presbyterian church (built ca. 1832) with Gothic windows similar to those in the Kirtland Temple. Kinsman, Ohio.

Photo by author.

**2-12.** Gothic windows in a Congregational church, Atwater, Ohio (1837–41). The windows are the only departure from the church building's Greek Revival style.

public structure in the late-eighteenth and early-nineteenth centuries. The specification of Gothic windows merely tells us that Joseph Smith and his associates shared a common culture with their contemporaries.

Joseph Smith also described the main volume of the structure—occupied by the two congregational spaces one on top of the other—in terms of traditional church design. Most contemporary churches had an entry vestibule that led into the main sanctuary, a feature also of the Independence Temple plans. In these church buildings, stairs at the sides of the vestibule led to an upper gallery, or balcony, which was above the sanctuary and supported on columns. Often these balconies were U-shaped, leaving a full double height in the center of the room. However, the Independence Temple specifications stated, "There will not be a gallery but a chamber [in] each story to be 14 feet high arched over head with an eliptical arch [in] each of the stories."[15] Joseph Smith and his counselors described the temple in terms of its divergence from well-known traditional forms.

## Pulpits and Pews

The written specifications for the Independence Temple dealt with the pulpits and pews in the greatest detail. Such detail was necessary since these arrangements were novel and the builders could not rely on a shared understanding of the intent. First, each end of the congregational spaces, or upper and lower courts as they are called in the revelation, has raised seating for twelve persons: three upper rows of three "stands," or pulpits, and a fourth (lower) row of three seats behind a "swing table" for the sacrament. In the corners of the room adjacent to these pulpits, additional raised seating provides space for choirs.

The rows of pulpits and seats at the west end were designated for the Higher, or Melchizedek, Priesthood, with the uppermost tier for "the president and his council" (Joseph Smith and his counselors, Sidney Rigdon and Frederick G. Williams). The next tier of pulpits was for "the Bishop and his council" (in Independence, Edward Partridge and his two counselors; in Kirtland, Newel K. Whitney and his two counselors), and the third tier was for the high priests. The lowest seats, those without pulpits, were for the elders.[16] On the east end of the building, the tiers of pulpits and seats were designated for the presidency of the Lesser, or Aaronic, Priesthood and then for members of each of the three offices within the Lesser Priesthood: priests, teachers, and deacons.

Each row of pulpits was to be raised above the previous row, with the central pulpit higher than the flanking ones. The specifications on both sets of drawings for the Independence Temple state that the central pews in each row should rise in twelve-inch increments, while the pulpits to each side should increase in eight-inch increments. The intent of this directive was probably to elevate the central pulpits four inches above the flanking ones. However, if the pulpits were built as described on the drawing, the uppermost central pulpit would be four times four inches, or sixteen inches, above its flanking pulpits and would require two steps leading from the side to the central pulpit. Unfortunately, lack of space would run such steps into the adjacent pulpit. Perhaps this unresolved problem led carpenters to dispense with making the central pulpit higher and to build all three pulpits in each row at the same elevation.

The pulpits' location, number, and rise are spelled out, but the specifications designate no other architectural detail or style beyond the general direction that "the pulpits . . . are to be . . . [done] off with pannel work."[17] As mentioned above, this general statement does not indicate a lack of interest in the form of the pulpits, but rather implies a common understanding as to what was intended.

The unusual plan of the Independence and Kirtland Temples also modified traditional congregational seating. Even today, most congregational spaces use fixed benches that face forward. The temple's east- and west-facing pulpits required that the congregation be able to comfortably face either direction. The Independence Temple drawing specifications describe a clever solution to this problem:

> Observe, that as there are pulpits in each end of the house, to avoid the necessity of the backs of the congregation being towards the speaker at any time, the house must be finished with pews in[s]tead of slips. The seats in the pews must be so constructed that [the]y can be slipped, or moved from one side of the pew to the other at pleasure, and then the congregation can without trouble change their position at any time, and always face the speaker.[18]

With these movable benches set in the pew boxes, congregants could face either the Melchizedek or Aaronic pulpits, depending upon who was officiating during the meeting. Most meetings were held facing the west or Melchizedek pulpits—an arrangement that would have been far more practical for latecomers, who could then slip in the eastern doors without disturbing the western-facing congregation.

Specifications for the Independence Temple also dictated that sections of pews were to line up with the doors and windows in the west facade. The central block of pews was to have a four-inch gap dividing it lengthwise into two equal parts. In addition, the central and the lateral blocks were to be divided widthwise by another four-inch gap. These gaps allowed curtains, or "vails" [sic], to be unrolled from the ceiling and pass to the floor, thereby quartering the congregational area. Each of the quarters was to have a "gallery," or passageway, running from front to back.[19] The pulpits were to be fitted with curtains as well:

> As you see the pulpits are to have four seats one raising above another for instance the Elders seat is the lowest next comes the high Priests next the Bishop so each of these must have a vail that is suspended to the uper ~~ceiling~~ floor so to be let down which will at any time when necessary be let down and shut off each stand or seat by itself.[20]

Hooks were originally fixed in the ceiling of the lower court of the Kirtland Temple to accommodate these "vails," but an ingenious roller system was devised for the upper court (see chapter 6).

## Vestibule

The Kirtland Temple also required complex planning of the entry foyer, or vestibule. The unusual arrangement of two vertically stacked assembly rooms creates difficulties in lighting the spaces, especially with double sets of pulpits in each room. In traditional late-eighteenth- and early-nineteenth-century American church interiors, a large window (usually a "Palladian motif" or "Venetian" window) was located behind the pulpit and altar to focus sight on that area of the church. The western ends in the upper and lower courts in the Kirtland Temple follow this

Photo by author.

2-13. Vestibule, Kirtland Temple, looking north. Light passes from the central window on the facade through the open balcony to the large window in the vestibule wall on the left.

traditional arrangement, but the eastern end required some modification. On the eastern end, the second floor is cut out above the vestibule, creating a second-floor balcony. Symmetrical staircases rise to the balcony from each side of the vestibule. The vestibule wall and stairs block the east light that otherwise would have brightened the main congregational space (figs. 2-13, 2-14).

Joseph Smith, Sidney Rigdon, and Frederick G. Williams solved this lighting problem in the Independence Temple design and the final Kirtland Temple plan by placing a large window in the center of the east facade and two windows, similar to the two exterior windows on the western end, in the interior vestibule wall. Light from the central facade window passes through to the interior windows behind the eastern pulpits, illuminating the eastern side of the main rooms.

Courtesy Library of Congress.

**2-14.** Vestibule, Kirtland Temple, looking south. The door built into the the stair kept small children from going upstairs while worship services were being held in the lower court. (In this view, the door is open and against the wall on the left.) Photographed by Carl F. Waite, April 1934.

This arrangement is accurately described in written specifications for both the first and revised sets of Independence Temple drawings: "This middle window is desighned [sic] to light both above and below as the upper floor as to be laid off ~~presently~~ in the same way as the lower."[21]  The balcony is described in more detail in the specifications accompanying the revised set of drawings: "Note 2. There is to be a window as large as necessary, directly over the east pulp[i]t, to convey the light from the outer court through to the inner court. . . . There will be a rail[i]ng over the lower petition [the balcony on the second floor] far enough east to give room for a sufficient aisle"[22] (fig. 2-15). In other words, the balcony on the second floor was not to block circulation in the vestibule; rather, it was to be fitted with a railing and to leave enough floor area in the ten-foot-wide space to permit passage from one side to the other. This window and balcony arrangement in the vestibule is an original solution to an unusual spatial problem and indicates fairly complex three-dimensional thinking on the part of Joseph Smith, Sidney Rigdon, and Frederick G. Williams.[23]

*Courtesy Library of Congress.*

**2-15.** View of the balcony in the upper level of the vestibule, Kirtland Temple. The balcony design allowed light from the exterior window to pass through the interior window and illuminate the main rooms. Photographed by Carl F. Waite, April 1934.

## Conclusion

While the vestibule arrangement, which required sophisticated three-dimensional insight, is described in accurate detail, both the first and revised sets of drawings overlooked the obvious need for physical space for the elliptical vaults. This contrast can perhaps be explained by the nature of the experience through which Joseph Smith, Sidney Rigdon, and Frederick G. Williams developed their plan for the Independence and Kirtland Temples. Their vision of the completed temple was the pattern for the temple's essential design. That the design was communicated visually would explain why the interior arrangement was spelled out in such detail while the physical structure was barely mentioned in plans and specifications for the companion temple in Independence.

Joseph Smith, Sidney Rigdon, and Frederick G. Williams were aware of their shortcomings. They noted on the Independence drawings that "the size form and demisions [dimensions] of the house were GIVEN US OF THE LORD,"[24] implying that everything else was their attempt to combine these defined elements into a functioning structure. These three men had a visual idea of what they wanted, but they knew neither how that idea should be implemented nor how various pieces should fit together. Their errors in the drawing sets are consistent with the claims concerning the plans' provenance. The advice of experienced craftsmen must have been invaluable as the Presidency's vision was translated into stone and lumber.

## Notes

[1]Sorensen, "Schools of the Prophets," 3:1269. *History of the Church*, 1:352, states that the temple was for worship and for the School of the Prophets. Only two rooms were planned; no description of the Independence Temple mentions the attic story. Therefore, I have concluded that Joseph Smith, Sidney Rigdon, and Frederick G. Williams did not realize there would be additional space in the attic. Because two functions were designated and two rooms were planned at this time in the temple building, I have assumed one function per room.

[2]On Saturday, June 3, Joseph Smith stated that he had received the dimensions of the temple (D&C 95) but that he, Sidney Rigdon, and Frederick G. Williams were "to obtain a draft or construction of the inner court of the house" (*History of the Church*, 1:352). Since Joseph Smith described the building to a meeting of brethren on Sunday, June 4, the vision had to have occurred sometime during the evening of June 3 or the morning of June 4.

[3]Truman O. Angell, "Journal." Truman Angell also wrote:

> F. G. Williams came into the Temple about the time the main hall first floor was ready for dedication. He was asked, how does the house look to you. He answered that it looked to him like the model he had seen. He said President Joseph, Sidney Rigdon and himself were called to come before the Lord and the model was shown to them. He said the vision of the Temple was thus shown them and he could not see the difference between it and the House as built. (Angell to Taylor and Council, 1–2)

One may argue that Angell's recounting of the vision was not written down until the 1880s and that Angell may have taken liberty with the facts. However, a study of Angell's diaries makes the latter interpretation very unlikely, as he presents a rather frank and clear picture of his life history.

Orson Pratt's April 9, 1871, statement from the pulpit echoes the generally accepted ideas concerning the authorship of the temple's design:

> When the Lord commanded this people to build a house in the land of Kirtland, . . . he gave them the pattern by vision from heaven, and commanded them to build that house according to that pattern and order; to have the architecture, not in accordance with architecture devised by men, but to have every thing constructed in that house according to the heavenly pattern that he by his voice had inspired to his servants. (*Journal of Discourses*, 14:273)

[4]"Ring without end or beginning (column top) is believed a symbol of Creator." *Kirtland Temple*.

[5]*History of the Church*, 1:363. The Independence Temple drawings were sent to Edward Partridge, the bishop in Independence. These drawings were then carried west and were eventually given to the LDS Church Historian's Office on June 29, 1865, by Edward Partridge's widow, Lydia. Independence Temple drawings, unsigned set.

[6]"Those patterns previously sent you, per mail, by our brethren, were incorrect in some respects; being drawn in grate haste. They have therefore drawn these, which are correct." Independence Temple drawings, signed set.

[7]Lucy Mack Smith, *History of Joseph Smith*, 64

[8]Note that Williams was placed in charge of brickmaking in April 1833 at the French farm, indicating he had at least some knowledge of building trades. *History of the Church*, 1:336.

[9]"There being an error in putting the upper windows too low, it was thought needless to finish the plan; you will therefore put the four common windows above, the proper height." Independence Temple drawings, signed set.

[10]*History of the Church*, 1:361.

[11]This drawing was not "sketchily done in freehand" as Andrew asserts but is a hard-line drawing by one without drawing skills. See Andrew, *Early Temples of the Mormons*, 33.

[12]Independence Temple drawings, east elevation, signed set.

[13]Andrew, *Early Temples of the Mormons*, 43–46.

[14]Other examples of churches in the Western Reserve displaying combinations of Greek and Gothic details are the Congregational Church in Claridon, Ohio (1831); the Christ Episcopal Church in Windsor Mills, Ohio (1832–34); and the now-destroyed St. Mary in the Flats in Cleveland, Ohio (1838).

[15]Independence Temple drawings, unsigned set. See also the transcription in *History of the Church*, 1:359–61. Note the small discrepancies between the transcription and the original document.

[16]Although these specifications list the intended seating arrangement, in practice Joseph Smith Jr. usually occupied the second highest tier of pulpits, apparently deferring to his father, Joseph Smith Sr., who often occupied the highest tier as Patriarch to the Church. Jessee, "Kirtland Diary of Wilford Woodruff," 372.

[17]Independence Temple drawings, signed set.

[18]Independence Temple drawings, signed set. Note that the explanation of pew arrangement is less clear in the first set of drawings sent to Independence. Independence Temple drawings, unsigned set.

[19]The assertion that the two-door arrangement has to do with the separation of men and women during the temple ceremony does not match with the facts of the development of the design. See Andrew, *Early Temples of the Mormons*, 50–51. The east doors and internal passages between the pews were specified to line up, and the double sets of pulpits precluded any possibility of a central passageway in the congregational spaces. In a presentation at the Kirtland Temple, June 7, 1997, Paul Anderson pointed out that Joseph Smith undoubtedly knew of and the Smith family probably worshipped at the first meetinghouse built in Palmyra. Built in 1811 and dedicated in 1812, it was known as the Union Church, because several Protestant denominations met there. This meetinghouse had two entry doors. See Jacobs, *Wayne County*, 206. While some of the fast meetings in Kirtland did separate men and women into different quadrants of the lower court to conduct independent sessions of the meeting, no special ceremony in Kirtland included women. All washings and anointings conducted in Kirtland involved the male priesthood members only.

[20]Independence Temple drawings, unsigned set.

[21]Independence Temple drawings, unsigned set.

[22]Independence Temple drawings, signed set. Note that the implication here is to leave another open balcony on the attic office level, as reference is made to "the lower petition." As built, the third floor has no opening to lower floors. However, it does have a heavy trapdoor that allows the bell to be hoisted up through the interior. This might have been a later addition since a letter written in 1841 talks about laying a new bell deck. It could be that the original intention was to leave the space open through the attic office floor. See Jenson, Journal History, October 19, 1841, 1.

[23]This concern for proper interior illumination was also evident in the specifications on the first unsigned set of drawings for the Independence Temple (figs. 2-2 and 2-3), where all the doors and windows on the facade were to have "venetians," meaning sidelights, to increase illumination, although this was not carried out in Kirtland. The transcription in *History of the Church*, 1:359–62, erroneously changed "venetians" to "venetian blinds."

[24]Independence Temple drawings, unsigned set.

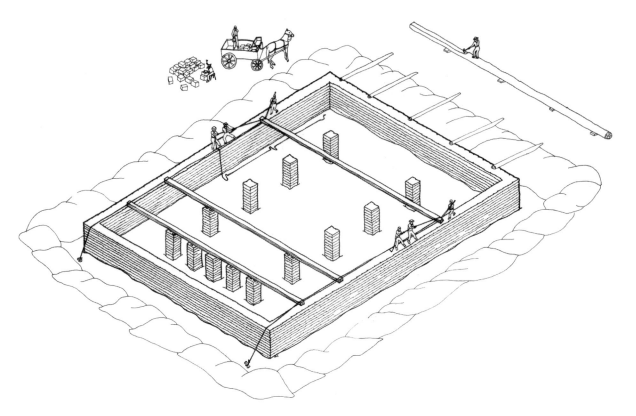

**Fig 3-1.** Axonometric view of building site circa early 1834. The representative construction phases illustrated here would probably not have occurred simultaneously as shown, but they have been included to show the range of tasks required in construction.

Chapter 3

# The First Campaign of Construction, Summer–Fall 1833

On June 1, 1833, Joseph received a revelation which caused a sudden flurry of temple-building activity during June 1833. In this revelation, the Lord "chasten[s]" the members of the Church, "for ye have sinned . . . a very grevious sin, in that ye have not considered the great commandment in all things, that I have given unto you concerning the building of mine house." Furthermore, in this revelation, the Lord gives specific instructions about the dimensions of the temple and promises to "show unto three of you" the manner in which it should be built (D&C 95:3, 14–15).

On the day Joseph Smith, Sidney Rigdon, and Frederick G. Williams saw the Kirtland Temple in a vision, Joseph Smith convened a council meeting and asked each participant to propose the type of structure for the temple. Lucy Mack Smith, Joseph Smith's mother, later recorded:

> Some thought that it would be better to build a frame others said that a frame was too costly kind of a house and the majority concluded upon the putting up a log house and made their calculations about what they could do towards it building it—Joseph rose and reminded them that they were not making a house for themselves or any other man but a house for God. ["]And shall we brethren build a house for Our God of logs. No brethren, I have a better plan than that I have the plan of the house of the Lord given by himself you will see by this the difference between our calculations and his Ideas[."] He then gave them the plan in full of the house of the Lord at Kirtland.[1]

Clearly, the concept of a substantial masonry structure was beyond the expectation of most in the group. But Joseph's proposal was enthusiastically embraced, and after the meeting's close, council members walked to the building site. Lucy Mack Smith recorded that, while the group viewed the site,

> Hyrum [Joseph's older brother] ~~came~~ ran to the house and caught the sythe and was about returning to the place without giving any explanation but I stopt him and asked him where he was going with the sythe he said we are preparing to build a house for the Lord and I am determined to be the first at the work In a few minutes the fence was removed the young wheat cut, and the ground in order for the foundation.[2]

Construction of the temple began in earnest the following Monday, June 5, 1833, with Hyrum Smith and Reynolds Cahoon digging the trench for the foundation and Harry Stanley and George A. Smith hauling the first load of stone.[3]

The scale of the intended building must have seemed ludicrous to those viewing the construction site, for Benjamin F. Johnson records, "Such was the poverty of the people at the time of breaking ground for its foundation, that there was not a scraper and hardly a plow that could be obtained among the Saints."[4] Without scrapers, effective use of draft animals in the excavation would have been difficult. Hyrum Smith's enthusiasm must have been vital to the completion of the project, for he and Reynolds Cahoon excavated the foundation by hand.

Despite these difficulties, the excavation was ready for the cornerstones by July 23, following about six weeks of labor.[5] Just as the Saints had lacked sufficient tools for digging the foundation, they also lacked sufficient personnel for the cornerstone ceremony. Twenty-four Melchizedek Priesthood holders were needed (or desired) to officiate, but the group of Saints was so small that a sufficient number could not be assembled on the required day. Joseph C. Kingsbury and Don Carlos Smith, still in their teens, were quickly ordained to the proper priesthood office in order to expedite matters.[6] Despite this serious lack of both men and proper equipment, to say nothing of the staggering debt already incurred by Joseph Smith on behalf of the group,[7] construction moved ahead.

This dogged determination to complete the building in the face of continuous obstacles is a leitmotif in the history of the building. Whatever motives might be ascribed to Joseph Smith and his associates, the building history of the Kirtland Temple clearly underscores their vision of what the Mormon community was eventually to become. At the time construction began, only about 150 members of the faith lived in Kirtland.[8] Not until well after the Kirtland Temple was finished and most Saints had left Ohio did large numbers of English converts dramatically increase the size of the Church. Given these rather inauspicious beginnings—especially considering local opposition to the group—the faith in the future exhibited by Joseph Smith and his associates is all the more remarkable.

## Construction of the Foundation Walls

From late July through October, construction on the foundation walls progressed under the direction of Reynolds Cahoon and Jacob Bump, a plasterer and carpenter from a Lake Erie harbor town in New York state.[9] Workers continued to haul sandstone from Stannard's Quarry, located about two miles south of the building site. Though not deep, this quarry consists of a sandstone bed exposed by the small stream running over it (fig. 3-2). The neat, regular drilling holes still visible in the quarry probably do not date from the Mormon excavations, for the majority of the stone in the temple walls is far more irregular in shape. Workers most likely used wedges to split out irregular blocks of stone along natural fissures.

Typical residential foundations in the 1830s had cut-stone or rubble-stone walls and extended into the soil below frost level—deeper if root cellars were to be located under the structure. In most soils, wood-framed houses do not require wide foundations to spread out their relatively modest weight, and such simple foundations perform satisfactorily.

Like these residential foundations, the Kirtland Temple foundation is formed of large cut-stone blocks to the outside, with rubblestone completing the thickness of the wall. However, the Kirtland Temple, more than ten times the volume of most residences and constructed of thick masonry walls, requires a far more substantial foundation than a residence. Though the temple's foundation walls are twenty-eight inches wide—approximately double the width of most residential foundations—they have no footing, or flared base, to spread out the weight on the soil. As none of the workers involved with the project up to this point had experience with such large-scale buildings, they did not sufficiently broaden the foundation. Consequently, the building has settled about two inches since its construction, causing the walls to crack visibly.[10]

Photo by author.

**Fig 3-2.** Stannard Quarry, Lake County Metroparks, Kirtland. The neat, regular excavation markings probably date from later quarrying activities.

## Rough-Worked Girders

Bump and Cahoon likely supervised placing the girders that go on top of the foundation walls, for these girders exhibit characteristics typical of relatively unskilled craftsmen. The oak girders show a large number of knots; apparently no special effort was made to obtain timbers free from defects. The surface of the girders is roughly worked, showing a pockmarked pattern where chips of wood were crudely split off (fig. 3-3). Either the workers did not have an adze at their disposal, or they did not know how to wield one effectively.

The orientation of the girders also reveals the workers' lack of experience constructing large buildings. The girders have a scantling, or cross section, of about nine inches by twelve inches oriented flatwise—that is, with the twelve-inch dimension horizontal and the nine-inch dimension vertical. This orientation cuts the bending strength nearly in half compared to that of a vertically oriented girder.[11] This construction practice is typical of the eighteenth century, as builders preferred leaving substantial beam widths in order to accommodate mortises, or joist pockets, which were carved into the sides of the beam. This practice was also adequate for residences, which typically have smaller spans and floor loads than public assembly buildings.

Fig 3-3. Detail of girder and pier supporting floor of lower court. Also visible are the masonry pier supporting the girder and joists framing into the girder. Modern additions include the insulated ductwork.

However, with the building designed to house large public assemblies and with the span between support piers close to twenty-five feet, the horizontal orientation of support girders is woefully inadequate.

After its completion, the temple regularly hosted meetings with about one thousand people in attendance.[12] Given the weakness of the girders supporting the floor of the lower court, the floor must have creaked and groaned during the services. The girders possess only about one-sixth of the modern code-required strength. Of course, today's codes have a generous safety factor built in, and wood will safely carry moderate overstresses for

# Foundations

Proper foundations are essential to the long-term stability of a building. If some sections of a building sink into the ground farther than others, walls can crack. These cracks may not themselves be dangerous, but they allow moisture to penetrate the walls, causing wooden elements to rot. In colder climates, cracks can cause freeze-thaw damage due to the expansion that occurs when water freezes. In more serious cases of settlement, walls can rotate or lean dangerously, threatening the stability of a structure.

The best foundation is one established directly on bedrock. In that instance, builders merely extend the walls down to the rock strata. However, bedrock is rarely found conveniently close to the surface, so to prevent the building from sinking into the soil, foundations must spread out their load much as one wears snowshoes to prevent floundering in deep snow. Techniques used in preindustrial America to build adequate foundations for larger structures included stepping out the foundation at each course, thereby widening the contact area between the foundation and the soil, and laying stout timbers crosswise underneath the wall to spread out the weight. However, the builders of the Kirtland Temple, who did not employ these techniques, did not fully appreciate the substantial weight of the structure, nor did they realize how poor the underlying soil is for building.

The soils under the Kirtland Temple are glacial deposits that vary a great deal at different depths. The foundation walls bear directly on reasonably firm soil. However, when the building is fully occupied, the relatively narrow width of the foundation walls stresses the soil to nearly three times the level recommended in modern engineering practice. Exacerbating this situation is a layer of loose sand and silt, which has a very low bearing capacity, about ten feet below the foundations. This soil profile presents some paradoxical problems.

The downward pressure of foundations can cause sandy soils such as those under the temple to flow upward and away from the bottom of the foundation, much like what happens when one steps in firm mud and it oozes up around the foot. This problem is avoided in modern practice by burying foundations deep enough that the weight of the soil above holds the lower soil in place.

The foundations of the temple have almost no embedment in the soil. The dirt floor of the basement is just inches above the bottom of the foundation, so excessive weight on the foundations could cause an uplift of soil in the basement floor. However, if builders had tried to solve this problem by burying the foundations deeper, the area affected by the foundation's pressure would have come dangerously close to the loose stratum of soil lying about ten feet below.

As it currently stands, the Kirtland Temple is delicately balanced on insufficiently wide and insufficiently embedded foundations perched above a loose layer of soil. The west wall has rotated outward slightly, probably because of the foundations' settlement. Some joist ends have nearly pulled out of their pockets in the wall, and one of the piers under the vestibule wall has rotated a significant amount. However, the foundation wall is so thick that the current amount of rotation is not a cause for concern. Recent stabilization of the soil by pressure grouting will hopefully secure the structure for its long-term preservation.

shorter duration loads (such as three- or four-hour meetings). However, the stresses in the girders underscore the extreme good fortune that the floor of the lower court did not collapse during the temple's dedicatory services.

Later occupants were not so lucky. The westernmost girder supporting the lower court floor has a large defect in the wood that eventually caused it to split and fail. Luckily, the floor did not completely collapse. It probably gave a loud crack and dropped a few inches in midspan. Total collapse of the girder likely was prevented by both the quick reaction of people standing above the failure and the thick floorboards, which spread the load over to sound structural members.[13]

Timber props to support the girders at their midspans and reduce the tremendous overstresses present in the original design were placed in the basement in about 1883 (fig. 3-4).[14] These provisional supports have adequately supported the floor of the lower court over the years, and it is fortunate that these girders, oriented in their weaker flatwise position, were placed where they could be easily supported on the basement floor. Had such girders been used in the structure of one of the upper floors, propping them up without ruining the space below would have been extremely difficult.

## Walls of Rubble: The Arrival of Artemus Millett

The settlement and subsequent cracking of the temple's walls might have been reduced if the temple had been built of brick as originally intended.[15] Common brick weighs about 15 percent less than most stone, and less weight would have resulted in a smaller degree of settling. On April 2, 1833, Frederick G. Williams was placed in charge of a brickyard located on the recently purchased Peter French farm. Although the stated justification in the *History of the Church* for

Photo by author.

**Fig 3-4.** Timber prop supporting the lower-court floor girders at midspan. Note that the foundation of the timber prop is merely a block set on the dirt floor. In addition to the piping, wiring, and conduit visible in the photograph, a paint spot on the wooden girder identifies a surveying point which is checked periodically to ensure that these provisional repairs are not settling on the dirt floor.

the brick kiln was merely that it "was essential to the building up of the city," workers in the brickyard recorded in their journals that they were "making brick for the House of the Lord then about to be built in that place." Workers labored through the summer until September 25, 1833, when brickmaking was abandoned, apparently because workers were unable to produce a sufficient quantity of usable bricks.[16] As a consequence, when the stone foundation was completed in October, no materials were available to continue work, and the building site was abandoned until spring.[17]

The failure in brickmaking must have been a severe blow to the community. Not only had construction on the temple halted, but the fruitless expenditure of time and effort in a community handicapped by limited resources must have created great discouragement for both Church leaders and members. Of course, beginning in late 1832, brick was locally available for purchase in sufficient quantity to build the temple, but the impoverished Mormon community likely could not bear the expense of such a large purchase.[18]

This materials crisis was most likely solved by Artemus Millett, a builder of mills, chimneys, and foundations from Ontario, Canada. Apparently on the recommendation of Brigham Young, who had converted Millett in January 1833, Joseph Smith requested that Millett come to Kirtland to work on the temple.[19] Fortunately for the Saints, Millett had large-scale building experience: he had built a brewery in New York state around 1825 and two three-story flour mills in Canada in 1830.[20] Since brickmaking attempts were abandoned in September, Millett must have observed considerable anxiety over prospects for completing the temple when he arrived in Kirtland later that fall. His contribution during his short stay was the suggestion to use rubblestone walls covered with a stucco finish in place of brick.

Because of Millett's building experience in Canada, he was familiar with the rubblework-and-stucco building technique common in the provinces of Ontario and Quebec. During the early nineteenth century, buildings of rubble construction in the United States were quite rare, primarily because wood framing was so inexpensive in contrast with solid masonry walls. When a masonry building was desired, it was almost always constructed of brick. However, in Ontario and Quebec, rubblework construction was very popular, especially for public buildings. This popularity is probably due to Canada's closer ties with England and France, where stucco-covered, rubble-walled buildings are common. The northern shore of Lake Ontario, where Millett had worked, still has many examples of churches built using rubblework construction techniques during the late eighteenth and early nineteenth centuries.[21]

Millett was also familiar with American variations on traditional masonry. During the War of 1812, he worked as a "huckster," hauling supplies

**Fig 3-5.** Russell Quarry in Kirtland. The regular bedding planes and exposed sandstone bed would have enabled roughly rectangular stones to be quarried with a minimum amount of effort. This site is one of several on the Russell property.

Photo by author.

for the army at the Sackets Harbor, New York, army post.[22] The buildings in this military installation are some of the few examples of stone construction in this region of the United States. The Madison Barracks (1816–1819), constructed just after the war in the area where Millett worked as a mason, have narrow decorative stones at the corners. These quoins are unusually long and narrow and are similar to those found on the Kirtland Temple.[23] Millett may have picked up this local variation on quoin design and used it in Kirtland.

Millett's suggestion to use the sandstone readily available from local quarries must have brought tremendous relief to Joseph and members of the building committee, who were trying to raise the necessary funds to build the structure. For the stone of the upper walls, Millett selected a nearby quarry whose sandstone was reportedly soft when quarried and later hardened when exposed. This was probably the Russell Quarry, located south of the temple site (fig. 3-5). Like the Stannard Quarry, the Russell Quarry is a ravine where the streambed has exposed a stratum of sandstone that can therefore be easily removed.[24]

## Spacing of Piers and Windows

In addition to solving the materials problem in Kirtland, Millett superintended the construction site. What Millett saw in October 1833 was an excavation four to five feet deep, with the stone foundation wall completed and probably at least some of the floor girders in place. This situation would have presented a number of difficulties for Millett. First, Millett had no way to provide for quality control on the foundations, which had been built by workers who lacked large-scale building experience. If Millett was concerned about the narrowness of the foundations and the weight of the walls bearing on them, one wonders if he would have been able to order substantial changes as a newcomer to the building. It would have been very awkward for him to walk onto the site and criticize the work, and in fact no record mentions any such discussions. Of course, spotting building problems after damage has occurred is much easier than anticipating their occurrence, and Millett may not have had the necessary expertise to recognize the inadequacy of the foundations.

The second challenge facing Millett was the spacing of piers and windows. Once foundations are built, they are not easily moved. Unless workers had been willing to go to great labor and expense in dismantling and moving the foundations (an unlikely step for the financially strapped Saints), no changes could have been made in the size of the building. Of course, since the dimensions of the structure were determined by revelation, the foundation walls could not be moved for theological reasons either. Most critical for Millett, the foundation walls and masonry piers determined the location of the interior columns and girders. Interior columns should be located between the windows so the girders (the main horizontal supports) that run between the columns and outside walls are supported on the exterior by solid masonry and are not immediately above a window. However, when Hyrum Smith and Reynolds Cahoon started digging the foundation trenches—and, consequently, determining the size of the building and the location of columns—details such as window placement were not fully worked out.[25]

The difficulty for Millett, who eventually built the masonry walls, was to create a regular exterior shell around an irregular internal structure. The plan by Joseph Smith, Sidney Rigdon, and Frederick G. Williams specified a ten-foot-wide vestibule (fig. 3-6). Since the vestibule wall (and tower above) determined the location of the easternmost line of masonry piers, the remaining lines of piers would logically continue at even, ten-foot intervals. However, the revelation also determined the length of the courts as sixty-five feet—a number not evenly divided by ten—making a series of ten-foot intervals between windows on the exterior impossible.

Rather than building the piers at five even intervals of thirteen feet, builders varied bay spacing across the building. This irregular spacing is visible in the longitudinal section of the temple as built (fig. 3-7; transverse section shown in fig. 3-8). Starting at the east end, bay spacings begin with the required ten feet in the vestibule, then jump up to just over twelve feet

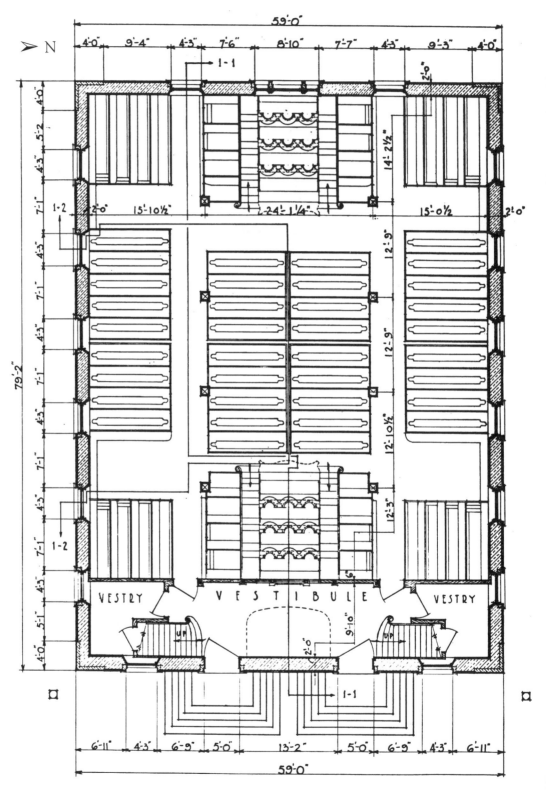

**Fig 3-6a.** Plan of the lower court, Kirtland Temple, drawn March 1934 by Veredon W. Upham. Courtesy Library of Congress.

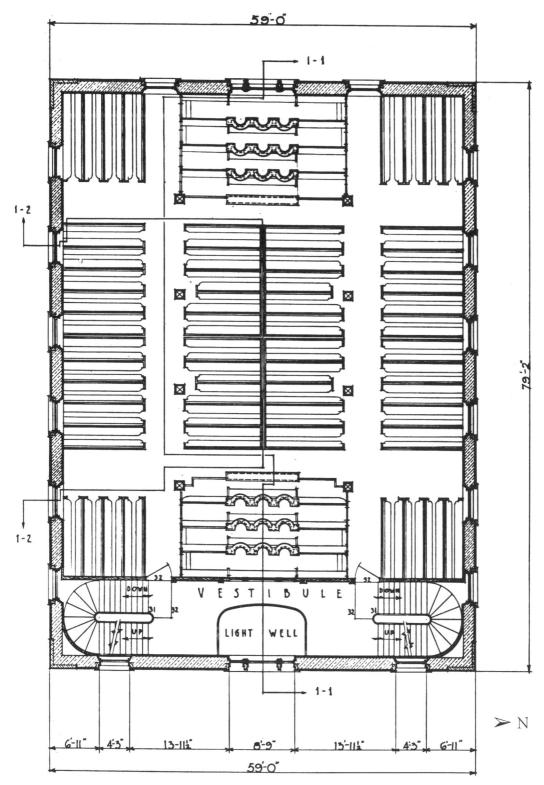

**Fig 3-6b.** Plan of the upper court, Kirtland Temple, drawn March 1934 by Veredon W. Upham. Courtesy Library of Congress.

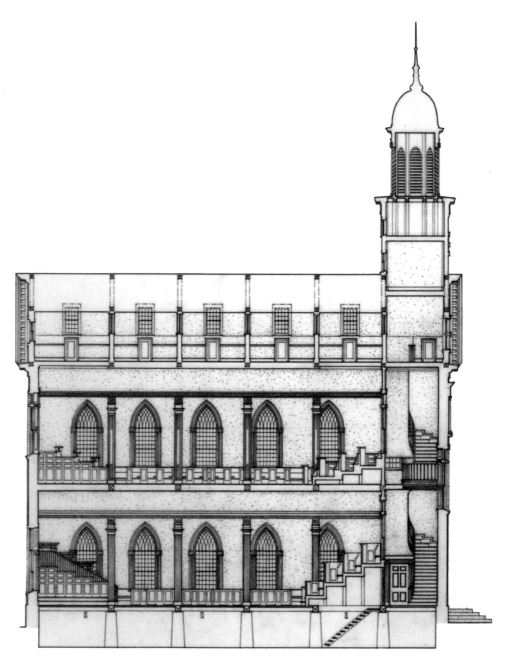

**Fig 3-7.** Longitudinal section, Kirtland Temple, drawn March 1934 by Verdon W. Upham. Courtesy Library of Congress.

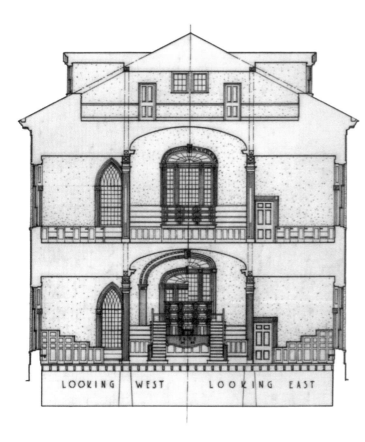

LOOKING  WEST    LOOKING  EAST

**Fig 3-8.** Transverse section, Kirtland Temple, drawn March 1934 by Verdon W. Upham. Courtesy Library of Congress.

in the courts and gradually lengthen as they approach the westernmost bay, with a maximum spacing of about fourteen feet, measured center to center. This irregular spacing creates a variety of problems, indicating that the builders who determined the bay spacing were unaware of its effect on the upper wall.

Columns and girders manage to miss the windows on the western half of the building, but unfortunately, the narrower bay spacing causes the easternmost girders (set into the vestibule wall) to frame into the masonry directly above a window. Although about eight feet of masonry separates the girder and the window opening (allowing the pressure of the girder load to spread out along the wall), stacking the girder and window puts unnecessary stress on the arch above the window.

In addition to adding structural stress, this uneven bay spacing causes the vestibule wall that separates the stairs from the lower and upper courts to cut awkwardly through a window opening (fig. 3-9). On the lower floor, raised choir seats in the corner would have further interfered with the window opening in the eastern corners. Later restorers simply chose to cover the window, boxing it in so it lights only the vestries (the small rooms located under the stairs). However, early descriptions indicate that

**Fig 3-9 .** Interior detail, upper court, showing the vestibule wall intersecting a window.

Photo by author.

the lower-court window was originally treated like that in the upper court, with an awkwardly shaped portion of the window peering into the corner of the room.[26]

Since the joists have the same cross section throughout the lower-court floor, the variation in spans in the joists—from twelve feet, center to center, at the east end of the court to fourteen feet, center to center, at the west—supporting the lower-court floor results in a 20 percent difference in bending stresses.[27] Even with the specified ten-foot bay under the vestibule, dividing the remaining sixty-five-foot court into even thirteen-foot intervals would have stressed the joists more uniformly and safely and would have avoided a girder framed above a window.

Further evidence of this lack of coordination between foundation construction and the design of upper sections of the temple is found in the three masonry piers built under the vestibule wall to carry columns supporting the belfry (figs. 3-10 and 3-11). The central pier is unused because the windows in the interior vestibule wall are directly above it. The column would run right through the center of the window, obviously an unsatisfactory arrangement. Remember that this window arrangement was clearly described in the specifications for the Independence Temple. However, just as Joseph Smith, Sidney Rigdon, and Frederick G. Williams were unable to anticipate the effect elliptical vaults in the ceiling would have on the total height of the structure, the builders who placed the foundations either did not understand the interrelationship between the foundation and the supporting walls and columns or, more likely, did not have the design explained to them in sufficient detail to avoid such errors.

## Conclusion

After his brief consulting visit in the fall of 1833, Millett returned to Canada to close his business and sell his holdings (on credit—he was never

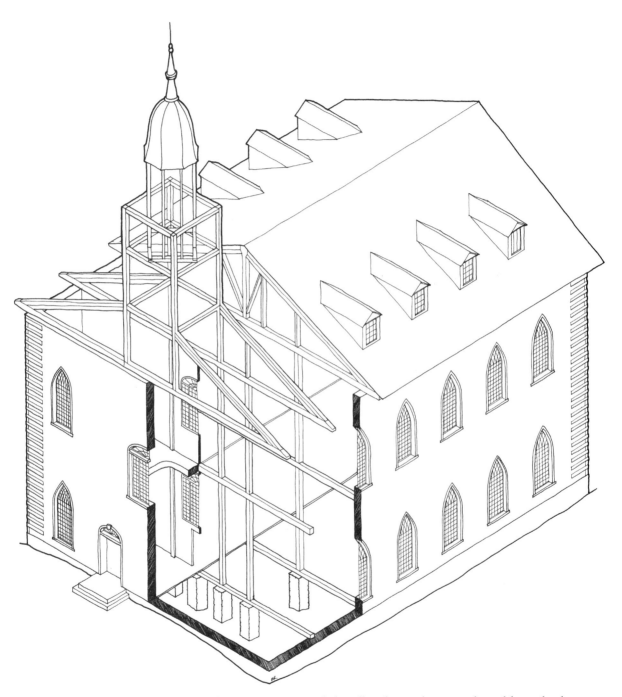

**Fig 3-10.** Cutaway axonometric showing the masonry piers, vestibule wall, and major framing timbers of the roof and tower.

fully paid).[28] Millett's journal does not state how long his initial visit to Kirtland lasted, but it probably was not long. Millett's son reported that Millett was sustained by vote as superintendent of the construction site, but that he left Jacob Bump and Reynolds Cahoon in charge while he returned to Canada. Since he arrived after the closing of the work site in October and would have returned to Canada before the icing over of the Lake Erie and Lake Ontario ports by late December, his visit could have lasted at most two months.[29] However, since he had over thirty masons working for him in Ontario,[30] he had to hurry back to supervise work in Canada and probably left in a matter of weeks. Except for workers stockpiling stone and seasoning timbers to be used the next year,[31] the work site was largely inactive until Millett's return the following spring.

Photo by author.

**Fig 3-11.** Detail of unused masonry pier directly under the window in the center of the vestibule wall. There is no physical connection between the pier and the girder above. Also visible are the large cast-iron pipe of the sprinkler system and smaller conduit carrying electric wiring.

## Notes

[1]Lucy Mack Smith, "History of Lucy Smith," 189. This written history was later edited and published as the *History of Joseph Smith by His Mother* with the corresponding passages found on p. 230 of the 1979 edition.

[2]Lucy Mack Smith, "History of Lucy Smith," 189–90. The edited version reads as follows: "In a few minutes the fence was removed, and the standing grain was levelled, in order to prepare a place for the building and Hyrum commenced digging a trench for the wall, he having declared that he would strike the first blow upon the house." Lucy Mack Smith, *History of Joseph Smith*, 231.

[3]*History of the Church*, 1:353: "Hyrum Smith and Reynolds Cahoon commenced digging the trench for the walls of the Lord's house, and finished the same with their own hands." See also George Smith, "Memoirs," 8.

[4]Benjamin Johnson, *Life Review*, 11.

[5]*History of the Church*, 1:400.

[6]"When the corner stones were laid in Kirtland, they had to pick up boys of fifteen and sixteen years of age, and ordain them Elders, to get officers enough to lay the Corner Stones." Brigham Young, in *Journal of Discourses*, 1:133, April 6, 1853. In November 1859, George A. Smith listed from memory the twenty-four elders who participated in the ceremony: Jacob Bump, Reynolds Cahoon, Gideon H. Carter, Jared Carter, Joseph Coe, Edmund Durfee, David Elliot, Levi W. Hancock, Solomon

Humphreys, Orson Hyde, Joel H. Johnson, Joseph C. Kingsbury, Sidney Rigdon, Harpin Riggs, Don Carlos Smith, Hyrum Smith, John Smith, Joseph Smith Jr., Joseph Smith Sr., Samuel H. Smith, Sylvester Smith, William Smith, Newel K. Whitney, and Frederick G. Williams. Jenson, Journal History, July 23, 1833, 1–2. (6a)

[7]The total debts incurred in 1836–37 by Joseph Smith and cosigners may have exceeded $100,000.00. Hill, Rooker, and Wimmer, "Kirtland Economy Revisited," 24–29. However, it should be noted that these authors concluded that if financial conditions had not changed in 1837 that Joseph Smith would have been able to pay his obligations.

[8]History of the Church, 1:366.

[9]"While the basement was going up Jacob Bump and Reynolds Cahhoon were left in charge of the work while Artimus Millett went back, finished his contract in Canada then returned bringing his family to kirtland." Joseph Millet, "Millet on C B Island," 92. Note that Artemus Millett's own account indicates that the foundation was finished before his arrival in Kirtland. Artemus Millett, Reminiscences.

[10]Petraus and Triggs, "Report of Subsurface Investigation."

[11]The strength of a beam in bending is proportional to its second moment of inertia, which for a beam of rectangular section is given by $I = bh^3/12$, where I = the second moment of inertia, b = the width of the beam, and h = the depth of the beam. For a vertically oriented girder with a 9" by 12" cross section, $I = (9)(12^3)/12 = 1296$ in$^4$. For the horizontally oriented girder, $I = (12)(9^3)/12 = 729$ in$^4$.

The Historic American Building Survey drawings prepared under the WPA program show slightly larger dimensions for the girders, but as with most long timbers, the dimensions vary along their length. Actual widths vary from 11 1/2" to 14", and depths vary from 7" to 9 3/4". However, the median measurements are approximately 9" by 12".

[12]History of the Church, 2:410.

[13]Graffiti on the prop supporting this failed girder dates from 1918, which serves as a post rem date. Repairs to the joists at the point of breakage use crudely cut plate steel with well-oxidized surfaces consistent with the 1918 date.

[14]Kelley and Blakesee, "Report of Committee on Kirtland Temple," 560.

[15]The specifications for the Independence Temple called for brick walls, and the same material was originally intended for Kirtland. Independence Temple drawings, signed set. See also History of the Church, 1:361.

[16]History of the Church, 1:336; Joel Johnson, "Journal or Sketch," 8. See also Benjamin Johnson, Life Review, 10.

[17]Ames, Autobiography and Journal; Williams to Saints in Missouri. Peter French, who sold the farm and kiln to the Saints, had previously built himself a two-story brick home. Holzapfel and Cottle, Old Mormon Kirtland and Missouri, 59, 60. Just what the problem with the brick manufacture was is not stated, but a likely possibility is that insufficient sand was mixed in with the clay, which results in excess shrinkage after firing causing crumbling, fractured bricks.

[18]Painesville Telegraph, May 1, 1832, 3. Painesville Telegraph, December 7, 1832, 4. A rough estimate of the number of bricks required to build the temple with twenty-four-inch-thick walls is thirty-five thousand.

[19]"In January 1833 I was baptized by Brigham Young in Loughborough—U.[pper] C.[anada] in the Summer Br. Hyrum Smith wrote to me that it was the will of the Lord that I should go and work on the Temple in Kirtland when I went the work was suspended, and I returned sold out on credit and took my family in April 1834 to Kirtland." Artemus Millett, Reminiscences.

[20]Artemus Millett, Reminiscences.

[21]One example among many such churches is the St. James Episcopal Church in Maitland, Ontario, built in 1826.

[22]Artemus Millett, Reminiscences.

[23]I am grateful to Priscilla Graham of Hudson, Ohio, for this observation.

[24]Joseph Millet, "Millet on C B Island," 92. See also Lumbard, "Family Chronicle," 9.

[25]The first set of drawings for the Independence Temple shows a side elevation (fig. 2-2) with five Gothic windows on each floor, while the revised set (fig. 2-6) has nine windows. Neither of these two plans was followed in the Kirtland Temple, which has six windows to each floor. However, both sets of

drawings show a regular spacing of the windows, clearly showing the intent of the designers to have as symmetrical a building as possible no matter how many windows were eventually placed on the structure.

[26]"The auditorium occupies all the rest of the first story, but one could wish that the wall which divided it from the vestibule need not have spoiled one of the beautiful windows at either end, thus leaving an ungainly half window in the auditorium." Mather, "Early Days of Mormonism," 209.

[27]The clear span of the joists in the vestibule is about 9 1/2' as opposed to 13 1/2' in the west bay, with corresponding center-to-center bay sizes of about 10' to 14'. Clear spans of the joists supporting the interior bays going from east to west increase from 12' 2 1/2" to 13' 6" along the south wall. Clear spans along the north wall are not as uniform because the central girder supporting the lower court is not parallel with the other girders, its north end being located approximately eight inches too far to the east.

[28]Artemus Millett, Reminiscences.

[29]Other trips made by Millett between Kirtland and Canada were taken by boat, see Millett, Reminiscences. Even when he had a wagon at his disposal, Millett only drove to the first port on Lake Ontario, avoiding the long journey around the lake. It was possible to walk across the ice, but Brigham Young's account of a six mile crossing across frozen Lake Ontario suggests that it was a risky proposition, see "History of Brigham Young," *Deseret News*.

[30]Joseph Millet, Record Book: "He had made lots of property there, in Earnesttown Upper Canada, Took contracts on Government roads, and Stone bridges, and building Stone houses, had employed over 30 Scotch masons."

[31]*History of the Church*, 1:353–54.

# Chapter 4

# Finishing the Walls and Roof, 1834–1835

In April 1834, Artemus Millett returned to Kirtland on what was probably one of that spring's first schooners to pass through the thawing waters of Lake Erie. During the winter months he spent in Canada, he probably had some time on his hands to sketch out plans for the structure of the Kirtland Temple. He probably also made some rough estimates of quantities of stone and lumber if estimates had not already been made during his brief stay in Kirtland a few months before.

## Zion's Camp and the Summer of 1834

Upon his return to Kirtland, Millett would have found the town in commotion over the impending departure of Zion's Camp. Hostilities toward Mormons in Missouri had peaked in 1833. Not only were plans for the Independence Temple abandoned, but mob violence in October and November had forced the Saints to leave Jackson County. In order to protect the rights and lives of the Saints once they were reinstated in Jackson County, Joseph Smith began signing up volunteers and raising money in February 1834 for an armed relief group. He then spent most of the month of March traveling through upstate New York visiting small congregations.[1] Much of the group that made up Zion's Camp left Kirtland on May 1, 1834, and Joseph Smith left on May 6.

Millett must have been a little bewildered upon his arrival in Kirtland since preparations for Zion's Camp were claiming most of the residents' energies and since Joseph Smith and Sidney Rigdon were out of town for conferences much of the time. Adding to the confusion was the recently concluded trial of Philastus Hurlbut for threatening Joseph Smith's life. In fact, Joseph's diary records only one meeting where the temple was discussed during the month of April.[2] Of course, Millett himself may not have had a great deal of time to discuss the building with Joseph Smith because Millett would have had to find lodging for his family and get them settled in.

Approximately 130 men—a significant portion of the population of Kirtland—left with Zion's Camp. As the *History of the Church* records, "We left but few men in Kirtland, viz.: Elders Sidney Rigdon, Oliver Cowdery, a few working on the Temple, and the aged."[3] Heber C. Kimball later described the impact this departure had on temple construction:

> Brother Cahoon and Br. Cutler can tell you how many hands worked upon that Temple at one time; I think there were not more than five or six. Father Cutler, and Elder Cahoon, can tell you that there was not left in Kirtland more than ten or fifteen men, when we left with the camp to go to Zion, to Jackson county.[4]

Millett did not record his emotions as he took over supervising the temple construction, but the sight of the small work crew laboring on the large structure in a town inhabited primarily by women and children must have evoked poignant feelings.

Millett must also have felt deep concern for the welfare of the families driven out of their homes in Missouri and for his own family. Ira Ames, who came to Kirtland in October 1833, recorded that the Saints there suffered their share of persecution: "Ever since my arrival in Kirtland I had stood guard at night in consequence of the Mob and persecutions we endured."[5] Opposition was less intense during the summer of 1834 because everyone expected the Mormon community to leave for Independence in the near future.[6] Nevertheless, Joseph Smith's life had been threatened, and Ames indicates the Saints still felt compelled to keep a guard posted at night.

But fortunately for Millett, Jacob Bump, who worked on the foundations and later did much of the woodwork in the temple, remained in Kirtland. Other workers were not as highly trained, but most men in the Western Reserve possessed at least rudimentary building skills. For example, Ira Ames, the only other worker of the summer of 1834 who left a journal, worked as a shoemaker but built a home for his family as well.[7]

Although at the time of Millett's arrival the temple's foundations and at least some of the girders were in place, the work crew made little progress during the summer. The small work crew was able to raise the walls only about four feet above the ground.[8] But even this small step would have eliminated any possibility of design revision. Any work above the foundation would locate window and door openings with finality and determine the width of the walls. Millett himself was probably occupied with carving the stone quoins, the lintels, and the architraves that encased the windows and doors. The remainder of the crew probably mixed the mortar, roughly shaped and placed the stone, and prepared scaffolding. The modest accomplishments of the summer crew suggest that relatively small amounts of stone had been stockpiled on the site during the previous winter. Given sufficient quantities of materials, a small crew could make significant progress laying stone, but if they first had to quarry and haul the stone, construction would be considerably hindered.

Perhaps this lack of materials and manpower is what prompted some women to participate in building activities that dress conventions alone would have made difficult. Aroet Hale, who lived in Kirtland as a young child, reported:

> The Prophet required all the Church to Work on the Temple. all that was not on mishons did work all most Constant from the time it was Commenced till it was Completed Some Women & Children Labord and tended mason. One Sister I have forgot the name drove two Yoak of Cattle and haled Rock.[9]

The extent of the women's involvement in the physical construction is not known, but such work complements a more stereotypical pattern of female support for temple construction. Heber C. Kimball later related:

> Women were engaged in spinning and knitting in order to clothe those who were laboring at the building, and the Lord only knows the scenes of poverty, tribulation, and distress which we passed through in order to accomplish this thing. My wife . . . had a hundred pounds of wool, which, with the assistance of a girl, she spun in order to furnish clothing for those engaged in the building of the Temple. . . . almost all the sisters in Kirtland labored in knitting, sewing, spinning, &c., for the purpose of forwarding the work of the Lord, while we went up to Missouri to endeavor to reinstate our brethren on their lands, from which they had been driven.[10]

These activities were probably only part of the support given by women. One strongly suspects that tending gardens, milking cows, and doing other farm chores also fell largely to them, not only during the absence of Zion's Camp, but also after its homecoming, when the men turned their attention to temple construction. As Heber C. Kimball reports, the women did "all kinds of work; they were just as busy as any of us, and I say that those women have borne the heat and burden of those early and trying days and God will bless them for evermore."[11]

Another consequence of the departure of Zion's Camp was that the building site could not be closely supervised by the three to whom the plan had been revealed nor could changes be preapproved, although Sidney Rigdon was present in Kirtland during the summer of 1834. Workers did modify the basic pattern as set down for the Independence Temple. The existing doorways on the Kirtland Temple feature raised elliptical panels instead of the rectangular ones drawn by Williams for the Independence Temple (compare fig. 4-1 with fig. 2-7). Although the elliptical fanlight above the door was very common in American building practice, elliptical panels on doors are not found in northeast Ohio or in New England but are found in Canada. One such Canadian example is found on the rubblework, stucco-covered

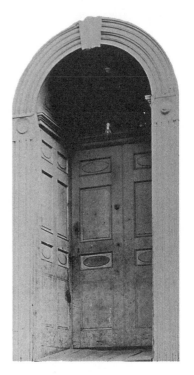

**4-1.** Raised elliptical panels on entrance door, Kirtland Temple. Elliptical panels are a feature found in Canada (fig. 4-2) but not in Ohio or New England. Photo by author.

**4-2.** Detail of entrance door, L'Assomption, Quebec, from Frary, *Early American Doorways*, 1937. Note the raised elliptical panels.

church of L'Assomption, Quebec (fig. 4-2).[12] The use of a Canadian building motif in the Kirtland Temple can probably be attributed to Artemus Millett.

To increase the temple's aesthetic appeal, Millett made other alterations to the exterior design of the temple, changes that differ from the Independence Temple drawings. Apparently not feeling the need for additional lighting in the vestibule, he eliminated the sidelights, or narrow windows flanking the doorways. He followed traditional architectural convention and replaced the "Gothic tops" prescribed for the doors in the Independence Temple drawings with elliptical ones. This decision remedied the awkwardness of the pointed Gothic arches above the wide doors and even wider "Venetian" windows without radically altering the existing design.

Most of these decisions regarding the form of the doors, the width of the masonry openings for the doors, and the location of the windows were made during the summer when Joseph Smith and the main body of the Mormon work force were absent from Kirtland. The faithful service of the temple workers during his absence must have been especially gratifying to the Prophet. Ira Ames's journal statement succinctly sums up the situation: "And when Joseph returned from Missouri he praised us much for our diligence."[13]

## Completion of the Walls and Roof

The return of Zion's Camp in the summer of 1834 made available the work force necessary to make substantial progress on the building. As he had done during the fall of 1833, Joseph Smith personally labored in the quarries, where he also acted as foreman:

> When we arrived in Kirtland, Joseph said, "Come, brethren, let us go into the stone-quarry and work for the Lord." And the Prophet went himself, in his tow frock and tow breeches, and worked at quarrying stone like the rest of us.[14]

In his diary, Joseph Smith wrote that he was acting "as foreman in the Temple stone quarry, and when other duties would permit, labored with my own hands."[15] This personal attention to construction indicates the priority placed on the temple's completion. About five hundred tons of stone had been required to build the foundation and start on the walls of the temple. To finish the walls, the Saints needed to haul about double that amount to the site. Consequently, working the quarries and hauling stone were high priorities during the fall months.

As the walls of the temple rose during the fall, large numbers of workers would have been necessary. Accounts of the construction make no mention of cranes or pulleys, and the poverty-stricken Saints probably had to get along without them. The use of cranes could be avoided by employing large numbers of workers for lifting and by using each floor as a staging area for the next higher level. For example, placement of the main girders supporting the upper court floor would have required many workers and ropes. The fifty-five-foot girders weigh just over one ton and would require about fifteen men lifting approximately 150 pounds each to maneuver the girders around the site (fig. 4-3). These girders had to be lifted twenty-two feet from floor to floor, thus the need for temporary staging for workers and levers. Manpower did not require "hard money" as did equipment, and the lumber used for staging could be reused in other areas.

Such endeavors would also require careful coordination in order to avoid injury. Additional safety could be provided by tying ropes to each end of the girder and passing them over the top of the masonry wall. Draft animals on the ground could hold the girder in place using the friction of the rope as it passed over the wall as a safety brake.

As the height of the walls increased, the scaffolding enclosing the building had to keep pace. Scaffolding was usually constructed of long vertical poles that were too thin to turn into usable planking. These poles were lashed together level by level as needed. Of all the construction site dangers, scaffolding presented the greatest to workers, as Millett himself well knew; he had previously experienced several accidents involving falling from a building or being struck by stones dropped by a co-worker from the scaffolding, accidents that were so serious "my life was despaired of."[16] Millett's son Joseph

**4-3.** Masonry wall above the upper-court ceiling and below the attic-office floor, one of the few places in the temple where the roughly shaped sand-stone blocks can be seen.

Photo by author.

recalled that "when Artemus Millett was working on the Kirtland Temple he fell from off the top of the Temple down in a pile of rocks and broke his sholder blade. but kept on working. I can remember it was bigger than the other[.] one Side was natural. a hump on the other."[17] In addition, another observer reported, "I think it was Father Fisher, who, by some accident, fell from the scaffold, and was disabled for performing manual labor."[18] Such mishaps were part of the hazards of nineteenth-century construction sites.

## Contrasting Upper- and Lower-Court Girders

Construction apparently proceeded steadily, for by February 1835, the walls were "up to the square," and the roof was being put on.[19] Therefore, the walls must have reached the level of the upper court by about November 1834. Consequently, the girders supporting the upper court would have been placed at that time, and those supporting the attic office on the top of the masonry wall would have been placed in January or February. Although similar in size and hewn from the same species of wood, the upper and lower sets of girders show some unusual differences, suggesting that, consistent with the influx of new Church members and the practice of calling men on missions, personnel on the job site had shifted.

In contrast to the roughly finished girders supporting the lower-court floor (see chapter 3), the girders supporting the upper-court and attic-office levels are more skillfully worked and are oriented properly. These girders were more carefully selected for freedom from defects, an important factor that can make the timbers twice as strong as those with many knots and checks. The upper girders are more carefully adzed and have depths that average roughly between 13 1/2 and 14 inches as opposed to the 9-inch depths on the lower girders. Although the depths of the girders supporting the two courts differ by only a few inches, the strength of a rectangular beam is proportional to the cube of its depth, meaning that just a few inches (or fractions of inches) can result in significantly different strengths. Selected and hewn under Millett's supervision, the girders supporting the upper-court floor demonstrate his good intuitive feel for structure. The girders also demonstrate that his experience and resultant skill exceeded that of Reynolds Cahoon and Jacob Bump, the supervisors of the lower-floor girders.

Millett's first critical decision regarding these girders was to make them continuous. Like the girders supporting the lower-court floor, Millett's girders span fifty-five feet between the masonry walls and are supported by wooden columns at two intermediate locations. The locations of the supports result in spans of about fifteen, twenty-five, then fifteen feet. Although three separate girders would have been easier to find, prepare, transport, and hoist into place, discontinuous girders would never have developed sufficient strength to support the expected loads. Continuous girders resist bending not only at the center of the span, but also at the supports. This resistance spreads the bending stresses across a greater portion of the girder, thereby increasing the load it can safely carry. In addition, the upper girders are fitted at the interior supports with knee braces (fig. 4-4) that significantly

**4-4.** Detail of structure showing knee braces supporting the girders under the upper-court floor. The photograph was taken in the interstitial space between the ceiling of the lower court and the floor of the upper court. Note the framing for the elliptical ceiling on the left of the photograph. Modern items include stacks of upholstered pads for the wooden benches (lower right), piping for the sprinkler system, and an iron tie rod that was inserted to keep the west wall of the temple from leaning outward.

reduce the high stresses in the girders. These factors bring the girders very close to modern code requirements.

Although the main girders supporting the upper court and attic offices are of like material and are similarly tooled with adzes, the mortises cut into the girders for the joists vary. Likewise, the joist spacing of the attic-office floor differs from that of the upper-court floor, suggesting that different craftsmen under Millett's supervision worked on these different floor systems.

## Mortises and Tenons

After main girders are placed, smaller timbers, or joists, are spaced between them. In the early nineteenth century, builders joined girders and joists using *mortises* (pockets cut into timbers to accept a tongue, or *tenon*). The joint is then secured by drilling a hole through the joint and tightly fastening the tenon into the mortise by driving a peg into the hole. Common practice was followed in the temple construction by using pegs with a slightly polygonal shape so the pegs would jam securely into the round hole. While such connections are effective in tying the structure together, they weaken the timbers considerably by reducing the cross section both of the mortised member, which has a substantial pocket carved out of it, and the tenoned member, which is reduced to a small tongue. Newer construction methods join timbers with spikes or nails, which do not cut through wood fibers, and place joists on top of supporting girders, thereby preserving the full strength of the members.

In the Kirtland Temple, the mortises in the girders are relatively small, minimizing their impact on the strength of the girder. However, the trade-off is that the corresponding tenons are also very small, and in fact many of the joist tenons in the Kirtland Temple are too small to meet modern safety standards.

The considerable variation in mortise and tenon details throughout the temple (fig. 4-5) is a direct result of the work force changing during construction.

The girder-joist connection on the lower-court floor is a mortise cut into the upper half of the girder. This technique was common because the tops of girders are generally in compression. If a tightly fitting tenon is inserted into a mortise in compression, the girder is not weakened substantially, while the tenon is tightly bound in the mortise. However, the multiple-span, continuous girders of the temple have tension areas on the tops of girders at the intermediate supports, and mortises in these areas significantly weaken the girders. Bump and Cahoon, the craftsmen who likely placed these girders, did not make any adjustments to the mortise and tenon system near these intermediate supports, nor did the other craftsmen working on the upper girders. Such a level of structural understanding was well beyond the capabilities of common builders in the 1830s.

The depth of the mortises in the temple's lower girders is roughly equal to half the depth of the joist. This reduction in the cross section of the joist at the connection creates high stresses in the joist at the bottom of the tenon. Several joists in the temple have "failed" by splitting along the length of

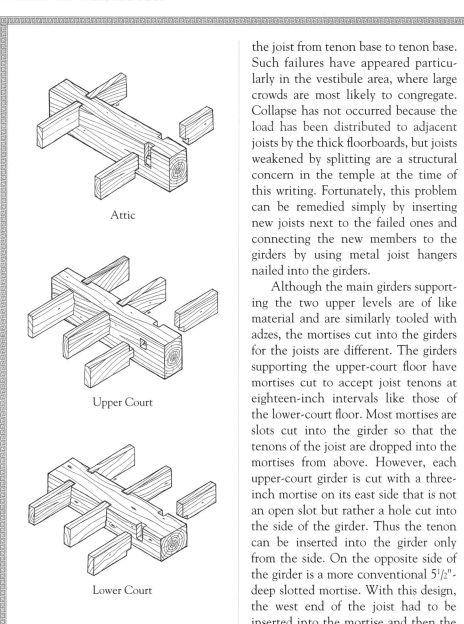

Attic

Upper Court

Lower Court

**4-5.** Detail of mortise-and-tenon joints for the lower-court, upper-court, and attic floors. Note that the tenons of the joists on the east end are extremely small. Also note that the mortises of the attic-office floor are "shouldered"—they have a second, shallow mortise intended to support the joist across its full depth.

the joist from tenon base to tenon base. Such failures have appeared particularly in the vestibule area, where large crowds are most likely to congregate. Collapse has not occurred because the load has been distributed to adjacent joists by the thick floorboards, but joists weakened by splitting are a structural concern in the temple at the time of this writing. Fortunately, this problem can be remedied simply by inserting new joists next to the failed ones and connecting the new members to the girders by using metal joist hangers nailed into the girders.

Although the main girders supporting the two upper levels are of like material and are similarly tooled with adzes, the mortises cut into the girders for the joists are different. The girders supporting the upper-court floor have mortises cut to accept joist tenons at eighteen-inch intervals like those of the lower-court floor. Most mortises are slots cut into the girder so that the tenons of the joist are dropped into the mortises from above. However, each upper-court girder is cut with a three-inch mortise on its east side that is not an open slot but rather a hole cut into the side of the girder. Thus the tenon can be inserted into the girder only from the side. On the opposite side of the girder is a more conventional $5^1/_2$"-deep slotted mortise. With this design, the west end of the joist had to be inserted into the mortise and then the east end dropped into place (fig. 4-6).

Unfortunately, the three-inch tenon on the west side of the joist is woefully inadequate to transfer the weight borne by the joist to the girder. Failure has not occurred because the upper court has not received the intensive use the lower court has, and—at least since their installation—the pews have prevented tightly packed concentrations of people such as occur in the vestibule area. However, this problem, too, is easily remedied by placing new joist hangers at the joist ends.

The girders supporting the attic-office floor are cut with simpler mortises $5^1/2''$ deep that are also stronger as far as the joists are concerned. These mortises are cut to accept a shouldered tenon on the joist, meaning that a shallow recess is cut into the girder the full depth of the joist. This shoulder supports the joist and thereby originally aided in shear transfer. Timber shrinkage has pulled many of the joists out of the shallow pocket so that they are no longer effective. But the two-pocket system does demonstrate the greater technological sophistication of the craftsman directing this work.

Unfortunately, technological sophistication does not necessarily accompany greater structural understanding; for example, the joists of the attic floor are spaced at every thirty-six inches instead of eighteen inches as on the lower two floors. This spacing effectively doubles the potential load on the joists, resulting in a floor half as strong and (from the viewpoint of modern codes) potentially unsafe. At the time of this writing, large groups have been excluded from the attic offices pending the insertion of additional joists to safely support the floor. Again, collapse has not occurred because large, tightly packed groups of people rarely congregate in the attic. The lively attic-office floor, which deflects and vibrates under foot, probably warned occupants to moderate the loads placed on it.

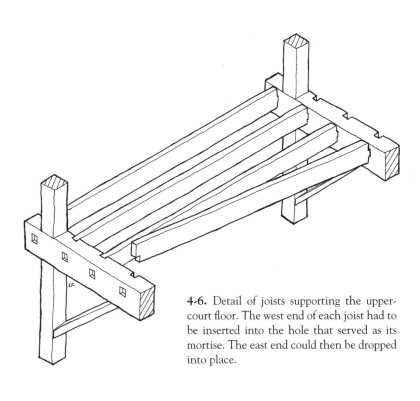

**4-6.** Detail of joists supporting the upper-court floor. The west end of each joist had to be inserted into the hole that served as its mortise. The east end could then be dropped into place.

# The Attic

Begun in February 1835, the roof structure uses a variation of the king-post truss (fig. 3-10 and glossary) and is from the same wood species, probably black walnut, that is used in the timbers in the lower court. Coinciding with the bays of the supporting columns, the trusses are contained in the walls that divide the attic into five separate offices. Although not mentioned in the specifications for the Independence Temple, the attic offices take advantage of the considerable space under the roof and between the roof trusses (fig. 4-7). No corridor

Photo by author.

**4-7.** Western office used by Joseph Smith, Kirtland Temple. The doors and windows on the interior wall are placed between the posts and diagonals of the roof truss.

joins the offices; rather, one has to walk through each of the offices in turn to access the westernmost office (fig. 4-8). This "shotgun" arrangement of spaces was not unusual in the nineteenth century, and it allowed for the maximum amount of floor space and light in each of the rooms. Joseph Smith and his counselors probably did not anticipate the large volume of space available under the roof since their previous experience was with smaller residential structures. The five large attic offices provided more than adequate space for the relatively small Church leadership, and plans for a separate structure for printing and other office functions were dropped (see D&C 94).

An unusual feature is the windows in the interior walls that divide the offices. The outer offices are lit by dormers. To help light the central offices when the doors between offices are closed, windows are fit between the diagonals of the roof trusses (as are the doors). Because of the manner the doorways and windows communicate between the rooms, the heavy structural members that support the roof are inconspicuous. Note that careful coordination was required to determine the location of the openings through the truss and of the run of stairs that terminates at the line of doorways (fig. 4-8). The mistakes that occurred during the early stages of construction, such as the awkward junction between the exterior masonry and the wooden structure, are no longer present. Artisans who had sufficient experience to visualize the three-dimensional location of stairs, doorways, and structure were now in control of the design.

## Persecution

After the masonry walls were in place and the roof framing completed, Millett no longer had direct superintendency responsibilities at the job site. Accordingly, in May 1835 he asked for permission to return to Canada to try to collect on debts still owed him. After nearly drowning while disembarking from a boat in the Kingston, Ontario, harbor, Millett collected some debts and sold his property. He then "returned to Kirtland where I continued working on the Temple as much as I could, my leg being occasionally troublesome."[20] Because of his faithful service, Millett was singled out in a special meeting where workers on the temple were given blessings.[21]

**4-8.** Doorways leading through the attic offices, photographed from the top of the vestibule staircase. The staircase is aligned to end where the line of doorways starts.

Photo by author.

As the substantial masonry walls rose above the Chagrin River valley during 1834 and 1835, opposition to the Mormons grew in seemingly proportionate amounts. Perhaps enemies of the Church were encouraged by the mobs in Missouri, who successfully drove out the Mormons without any reprimand by the state or federal government. Or maybe they became suspicious that with Jackson County no longer a possible gathering place the Church would continue gathering in Kirtland. Or perhaps the sight of the temple rising on the bluff symbolized a success that challenged local opposition. Referring to the effects such opposition had on the brethren working on the temple, Lucy Mack Smith later wrote:

> They suffered much from fatigue and uneasiness for as soon as the work was commenced our enemies began to swear that we should not finish it but the brethren were faithful to their charge and they would take turns in watching the walls. . . . but oh how many of those affectionate brethren ~~that spent so many~~ spent days and nights watching ~~by th~~ for the enemy least they should steal into the town unawares and murder the prophet and his counsill and tear down the~~ir~~ foundation of the house but they clung fast by the walls and gave no qu[i]et sleep to their eyes nor peaceful slumber to their eyelid untill they found a place for the Lord an habitation for the mighty God of Jacob.[22]

Heber C. Kimball, a worker on the temple, reported in a similar vein, "Our enemies were raging and threatening destruction upon us, and we had to guard ourselves night after night, and for weeks were not permitted to take off our clothes, and were obliged to lay with our fire locks in our arms."[23] That the temple became the focal point for the Ohio mob's fears and frustrations is only natural given its physical size and dominance of the nineteenth-century agrarian landscape.

According to the reminiscences of those who lived through this period, external pressures strengthened the commitment and resolve of some of the Saints in Kirtland, while driving others away. The increased determination of the faithful in the group compensated for whatever losses in resources the Mormon community suffered from defections.

## Notes

[1]*History of the Church*, 2:40–45.

[2]*History of the Church*, 2:50.

[3]*History of the Church*, 2:64.

[4]Heber C. Kimball, "Speech Delivered," 972.

[5]Ames, Autobiography and Journal.

[6]Doctrine and Covenants 51:16 states that Ohio was to be a gathering place "for a little season, until I, the Lord, shall provide for them otherwise, and command them to go hence." The community at large seems to have been well informed of the intentions of the Saints in Kirtland, for the article "Mormonism" in *Painesville Telegraph*, March 13, 1832, states: "A few, however, who are in lucrative business have a special permit from the prophet to remain [in Kirtland] for four or five years."

[7]Ames was certainly a willing laborer, but he must not have developed into a highly skilled craftsman since he worked through the summer and then eventually moved away from manual work into financial committees.

[8]Hales, *Windows*, 95–96.

[9]Hale, Reminiscences, 4.

[10]Kimball, "Extracts from H. C. Kimball's Journal," 867. Lucy Mack Smith also reported, "Mary ~~Fielding~~ Baily and Agnes coleby was then boarding with me they devoted their whole time to ~~the~~ making and mending clothes for the brethren who worked on the house. There was but one main spring to all our thoughts and that was ~~the~~ building the Lords house." Lucy Mack Smith, "History of Lucy Smith," 191.

[11]Heber C. Kimball, in *Journal of Discourses*, 10:165, April 6, 1863.

[12]See Frary, *Early American Doorways*, 191.

[13]Ames, Autobiography and Journal.

[14]Kimball, in *Journal of Discourses*, 10:165.

[15]*History of the Church*, 2:161.

[16]Artemus Millett, Reminiscences.

[17]Joseph Millet, Record book, 33. Artemus Millett's grandson, Joseph Millet Jr., recalled:

Artemus rezided in Spring Valley untill the Summer of 1872 engaged in Dairying. Assisted his wife Annie in milking cows. making butter & cheese. and raising chickens. and he done some mason work helping to build chimneys & etc. Tho not able to do any heavy lifting, as he had been badly crippled up in his younger days. had his back (& sevral rebbs) broken, one arm and one leg, While working on The Kirtland Temple. and was healed by faith. by the Prophet Joseph Smith & foot mashed, altho he did do much hard work, Principly Masoning & plastering and some carpenter work and gardening and basket making. he learned me how to mix mortar and to lay rocks, & told me mutch about his work on the Kirtland and Nauvoo Temples & how he made the hard finnish he put on them. (Joseph Millet, "Millet on C B Island," 3)

[18]Daniel Tyler, "Temples," 283.

[19]Young to Harvey, November 16, 1880.

[20]Artemus Millett, Reminiscences.

[21]*History of the Church,* 2:205. Note that the typescript copy of Millett's journal says that he returned to Canada in 1833, but that date must be in error, for he arrived in Kirtland only in October of 1834. The most logical date is 1835, since the masonry walls would have been completed in May and his presence would not be needed.

[22]Lucy Mack Smith, "History of Lucy Smith," 190. See also the edited version of this account, *History of Joseph Smith,* 231.

[23]Kimball, "Extracts from H. C. Kimball's Journal," 771. Although no record exists of individuals preventing building materials from reaching the temple site, George A. Smith recorded:

In the spring of 1835, a majority of the inhabitants of Kirtland combined together and warned all the Saints to leave town. This was done to prevent any of our people becoming a town charge in case of poverty. They then bought up all the grain that was for sale in the country around, and refused to sell a particle of it to our people. (George Smith, "Memoirs," 25)

# Chapter 5

# Interior and Finishing Work, 1835–1836

With the completion of the roof, interior woodworking began in earnest. During the fall and winter of 1834–35, workers had been busy felling timbers for seasoning while craftsmen drew detailed plans for implementing the rough outline of pews and pulpits indicated by Joseph Smith and his associates. Skilled workers in wood relied on previous building experience and carpenter's manuals to work out spatial and ornamental details and create a functional interior of distinctive beauty.

One of the first impressions one receives of the temple's interior is the expansive volume of the lower court. Coupled with the white reflective surfaces, the relatively large number of windows on all sides of the room introduces a great deal of soft, even light into the space. The elliptical vault in the ceiling immediately draws attention to the western pulpits and window, and the intricate carving on both the pulpits and the arch framing the west windows provides a visual focal point for the room (figs. 5-1, 5-2). Only after entering the center of the room is one fully aware of the tiers of pulpits on the east wall that step down into the space symmetrically. Along with the raised seating for the choir to each side, the pulpits create a sense of enclosure for those seated in the pews. This arrangement heightens the worshipful quality of the space by creating a feeling of removal from the world outside.

## Jacob Bump and the Lower Court

Much of the preliminary work on the interior of the temple and the design of the decorative motifs in the lower court should be credited to Jacob Bump. He, like Millett, was singled out for a special blessing in the March 1835 service for workers. Christopher Crary, an old Ohio settler who watched the Church come and go in Kirtland, credits Bump with the design and construction of the entire structure.[1] Though documents make it clear that Crary exaggerated the role of his longtime friend, Bump was indeed one of the most important craftsmen involved with the construction.

**5-1.** West interior
of the lower court
as it looks when
naturally lit.

Photo by author.

Bump's primary skills must have been limited to joinery and plastering, since the foundation and the girders supporting the lower court floor, which he and Reynolds Cahoon superintended, were inadequate for the size of the temple structure.[2] Not surprisingly, Bump's work previous to his arrival in Kirtland was limited to smaller residential-scale construction.[2] As Bump stayed in Kirtland during the march

## Carpenter's Manuals

Carpenter's manuals, also called pattern books, were an important part of nineteenth-century American artisans' equipment. Popular first in England, such manuals gave rules of thumb for structural design, explained principles of geometry, and showed how to build out of simple plank lumber ornate classical elements (columns, capitals, entablatures) originally intended for stone construction. Some American carpenters recognized the potential market for such manuals, and in 1797, Asher Benjamin published the first of seven pattern books that would make him one of the most popular American carpenter-authors.

The popularity of different pattern books tended to follow geographic lines. For example, as a New Englander, Benjamin was popular with other Yankees, and New England emigrants coming to the Connecticut Western Reserve brought his carpenter's manuals with them. On the other hand, Minard Lefever, another American writer of carpenter's manuals, was popular in central New York. Lefever's influence was rather small in the Western Reserve, but following general settlement patterns, variants on his designs are commonly found in southern Ohio. A number of pattern books were available for sale in the Kirtland vicinity, with Benjamin and Englishman Peter Nicholson being popular authors.[1]

[1]"NEW GOODS, JUST received at the Painesville Book Store, and for sale very low. . . . House Carpenters Guide. . . . Nicholsons Mechanic's companion, do operative Mechanic. . . . House Painters Guide." *Painesville Telegraph,* July 5, 1832, 3.

Courtesy Library of Congress.

**5-2.** West window and pulpits, lower court, Kirtland Temple, photographed April 1934 by Carl F. Waite. Flanking the pulpits are an organ and sacrament (communion) table, which have since been removed.

of Zion's Camp, he and Millett probably spent a good deal of time going over detailed plans and coordinating efforts between the masonry exterior and the wooden interior. Bump's later comments recorded in Millett's son's journal indicate the two men became good friends and respected each other's abilities.[3]

Bump and other skilled workers on the Kirtland Temple followed the general practice of American builders in freely using carpenter's manuals to develop designs and architectural ornament. Builders commonly combined elements from several different pattern books or changed elements intended for a particular usage or scale to fit the situation at hand. Kirtland Temple craftsmen followed these practices as they took a verbal description and plan outline for the interior and gave them three-dimensional form.

By the fall of 1834, Bump must have been busily engaged in seasoning timbers and obtaining molding planes for the woodwork in the temple. The multiple tiers of pulpits allowed for considerable standardization since the basic curved "stand," or pulpit, is replicated eighteen times in the lower floor and thirty-two of the windows share an identical design. Bump must have made a number of sketches to work out joinery details and compute quantities of lumber and molding profiles before the roof was completed. In fact, some interior ornament could have been produced earlier in the nearby mechanic's hall and set aside for later installation. However, a great deal of the work was done in the lower court, as a visitor to the temple in 1835 recorded: "The

**5-3.** Pulpits and west window, lower court. Fringed covers on the pulpits covered the graffiti-scarred tops until their sanding and refinishing in the 1960s. The upper arch is composed of egg-and-dart, bead-and-lozenge, and running-guilloche moldings. The lower arch has opposed Vitruvian scrolls and a series of transversely oriented half-round moldings. Photographed by Carl F. Waite, April 1934.

center pews only were finished, outside of these were the workmens benches the only seats we found. The floor was covered with shavings."[4]

The focal point of the lower-court interior is the great window behind the west pulpits (fig. 5-3). The upper arch of this window is formed from decoratively carved molding derived from classical precedents, with ornaments including a running guilloche, plain band, bead and lozenge, and egg and dart. The deeply carved molding and plastic curves of these ornaments are typical of Bump's style. The wide range of stylistic

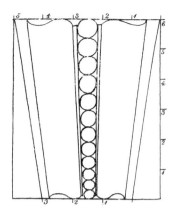

**5-4.** Possible pattern from which the beaded keystone of the west window, lower court, was adapted. Detail from plate 31, Benjamin, *American Builder's Companion*, 1806.

sources is also typical of Bump, a mature craftsman with years of experience. Each of these motifs is found in many pattern books, and identifying an individual source for the design would be virtually impossible were it not for the unusual beaded keystone placed in the center of the arch. These beads seem to be adapted from a design in Benjamin's *American Builder's Companion*, which was published in several editions between 1806 and 1827 (fig. 5-4).[5] Another ornament, the oval medallion with a stylized acanthus leaf divided by a starlike cruciform element on the interior columns in the courts, is also found only in Benjamin's *American Builder's Companion* (figs. 5-5, 5-6). Originally intended to be placed on a doorway, this oval is elongated slightly to fit the proportions of the pillars in the temple. Apparently, temple builders possessed at least one copy of this carpenter's manual.

Other decorative elements of the lower court reveal the particular edition of *The American Builder's Companion* that workers used. The lower arch framing the west window has a band of widely spaced reeds topped by opposing scrolls that appear to have been derived from the more common Vitruvian scroll. One of the few American sources for a Vitruvian scroll is *The American Builder's Companion*, plate 40 of the first (1806) edition (fig. 5-7);[6] this scroll was not included in later editions. The use of this early pattern book in the design of the interior of the lower court is consistent with Bump's age, as the 1806 *American Builder's Companion* would have been new when he apprenticed, a time he might have been purchasing reference materials for use in his career.

The pulpits share the same general articulation as the windows and pillars in that they are ornamented with fluted pilasters; a simple, Doric-like capital; a frieze with a running guilloche; and a dentiled cornice (fig. 5-3). A standard entablature, the horizontal element placed on a column or pilaster, would have looked too heavy on the relatively small-scale pulpits, and so Bump eliminated the architrave, or lowest section, that is normally prescribed by classical canon. In addition, Bump reduced the capital to a simple

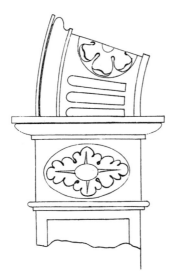

**5-5.** Possible pattern for an ornament on interior columns (compare to fig. 5-6). Detail from plate 30, Benjamin, *American Builder's Companion*, 1806.

**5-6.** Detail of column capital, lower court.

Photo by author.

## Altering Classical Column Forms

The classical orders were the stylistic basis for the architecture of the Georgian, Federal, and Greek Revival periods, the stylistic periods on which the Kirtland Temple was based. Carpenter's manuals taught American builders how to proportion, frame, and assemble in wood the five classical orders: Tuscan, Doric, Ionic, Corinthian, and Composite. However, in practice the latter two orders were too ornate and complicated for most American builders and were rarely used. And since the Tuscan order is largely an unfluted version of the Doric order, the distinction vanished when these forms were abstracted and simplified by American builders. Hence, the primary orders used in American practice were the Doric and Ionic.

As used by the Greeks, Doric and Ionic columns consist of a column shaft and a capital (the widened portion on top of the column shaft). On top of the column shaft and capital sits the entablature, a horizontal lintel composed of three parts: the architrave, frieze, and cornice. The Romans adopted the Greek system of the orders, but oftentimes used the columns not as freestanding elements, but rather as rounded attachments to wall surfaces. These half-columns placed on wall surfaces are called engaged columns. Another variation was the pilaster, a flattened version of the engaged column. Pilasters were most popular with American craftsmen, as they were easily formed from sawed planks of lumber.

**5-7.** Detail showing Vitruvian scrolls, from plate 40, Benjamin, *American Builder's Companion*, 1806, one of the few American sources for this ornament.

series of moldings supported by double reeds and rosettes. The three tiers of triple pulpits are well executed, and the manner in which the doors to the pulpits are cut to accommodate the radius of the swing testifies to the skill of Bump and his workers (fig. 5-8).

Bump also modified standard elements in the piers that support the lower-court ceiling. These eight fluted piers have simple Doric capitals. Each capital is capped by discontinuous sections of an Ionic architrave and frieze, with an Ionic cornice running the length of the room defining the edge of the plaster vaulted ceiling.

The practice of mixing Doric and Ionic elements is common in early American building practice, as is the practice of including only small sections of the architraves and friezes. The academically correct classical column is topped with an entablature composed of an architrave, frieze, and cornice. This arrangement works well for the proportion and scale of Greek temples, but when classical orders are used in other situations, such as in interior columns or other woodwork, the standard arrangement often has to be altered either to fit within available space or to remain simple enough to complement other elements of the design.[7]

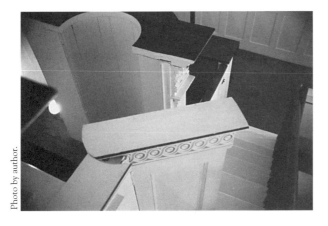

Photo by author.

**5-8.** The skill of the workers is shown in the way this pulpit door is cut to provide clearance for the door to swing. Lower court, Kirtland Temple.

In this instance, Bump had several reasons for changing the standard classical arrangement. One reason was to keep the capitals on the supporting piers at the same height as those on the pilasters supporting the decorative arch above the big west window. Another reason was to make as simple a transition as possible from the flat ceiling over the side aisles to the elliptical ceiling. Inserting full architraves and friezes above the interior columns would raise the level of the elliptical ceiling's springing, raising the height of the temple another four feet. Finally, the height of a classical column is proportionate to its base diameter; in other words, the width of the column must change with its height. However, architects can "adjust" this system by either placing a column on a pedestal or, as in the Kirtland Temple, by inserting pieces of an architrave and frieze on top of the capital. Using these devices, Bump designed an interior that followed (more or less) accepted rules of design while still fitting within the predetermined structure and walls.

## Truman Angell and the Upper Court

The east window in the lower court (fig. 5-9) presents a sharp contrast to Jacob Bump's deeply carved, plastically molded ornament on the lower court's west window. Bump's west-window moldings are formed from simple, but bold, half-round projections and recessions that are formed from a set of

**5-9.** East window, lower court. Light from the exterior window, visible through the fanlight, was a source of illumination for the lower court.

Photo by author.

inner moldings

(a)

(b)

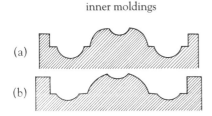

inner moldings

(a)

(b)

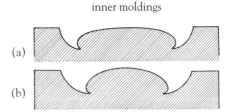

outer moldings

(a)

(b)

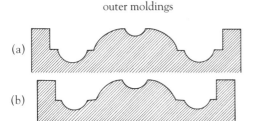

outer moldings

(a)

(b)

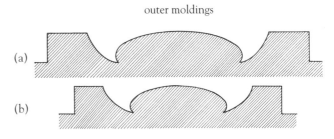

**5-10.** Cross-section profiles, shown at 25 percent, west windows, upper court (a) and lower court (b).

**5-11.** Cross-section profiles, shown at 25 percent, east windows, upper court (a) and lower court (b).

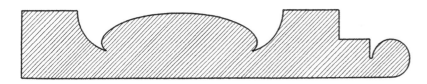

**5-12.** Molding profile. Plate 47, from Benjamin, *Practical House Carpenter*, 1830. Compare to fig. 5-11.

two molding planes that cut simple circular grooves into the wood (fig. 5-10), while the east-window moldings are wide, flattened, elliptical shapes whose curvature is far more complex (fig. 5-11). These latter moldings are taken directly from another of Asher Benjamin's books, *The Practical House Carpenter*, published in 1830 (fig. 5-12). Instead of classical ornaments (guilloche, egg-and-dart, Vitruvian scroll, etc.), the east window has simple, diamond-shaped insets of reeds flanked by fillet moldings set into the flattened curve of the elliptical molding. The east window's keystone is a perforated box, diametrically opposed to the plastically carved, beaded keystone to the west (fig. 5-13). This east window, which differs stylistically from the rest of the lower room and which shares a similar architrave molding as the window in the upper room, is the work of Truman Angell, who later worked on the Nauvoo and Salt Lake Temples. Though the upper and lower courts follow a similar layout, many ornamental details in the upper court are abstractions or simplifications of more-ornate elements found in the lower court.

The abrupt change in style in the lower-court interior occurred because of Bump's "open rebellion" against Joseph Smith in August 1835.[8] It

Photo by author.

**5-13.** Keystone with perforated-box ornament, east window, lower court. Compare to the west window keystone, fig. 5-3.

must have been yet another serious setback for Joseph Smith and the building committee to have one of their chief carpenters leave the group, especially since Bump's absence coincided with the period of greatest building activity on the temple. Since skilled workers were few in the Mormon community, the fall 1835 arrival of Angell, who had been a carpenter's apprentice and joiner in Providence, Rhode Island, was likely viewed as providential.

In his journal, Angell states that he finished "the second, or middle Hall of the Temple; including the stands &c."[9] One of the distinguishing characteristics of Angell's work in the upper court was his reliance on *The Practical House Carpenter*. Since the book was available locally, several craftsmen may have owned copies. Another factor encouraging the use of *The Practical House Carpenter* was the commercial availability of its moldings. "Benjamin's Mouldings of 1833" were advertised for sale in nearby Portage County in 1835,[10] and with the Ohio Canal operating nearby, such products would have been available in neighboring Geauga County (now Lake County) as well.

## Rush to Complete the Temple

Other defining characteristics of Angell's work on the temple were determined by the rush to complete the temple. During the fall and winter of 1835–36, the Kirtland community rallied together to complete the temple as soon as possible. Temple construction became a work project for those converts arriving in Kirtland without financial resources, and as W. W. Phelps recorded, the number of laborers increased markedly: "Very great exertions have been made to finish the House of the Lord this winter. I suppose for the last fortnight, that nearly fifty men, as carpenters and joiners, masons, mortar makers, etc., have been laboring on the house."[11] As more men were put to work on the temple, more unskilled workers were necessarily included in their ranks. Caroline Crosby candidly wrote in her autobiography, "My husband worked 3 months on the temple before it was dedicated, which was nearly the first he had ever done at the business."[12]

The men working on the temple had personal reasons for desiring its speedy completion. A number of them had left their families elsewhere, likely to avoid Kirtland's cost of living, which was extremely high due to land speculation following the completion of the Ohio Canal. Others were in Kirtland only temporarily, called there by Joseph Smith. For example, W. W. Phelps wrote to his wife, Sally, whom he had left behind in Missouri, "Don't reckon too much on my coming home in the spring. You may not see me until a little later. Keep up your faith and pray for the endowment. As soon as that takes place, the Elders will anxiously speed toward their families."[13]

Thus the great push to finish the structure was motivated not only by impatience, but also by the desire to receive the "endowment," or blessing, the Lord had promised upon completion of the structure. This promise was first mentioned in 1831, when the Saints were commanded through Joseph Smith to "go to the Ohio . . . and there you shall be endowed with power from on high" (D&C 38:32).[14] Three years later, while Joseph Smith was undoubtedly preoccupied with Zion's Camp, he received the instruction that "the first elders of my church should receive their endowment from on high in my house, which I have commanded to be built unto my name in the land of Kirtland" (D&C 105:33). The Saints were naturally anxious to receive such a bestowal of God's presence and power.

Hastening the completion of the temple involved simplifying in the upper court (fig. 5-14) many of the elements found in the lower court. Workers formed most of the upper floor's ornament by nailing on strips of wood instead of carving into the base material as was done in the lower court. A good example of this ornamentation technique is found in the piers supporting the ceiling in the upper court. These are not fluted as in the lower story but are decorated with a fret variation of strips of wood nailed to the plank, as shown in Benjamin's *Practical House Carpenter* (figs. 5-15, 5-16). Likewise, the pulpits on the upper story do not have fluted pilasters but rather have applied reeds. The reeding technique was widely used in New England in the first decade of the nineteenth century and was used in the Western Reserve area as well.[15] Nailing strips of wood to the planks is far easier than carving the long, deep flutes used on the lower story and resulted in significant savings of time.

Of course, it could be that Bump owned the molding planes used to produce the flutes in the lower court, and interior ornament in the upper court may have been changed to avoid purchasing additional tools in the

**5-14.** Pulpit-to-pulpit view, upper court, facing west. Photographed by Carl F. Waite, April 1934.

wake of Bump's departure. However, the reliance on a different pattern book and aesthetic suggests that the different design traditions of the respective craftsmen in charge of the lower and upper courts and the rush to complete the temple were the primary reasons for the change in architectural ornament.

The use of the applied reeding in the upper room also indicates that many workers were not skilled joiners. While the fluted ornamentation in the lower court and the reeds used on the upper court produce similar visual effects of light and shadow, reeding can be done by a worker with little skill. This shift in technique allowed skilled craftsmen like Angell to direct many other workers, accelerating progress on temple construction.

The pulpits built by Angell in the upper court follow the general arrangement of Bump's pulpits in the lower court but are simplified to accommodate unskilled workers and a hurried schedule. Their ornamentation is loosely derived from Benjamin's design for a pulpit in *The Practical House Carpenter* (fig. 5-17). Spiral frets top each of the vertical supports, and

**5-15.** Illustration of fret moldings. Plate 28, from Benjamin, *Practical House Carpenter*, 1830. Compare to fig. 5-16.

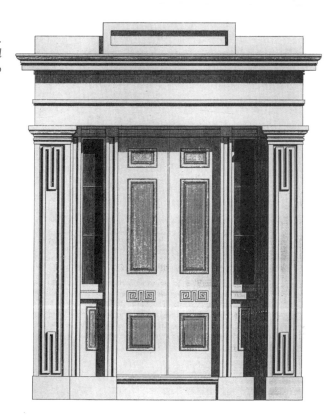

although reeded pilasters are substituted for the molding profiles in Benjamin's design, his molding profiles are used in the window architraves immediately behind the pulpit. The two upper ranges of pulpits are also simplified because the rise from stand to stand is not as great and there is very little of the pulpit body that extends above the back of the bench below (fig. 5-18). By changing the height of the pulpits and rise of the stands, Angell eliminated a significant amount of joinery. Additional savings were realized by eliminating the doors leading into the pulpits. This practical approach to design by Angell, however, does not mean that he was incapable of more intricate work. His east window above the pulpits, for example, has a single arch with a carved running-vine motif that is gracefully handled (fig. 5-19).

The most common decorative motif used throughout the temple is the Greek fret. Frets are easily formed from pieces of sawed lumber and do not require a high level of skill to produce. Greek frets are published most extensively in eighteenth-century English pattern books by authors such as Gibbs, Langley, and Paine. Exact copies of many of these frets are found in the temple, but so many different pattern books illustrate them that identifying a single source is not possible.[16] On the other hand, some of the frets in the temple seem to be unique compositions created by the builders, who at times added additional loops to the frets (fig. 5-20) and at other times expanded square forms to a rectangular format by inserting an additional horizontal run to the frets (fig. 5-21).

**5-16.** Detail of pier, upper court, with fret ornamentation similar to that illustrated in *Practical House Carpenter*. Nailing strips of wood to the plank instead of carving the design saved considerable time and effort.

Photo by author.

**5-17.** Design for a pulpit, plate 63, from Benjamin, *Practical House Carpenter*, 1830. The ornament for the pulpits in the upper court was adapted from this design. Compare fig. 5-18.

**5-18.** Detail of pulpits in the upper court, photographed April 1934 by Carl F. Waite. Simplified versions of the pulpits in the lower court, these pulpits have no entry doors and a reduced rise from stand to stand.

**5-19.** An arch with an intricate, carved, running-vine motif. East window, upper court. Designed by Truman Angell.

**5-20.** Greek fret composed of two spirals topped by an additional loop. Located at the springing of the arch over the west window, upper court. Compare the moldings to fig. 5-10.

**5-21.** Two Greek frets on the east window, upper court. Note how the more common fret on the left has been modified on the right by extending it to a rectangular format, creating a new diagonal axis through the design. Compare the moldings to fig. 5-11.

**5-22.** East gable end and tower of the Kirtland Temple showing simplified mutule beds on the raking cornice of the gable and properly formed mutule beds on the cornice of the tower. Photographed early 1993.

## Exterior Ornament

As with interior details, the exterior ornament on the gable ends and tower shows the influence of different artisans who worked to complete the job as efficiently as possible. Although some of the wooden ornament on the cornice and tower is probably original, all the wooden siding on the gable ends has now been replaced. In the gable, the mutule beds (the square blocks attached to the underside of the projecting cornice) show a shortcut technique of drilling holes into a block of wood (fig. 5-22) instead of laboriously fitting pegs as was done in Greek architecture. The artisan who built the gable was familiar with common building tradition and did not rely on pattern books. He knew that since these mutule beds were about fifty feet above ground, a few hours' work with a saw and auger would look nearly the same as several days' work turning the pegs on a lathe, then fastening them into their bases, then building the enclosing box around them. The "homespun" training of this builder is further evidenced by the small windows in the west pediment, which have a small rosette in each corner, a motif found locally in the Western Reserve (figs. 5-23 and 5-24).[17] The identity of the craftsman who worked on the gables is not immediately clear. Millett may have been directly involved, although his direct superintendency seems to have ended with the completion of

**5-23.** Rosette motif on doorway in Bloomfield, Ohio. From Frary, *Early American Doorways*, 1937.

**5-24.** Rosette motif on window in west gable, Kirtland Temple. Compare to fig. 5-23.

**5-25.** Tower and belfry, photographed from the west. Photographed early 1993.

Photo by author.

the masonry walls. Another possibility is John Corrill, who directed the work in late 1835,[18] although his written history suggests that his primary involvement was supervisory and not design related.[19]

In contrast to the simplified decorative elements found on the gables, the tower and belfry have properly formed classical elements taken from pattern books (fig. 5-25). The overall design of the square base and octagonal belfry stems from the New England tradition of forming church towers from superimposed classical temple forms.[20] This tower is similar to scores of other church towers, one notable example being Charles Bullfinch's Congregational Church in Pittsfield, Massachusetts, which has an open, circular, classical tower on a square base.[21] Instead of a crude slab of wood drilled with a grid of holes as found in the gable ends, the mutule beds on the tower have individual pegs set into a box, exactly as illustrated in pattern books. In addition the entablature below the cornice of the tower has the properly formed classic triglyphs (three slots carved into a wooden block) and metopes (the flat spaces between them) derived from Greek Doric temples as found in the pattern books. The Ionic pilasters on the upper stage are a crude adaptation of the Roman Ionic order found in many pattern books, including *The Practical House Carpenter* (figs. 5-26 and 5-27). Typical of American practice, the spiral volutes are etched in a flat plank of wood instead of carved from a solid block.

One of the more interesting details of the tower is the awkward use of a quarter-round egg-and-dart molding just below the spiral volutes. Quarter-round moldings, which in cross section are one quadrant of a circle, are normally used at overhangs to make the transition between vertical and horizontal surfaces. In locations without an overhang, such as under the spiral volutes, a half-round molding, with the circular profile facing outward and the flat surface on the back, is normally used. This unusual use of quarter-round moldings implies that the builders used leftover pieces of precut

**5-26.** Illustration of Roman Ionic capital, plate 9, from Benjamin, *Practical House Carpenter*, 1830.

**5-27.** Belfry capital adapted from the Roman Ionic order. Compare to fig. 5-26.

Photo by author.

moldings in this lofty location where no one would notice the difference. As precut moldings were available for sale in the vicinity, these and other intricate moldings were presumably purchased.

The design of the dormers shares with the tower a dependence upon pattern books. However, instead of incorporating just a few details from the manuals, the entire dormer design is copied directly from Benjamin's *Practical House Carpenter* (figs. 5-28 and 5-29). Although Truman Angell depended heavily on Benjamin's pattern books for his design work, he was not necessarily responsible for designing the dormers. He would have had plenty of work to do finishing up the pulpits and, being a young man, was never part of the administrative leadership in the construction. Since the pattern books were widely available and since Angell was not the only one capable of following pattern book details, responsibility for designing the dormers could have fallen to any of a number of workers.

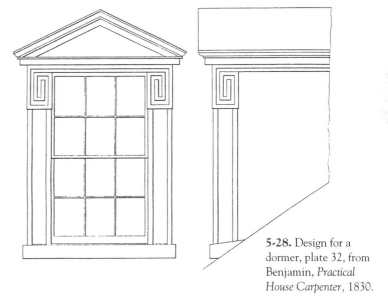

**5-28.** Design for a dormer, plate 32, from Benjamin, *Practical House Carpenter*, 1830.

**5-29.** Kirtland Temple dormer. The design was copied directly from *Practical House Carpenter*. Compare to fig. 5-28.

Photo by author.

## Final Finishing Work

A milestone in the construction of the temple was the installation of the windows in November 1835 by Brigham and Joseph Young. Brigham Young was a carpenter, painter, and glazier before coming to Ohio, and he did some carpentry in Kirtland as well.[22] The two brothers built the frames and installed and glazed the original windows, which are currently stored in the basement of the temple (fig. 5-30).[23] These windows show typical construction techniques of the 1830s, with the mullions and sashes joined by small mortise and tenon connections. The Young brothers were highly skilled craftsmen: the curved mullions and frames of the Gothic windows and the elliptical shapes in the windows on the facades must have been difficult to produce with simple hand planes.

Photo by author.

**5-30.** The original windows, which are currently in storage. The windows were made by Brigham and Joseph Young.

Once the windows were in place, the building fabric was weathertight, and final finishing work could begin in earnest. Jacob Bump was given the contract to plaster the interior for fifteen hundred dollars. Curiously, Bump's continuing disaffection with Joseph Smith did not permanently end his work on the building.[24] He was given the contract probably because no one else possessed the skill he did. Bump began plastering the interior on November 9, 1835, and worked steadily despite inclement weather.[25] Apparently, he built fires in the earthen crawl space below the lower-court floor to hasten the drying of the plaster, which would otherwise have taken weeks in the cold temperatures of November. Despite this advantage, such fires presented danger and no doubt were a source of much dirty soot. A solution was found, described by W. W. Phelps:

> The committee has made a contract with a man to warm the house until the 1st of April. Four stoves are placed in the cellar and they heat twelve cylinders, four on the court for the sacrament, four in the court for the school ~~for~~ of the Apostles and four in the attic school rooms. If this plan works well, it will save wood and save trouble as to fires. Again it will be of great service to warm the house for the men ~~that~~ who work on it this winter.[26]

Unfortunately, warming fires could not help Artemus Millett, Lorenzo Young, and their crew of young men who stuccoed the exterior of the temple beginning on November 2, 1835, and finishing on January 8, 1836.[27] Despite the difficulty of working outside in winter, they produced a durable finish. Workers mixed broken glassware into the finish coat of the exterior to make it glisten in the sun. Millett stated that the mixture for the stucco covering was inspired.[28] Whether he was referring to the inclusion of glassware and crockery or of weather-resistant natural cements that had recently been discovered and used in building the nearby Ohio Canal is not clear. In any event, the mixture he used was new to him and lasted (with repairs) until 1955.

Later tradition states that women donated their best glassware and china to be broken up and mixed in the stucco. This belief conflicts with the recollection of the son of Artemus Millett that "Artemus sent men and boys to the different towns and places to gather old crockery and glass to put in the cement."[29] On the other hand, given the importance the building had as a symbol of the Mormon faith and the degree to which the Mormon community sacrificed to build the temple, it would not be out of character for families to select a special piece of glassware or china for inclusion. However many families may have made such contributions, the lion's share of the glassware in the stucco came from discard piles and not parlor shelves.

After Millett and his crew finished applying the "hard finish" to the outside of the temple, Joseph Young painted blue shadow lines to imitate cut-stone masonry.[30] The Saints wished to build a structure that presented a neat and tidy appearance. This aesthetic was also evident on the original roof. Instead of the current split shakes with their rough, irregular texture, the temple roof was originally covered with painted wooden shingles. These were either sawed pine shingles, which were commercially available in the area, or shingles produced locally using a machine patented by one of the early Saints.[31] The paint used to preserve the shingles was probably red lead pigment dissolved in linseed oil, as it was readily available in large quantity and was not prone to fading in sunlight like some pigments.[32] This painted roof, which would have had very little visible texture, would have blended nicely with the regular rhythm of the painted joint lines on the walls.

As the temple neared completion, finished portions were pressed into service. The main rooms were used for Sunday services and for special meetings (such as the one where workers on the temple were blessed) even before workers finished occupying the space.[33] Due to their lack of ornament and carved fittings, the attic offices were finished first. On December 31, 1835, Joseph Smith gave some final directions concerning these offices, designating the west office as his private study. The attic was also used, starting on January 4, 1836, by the School of the Prophets, a group of Church leaders who studied theology, languages, and other subjects (fig. 4-7).[34] The attic would not have been an ideal meeting place with all the hammering in the rooms below, but given the tight housing situation in Kirtland, any available meeting place must have been greatly appreciated.

The upper and lower courts were ready to be painted on February 22, 1836, with Brigham Young acting as superintendent.[35] During this time, Joseph Smith and various councils used the attic offices almost daily.[36] It must have been with no small excitement that the Saints began preparations for the dedication ceremony.

## Notes

[1]"Jacob Bump was the master mason, and the Temple will stand for unnumbered ages as a monument to his skill and genius." Crary, *Pioneer and Personal Reminiscences*, 32.

[2]See "Early History of Hanover," 1.

[3]Joseph Millet wrote, "Next morning [March 3, 1853] on foot to Kirtland. . . . to Jacob Bump (Brother Nelsons Milletts Father in law) they all seemed glad to See me, to hear about Nelson and Augusta and the Children. and to hear about Utah many questions to ask about Father. and other Old acquaintance &c. Ses he if your Father had staid here hem and me wold have owned all Kirtland now" Joseph Millet, "Millet on C B Island," 16–17.

[4]Goldsmith, "Rigdon the First Mormon Elder."

[5]Editions of Benjamin's *American Builder's Companion*, appeared in 1806, 1811, 1816, 1820, 1826, and 1827. Although there was considerable change between the editions, the plates illustrated in the text are common to all of them.

[6]Some of these English examples are Batty Langley's *City and Country Builder's and Workman's Treasury of Designs* (1750), which shows various Vitruvian scroll designs, and William Chambers's *Treatise on the Decorative Part of Civil Architecture* (1791), which shows two opposing dolphins on a mantelpiece, which the reversed scrolls resemble.

[7]Note that Greek usage of entablatures varied as well. For example, Ionic entablatures in the Ionian Islands generally did not have a frieze. However, that is largely irrelevant for American builders because they were following standards set out in their pattern books, not actual classical usage.

[8]Mary Young to Brigham Young, 2. See also William Huntington, Reminiscences and Journal, 3: "Jacob Bump . . . a disipated dishonest Decentor."

[9]Angell, Autobiography, 13.

[10]*Ohio Star* 6 (January 15, 1835): 4.

NEW FIRM—The Joiner's Tool Manufactory heretofore carried on by A. S. Collins will be hereafter carried on by A. S. & F. K. Collins. The subscribers will continue to carry on the above business with all its branches, at the old stand, a few rods south of the Court house. Being thankful for the support that has been extended to this establishment, the subscribers solicit a continuance, and an increase of public patronage. They are now offering to the public Benjamin's Mouldings of 1833, new and splendid articles. We invite our friends to call and examine them. . . . Ravenna, Oct. 16, 1834.

[11]Quoted in Fields, "History of the Kirtland Temple," 22.

[12]Caroline Crosby, Memoirs and Diary. Note that this labor was for board; see Jonathan Crosby, "Biographical Sketch," 14: "The 12th Janu 1836 I went to work on the Temple for our board untill it was dedicated."

[13]Phelps to Phelps, December 18, 1835, 4.

[14]Note also that verse 38 alludes to the fact that men will be sent forth after they are "endowed with power from on high."

[15]New England examples of the reeding technique include the mantel from the Nathan Read House, Salem, Massachusetts (1790), and the Christopher Ryder House, Chathamport, Massachusetts (1809). Two Ohio examples are the Whedon-Farwell House, Hudson, Ohio (1826), and the John Johnson House, Hiram, Ohio (1828). Note that John Johnson worked on the temple as a laborer.

[16]A common fret used in the temple is the single fret doubling back on itself. This form is more commonly found in English books, while American pattern books tend to illustrate simple spiral frets. While this fact might suggest that those working on the temple had other pattern books available to them, these frets are so simple and commonplace that it more probably reflects the fact that the craftsmen had a great deal of collective experience among them.

[17]A house near North Bristol, Ohio, has this same spiral rosette. See Frary, *Early American Doorways*, 136.

[18]"Brother Corrill will drive the work as fast as he can, in order that he and his brethren may be enabled to visit their families." Phelps to Phelps, December 18, 1835, 4.

[19]"In the winter of 1834 and 5, all the principal elders in Upper Missouri went to Kirtland. Some of them spent the Summer there, while others travelled and preached in the eastern States, and some went to the south. I was appointed to take charge of the finishing of the Lord's house." Corrill, *Brief History of the Church*, 22.

[20]This tradition is not unique to New England; it was largely borrowed from British practice dating to the rebuilding of London following the 1666 fire, when Christopher Wren built over fifty church towers using various combinations of classical elements.

[21]Andrew, *Early Temples of the Mormons*, 41.

[22]Arrington, *Brigham Young*, 13, 17. "My father employed Elder Brigham Young, who had just moved into Kirtland, to lay his floor." George Smith, "Memoirs," 8.

[23]The original frames were stored in the basement of the temple, having been replaced between 1967 and 1972 with more energy-efficient copies to hold down energy costs. See Hankins, Reminiscences.

[24]Jackman to Beloved Wife and family.

[25]Jessee, *Papers of Joseph Smith*, 2:75.

[26]Phelps to Phelps, December 18, 1835, 5.

[27]*History of the Church*, 2:363.

[28]"Not that glass and crockery had any adhesive property but it had its use. Artemus Millett claimed that the secret was given him by revelation. Many have tried to solve the problem but have failed." Joseph Millet, "Millet on C B Island," 93–94. Elmeda Harmon recounted, "The Kirtland temple was finished in the Winter time and Briant and Jerry with other boys cut wood to keep the fires to dry the plaster. I, with other little children, gathered bits of glass and broken dishes which were broken up quite fine and mixed with the mortar used in plastering the temple." Maybelle Anderson, *Appleton Milo Harmon*, 168–69.

[29]Joseph Millet, "Millet on C B Island," 93–94.

[30]Gee to Millet, 34.

[31]*Painesville Telegraph*, November 15, 1833, 4; February 20, 1835, 3. "In the year of 1829 I invented and patented the shingle cutter machine now used for making or cutting shingles throughout the United States and Canada." Joel Johnson, Autobiography, 1.

[32]Perkins and Osburns Bill. See also *Painesville Telegraph*, October 25, 1833, 3.

[33]Goldsmith, "Rigdon the First Mormon Elder." See also Watson, *Orson Pratt Journals*, 57, "On the 26th of April [1835]. . . . I found a large congregation collected in the stone meeting house."

[34]*History of the Church*, 2:347; Jessee, *Papers of Joseph Smith*, 2:128–29.

[35]"The lower room of the Temple is now prepared for painting. Elder Brigham Young was obliged to leave the Hebrew class and superintend the painting of the lower room until finished." *History of the Church*, 2:399. See also Jackman to Beloved Wife and family, "The lower room is in the hands of the painters and I think in about three weeks it will be redy for meetings."

[36]*History of the Church*, 2:352–409.

**6-1.** View of curtain in lower court as seen from the east, Kirtland Temple. Although the curtain was part of an 1887 replacement system, the photograph shows how the original curtains might have looked. Because of the curve in the ceiling, this curtain could not be raised all the way up. Photographed by C. E. Miller, 1912.

# Chapter 6

# Religious Life and the
# Kirtland Temple, 1836–1837

## Dedication

As Joseph Smith had officially organized the Church of Christ on April 6, 1830, dedicating the Kirtland Temple by that anniversary must have been in the back of everyone's mind. The structure seems to have been ready with plenty of time to spare. Extant journals do not mention any last-minute anxieties or flurries of activity other than with the troublesome lumber kilns, which caught fire as workers rushed to dry out green lumber.[1] The only concern expressed by Joseph Smith was about the choir, which, as he charitably observed after listening to their rehearsal on March 16, "performed admirably, concidering the advantages they have had." By the time of the dedication on March 27, 1836, the choir seems to have patched up its difficulties, and Joseph Smith was able to describe it as "an excellent choir of singers."[2]

On that Sunday morning, the Saints began queuing at seven o'clock, until about five or six hundred were waiting outside. Inside, the pulpits were dedicated separately before the congregation was allowed to enter. After the doors opened, between nine hundred and one thousand people were seated. Those without seats filled the vestibule, while still others held a separate service in the schoolroom under the printing house to the west of the temple.[3] One verse in Joseph Smith's lengthy dedicatory prayer (D&C 109) summed up the feelings of the congregation:

> we ask the[e], O Lord, to accept of this house, the workmanship of the hands
> of us, thy servants, which thou didst command us to build; for thou knowest
> that we have done this work through great tribulation: and out of our poverty
> we have given of our substance to build a house to thy name, that the Son of
> Man might have a place to manifest himself to his people.[4]

All those in attendance must have felt hearty agreement with these words, for many had sacrificed a great deal in constructing the temple, and constant money worries were ample reminders of their collective poverty. (A full account of the dedication is in appendix C, pages 169–84, below.)

## Washing the Feet, Partaking of the Sacrament, and a Night of Prophesying: From the Ohio Journal of Joseph Smith

29 March 1836 • Tuesday

At 11 oclock A. M. Presidents Joseph Smith Jun Frederick G. Williams, Sidney Rigdon, Hyrum Smith, and Oliver Cowdery met in the most holy place in the Lords house and sought for a revelation from Him to teach us concerning our going to Zion, and other im-[p. 185]portant matter[s] after uniting in prayer, the voice of the Spirit was that we should come into this place three times, and also call the other presidents, the two Bishops and their councils (each to stand in his place) and fast through the day and also the night and that during this, if we would humble ourselves, we should receive further communication from Him.

After this word was received, we immediately sent for the other brethren who came. The presidency proceeded to ordain George Boosinger to the high priesthood and annoint him.

This was in consequence of his having administered unto us in temporal things in our distress. And also because he left the place just previous to the dedication of the Lords house to bring us the temporal means previously named.

Soon after this, the word of the Lord came to us through Presdt J. Smith Jun that those who had entered the holy place must not leave the house untill morning but send for such things as were necessary, and also, that during our stay we must cleans[e] our feet and partake of the sacrament that we might be made holy before Him, and thereby be qualified to officiate in our calling upon the morrow in washing the feet of the Elders.

Accordingly we proceeded and cleansed our faces and our feet, and then proceeded to wash each others feet.—president S. Rigdon first washed presdt J. Smith jun and then in [p. 186] turn was washed by him—after which president Rigdon washed presdt J. Smith Sen. and Hyrum Smith <prsdt> J. Smith Jun washed presdt F. G Williams, and then pres. Hyrum Smith washed president David Whitmer's feet and president Oliver Cowdery's, then pres D. Whitmer washed pres. W. W. Phelps feet and in turn pres Phelps washed pres John Whitmers feet.

The Bishops and their councils were then washed: After which we partook of the bread and wine. The Holy Slp]irit rested down upon us and we continued in the Lords house all night prophesying and giving glory to God.

This meeting initiated a week of spiritual experiences many of the Kirtland Saints recorded in their journals. At another meeting that night, 416 of the Saints heard a noise

> like the sound of a rushing mighty wind, which filled the Temple, and all the congregation simultaneously arose, being moved upon by an invisible power; many began to speak in tongues and prophesy; others saw glorious visions; and I [Joseph Smith] beheld the Temple was filled with angels, which fact I declared to the congregation. The people of the neighborhood came running together (hearing an unusual sound within, and seeing a bright light like a pillar of fire resting upon the Temple), and were astonished at what was taking place. This continued until the meeting closed at eleven p.m.[5]

The following Wednesday, March 30, at a meeting sometimes described as a pentecost, "the Saviour made His appearance to some, while angels minestered [sic] unto others."[6] These events must have justified the extreme sacrifices made to build the temple.

## The Temple's "Vails," or Curtains

A unique feature of the temple was the series of heavy canvas curtains that could be lowered from the ceiling to divide the rooms into smaller classrooms and chambers. Large curtains divided the main court into quarters while smaller ones enclosed the pulpits at each end so "a vail that is suspended to the uper ~~ceiling~~ floor . . . will at any time when necessary be let down and shut off each stand or seat by itself"[7] (fig. 6-2). A visitor to the temple in 1850 described the curtains as being of canvas, "heavy as sails to a ship. . . . fastened at [the] bottom to large rollers and rigged with ropes and pulleys at [the] top like curtains in theaters."[8] By rolling the curtains up or down, the Saints could configure the large lower court to serve several different functions. Though curtains were planned for both the upper and lower courts and though workers began installing a pulley and roller system for curtains in the upper court, that system was never completed, and curtains were never hung there.

The Saints' use of the term "vail" (veil) for the curtains demonstrates their desire to connect the temple with its Solomonic forerunner,[9] though dividers were not a new idea in Ohio architecture. For example, the Yearly Meeting House of the Society of Friends (Quakers) built in 1814 in Mount Pleasant, Jefferson County, Ohio, has an elaborate system of panels that could be lowered to divide the room in half lengthwise. However, even though Joseph Smith traveled nearby on the Ohio River while making his first trip to Missouri,[10] significant differences between the two sets of dividers make a direct influence of the meetinghouse on the Kirtland Temple unlikely.

# Wilford Woodruff Journal

November 25, 1836

We soon entered the village & I spent one of the happiest days of my life at this time in visiting Kirtland & the House of the Lord & the Presidents & Elders of the Church. I was truly edified to again strike hands with President Joseph Smith Jr. & many other beloved saints of God who are rolling on the mighty work of God & of Israel after being seperated from them for 2 1/2 years & amoung the rest I was filled with joy with the priviledg of again meeting with Elder Warren Parrish & also being made acquainted with his Companion Sister Parrish. There is an enjoyment in meeting our brethren & companions in tribulation that the world Knows not off because it flows from a Celestial Source.

After Spending a short time in Conversing With my friends A more important scene was now to open to my view that Kings ever saw or Princes ever Knew in this generation Which was to visit the Temple of the Lord & its contents. Elder Smoot & myself visited each appartment of the House accompanied by Elder Parrish & I must confess the scenery in indiscribable. When I entered the threshhold of the house & Passed into the lower room their was great Solemnity if not Awe immediately overwhelmed me. I felt indeed as if my footsteps were in the Temple of the Lord.

After walking into the Pulpets, erected for the Priesthoods & viewing the curtains [fig. 6-1] all bespeaking that grandure, solemnity & order that nothing Short of wisdom from God could invent . . . Many other important views I was Privileged with in the upper story the school rooms, belfry &c. all indicating great Architecture & wisdom.

November 29 [27], 1836

Upon this Lords day Elder Smoot & myself accompanied Elder Parrish to the house of the Lord for the first time to behold the Congregation of the Saints assembled within its walls for the Purpose of worshiping God. . . . After I entered the house & was seated I cast my eyes upon the Pulpits aranged in order for the High Priest I beheld the Patriarch Joseph Smith sen. standing in the upper Pulpet. & President Joseph Smith jr. & Elder Carter in the second one & in the third Elders Parley & Orson Pratt & W. Parrish was seated soon Elder Carter arose & opened meeting by Prayer & then Preached the gospel unto us & was followed by President Joseph Smith jr When meeting was dissmissed & after an intermishion of an hour we again met in the house of the Lord & I was called into the stand in company with Elder Smoot & requested me to Preach to the People. (Woodruff, *Journal*, 1:106–8)

Courtesy RLDS Church Archives.

**6-2.** Lower court, east pulpits and window, showing hooks in the ceiling above the pulpit. These hooks, which were removed before 1934, supported the curtains, or "vails," that could enclose each tier of pulpits. A four-inch space between the two sets of center pews served as a passage for one of the curtains dividing the congregational space. Photographed about 1888.

The first difference is that the wood-framed panels of the Friends' meetinghouse partition are far more substantial than the canvas curtains in the Kirtland Temple, and their greater weight required a totally different scale and level of technology for the lifting mechanism. In addition, the Friends' partition was designed to separate men and women attending the same service, while the temple's curtains were designed in part to accommodate concurrent meetings. Spatially, the Friends' meetinghouse was a large balconied hall. The partition could never create convenient classrooms, as in the temple, since the panels divided the room into long, proportionately thin sections overlooked by the balcony. Finally, the specifications written for the Independence Temple by Joseph and his associates never mention tracks and rollers, as are present in the Friends' meetinghouse, but instead specify that the curtains should hang from hooks and rings. If Joseph Smith had been aware of this Quaker precedent, the idea was so thoroughly reworked that study of the Quaker partition sheds little light on the Kirtland Temple curtains.

The "hooks and rings" called for in the Independence Temple specifications to support the curtains were removed sometime before 1934, but early interior photographs show rows of hooks on the ceiling above the pulpits (see figs. 6-1, 6-2, and 8-8). The original curtains were removed from the lower court probably before 1860, and a new curtain system was installed around 1887.[11] Photographs of this later system illustrate how the original curtains might have looked (fig. 6-1). Note that the large curtain hanging transversely across the room cannot be raised up to the surface of the ceiling because of the curve in the elliptical arch. Although the rolled-up curtain looks rather awkward hanging in the space, its convenience in dividing the room compensated for its aesthetic disadvantage.

A detail not covered in the Independence Temple specifications was how the curtains would be controlled. Thus, builders devised an ingenious system of concealed pulleys and cranks to operate the curtains with minimum difficulty. A contemporary description of this system states:

> The vails by which the house is divided into quarters, are of canvass, painted white, and are rolled up or drawn at pleasure, by means of cords which come down the pillars concealed, and are worked with cranks; also each official seat is completely vailed, both sides and front; these are also worked with cords which come to the seats concealed.[12]

Details of column construction made this enclosed pulley system possible (figs. 6-3, 6-10). The columns are made of timbers approximately eight-by-eight inches that sit atop the major girders below and support the girders some twenty-two feet above. The columns stand one on top of another, forming a continuous support from the masonry piers in the basement to the roof rafters. Inside the congregational spaces, however, wooden panels encase these eight-by-eight-inch timbers, giving them an apparent size of about fifteen by fifteen inches. This design leaves several inches of space inside the panels for the ropes and pulleys.

The lower ceilings to each side of the elliptical vaults are supported by horizontal beams that frame into the columns about fifteen feet above the floors. These secondary beams then frame into joists that support the plaster ceilings. This framing system leaves a gap on the outside faces of the columns for ropes to pass through into the five-foot-high interstitial spaces to the sides of the elliptical arches (fig. 6-3). The ropes then pass through pulleys that direct them horizontally to the curtains.

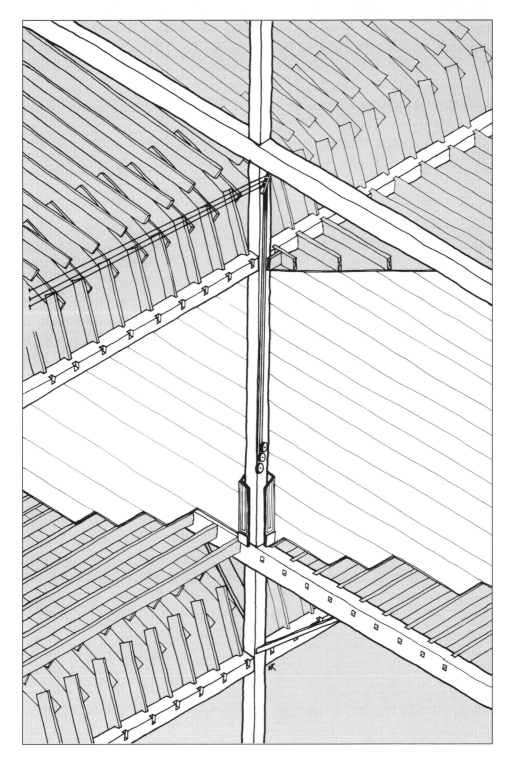

**6-3.** Drawing of the concealed pulley system for the upper-court curtains. The wood panels encasing the 8" x 8" columns are offset several inches, leaving room to hide the axle stubs for the crank, the winding drums, and the ropes. The ropes continue up the outside face of the column and are then redirected into the space at the side of the elliptical vault. Also see fig. 6-10.

The concealed pulleys of the system were made of cast iron and would have accommodated ropes about three-eighths of an inch in diameter. These pulleys were fixed into thick boards and attached to the central columns by machine-cut nails (fig. 6-4). The pulleys on the end columns were attached using thick wooden dowels. This stronger method was used because these pulleys were not attached on the flat side of the column, where they could be easily nailed in place, but rather were set on the corner of the column so the ropes could run diagonally to the curtains above the pulpits (fig. 6-5).

The curtains dividing the main rooms were controlled by cranks set into the central columns. This arrangement is still visible in the upper floor, where an iron axle protrudes from the column and a small access door opens to the wooden winding drum within (fig. 6-6). However, the cranks in the lower floor have all been removed. Large sections of the fluted planking of the columns have been replaced, as is evidenced by seams in the wood. Presumably the cranks were removed and the fluted planks replaced during one of the interior restoration phases. Some of the bracketing that held the winding drums must still be extant inside the columns.

In the lower court, the curtains enclosing the pulpits were controlled by cranks set under the benches behind the pulpits, one crank for each tier of pulpits (fig. 6-7). This system required the pulley ropes to travel from above the ceiling to below the floor, a path that would normally be blocked by framing timbers and girders. However, this difficulty was avoided by extending the raised podium of the pulpits over to the first set of columns at each end of the room. Ropes controlling the curtains passed down the interior of the columns and then exited in the narrow gap between the main floor level and the raised seating. Ropes then ran underneath to each tier of seating, up to the pulpits' raised floor, and through a hole to the drum and crank under the seat (fig. 6-7). This installation of the pulley system was rather difficult, for workers had to drill through the four-by-four-inch wooden supports in the rope's path. Clearly workers were not building this system from a well-planned set of drawings but were working out the details to the best of their ability as they confronted new situations.

In the lower court, rollers with a rope wrapped around each end were attached to the bottom of the curtains. The curtains were raised by pulling on the ropes, which wound the curtains around the rollers as they rose up. This system of having the roller at the bottom of the curtain was easy to build but had the disadvantage that the rope controlling the roller bore up to half the weight of the heavy canvas curtain; this distribution of weight made for laborious cranking.

In contrast, the upper-court curtain system was designed with the roller at the top of the curtain. This system was more difficult to build since

Photo by author.

**6-4.** Detail of broken remnant of pulley carrier above the upper court. The rope is attached to the drum and crank below for illustrative purposes. Note the wrought iron cut nails still imbedded in the column after the pulley carrier split and broke away.

Photo by author.

**6-5.** Detail of pulley carrier above the lower court. Note the wooden pegs used to attach the carrier to the wooden column.

Photo by author.

**6-6.** Columns of upper court, Kirtland Temple, showing open access doors.

Photo by author.

**6-7.** Winding drum located under pulpit seat in the lower court.

Courtesy Library of Congress.

**6-8.** Upper court, facing west, Kirtland Temple. Photographed April 1934 by Carl F. Waite. The rollers set against the ceiling were designed to carry canvas curtains that would divide the congregation's space into four separate rooms and and would partition the multiple pulpits into separate worship spaces. Note the slit in the elliptical arch, just visible in the upper left, and the slit in the aisle ceiling, visible in the upper right, which allowed the transverse curtains to slip down through the ceiling. Their rollers remained hidden in the interstitial space above. The stovepipe just visible to the right of the columns connected the stoves in the lower court to the chimneys above the attic offices.

rollers had to be installed on or above the ceiling (fig. 6-8), but it had the advantage of making cranking easier since the ropes did not carry the weight of the curtain. Despite this superior design, curtains were never installed in the upper court. Unlike the columns in the lower court, those in the upper court have not had the decorative planking replaced, and the metal shafts connected to the pulley system are still visible (fig. 6-4). This variant arrangement for the rollers was likely developed during the fall of 1834 since slightly more headroom above the upper court gives the necessary space for rollers above the elliptical ceiling and any decision to increase the headroom to accommodate the system must have been made before structural framing was completed. The amount of headroom available above the elliptical vaults (fig. 6-9) is controlled by the height of the masonry walls, length of the columns, and location of the beams supporting the elliptical vault and the flat ceiling.

The supporting rollers for the curtains in the upper court were of two basic types: those recessed into the space between the ceiling and the attic floor and those attached directly to the underside of the ceiling. Rollers set against the surface of the ceiling controlled the curtains that divided the room lengthwise down the middle. These rollers are clearly visible on the plaster vault of the upper court and utilize a rather ingenious system of control (fig. 6-8). Each curtain would have been supported by a double set of rollers. The larger roller would store the curtain, which would have passed from the larger roller over the smaller one while being lowered. Without the smaller roller, the curtain would have shifted position as the diameter of the rolled-up portion decreased. The ropes controlled by the crank in the column passed through the ceiling through turned wooden blocks. A special flat wooden ceiling was installed above the pulpits of the upper court to allow the rollers in that area to fit flush against the ceiling. Wrought-iron straps attached to the joists of the floor above would have supported the weight of many of the rollers and their curtains, thereby eliminating undue stress on the framing of the elliptical arch. These straps are still visible above the ceiling.

The recessed rollers work similarly to the ones set against the ceiling except that the curtains drape down through a slit cut in the ceiling. Recessing the rollers neatly avoided the problem of a large canvas cutting the elliptical arch in two (see fig. 6-1). The only curtains that can operate in this manner are those oriented transversely in the space, since the joists framing the flat ceiling and elliptical vault both run in that direction. None of the recessed rollers is still in its original position, as the later insertion of gas piping, electric wiring, sprinkler systems, air ducts, and alarm systems has necessitated their removal. However, several of the rollers are still lying on the joists between the upper-court ceiling and attic-office floor, and of course the slit in the ceiling is still visible, indicating their original position.

Although locating the pulleys at the top of the curtains would have made the system easier to manipulate, the pulleys were never completed, and curtains were never installed on the second floor. Journals specifically mention curtains in the lower court but not in the upper court, even as late as 1850.[13] The rollers still sitting in the dead space between the upper-court ceiling and attic-office floor show no evidence of tacks or brads to hold the curtains in place, and no wear is visible on the wooden bearings. Curtains were never installed in the upper court, despite the elaborate measures taken to provide for them.

## Functions of the Curtains

The curtains allowed the temple's limited space to be used for a variety of purposes.

*Visions.* Sometimes when lowered, the curtains above the pulpits seem to have partitioned off a "holy of holies" similar to those in Moses' tabernacle and Solomon's temple. Such a sacred area was appropriate for Joseph Smith's religious leadership, which began with a vision of God the Father and Jesus Christ, and the temple was intended as a setting for additional divine manifestations.[14] Joseph Smith and other associates received at least some of these visions while the curtains were dropped around the pulpits. On April 3, the Sunday following the dedication of the Kirtland Temple, Warren A. Cowdery recorded for Joseph Smith:

> He retired to the pulpit, the vails being dropped, and bowed himself, with O. Cowdery, in solemn, but silent prayer to the Most High. After rising from prayer the following vision was opened to both of them. . . . They saw the Lord standing upon the breast work of the pulpit before them. After this vision closed, . . . Moses appeared before them and committed unto them the keys of the gathering of Israel. . . . After this vision had closed, . . . Elijah, the Prophet, . . . also stood before them . . . to turn the hearts of the Fathers to the children, and the children to the fathers.[15]

*Prayer.* The curtained enclosures of the pulpits were used not only by Joseph Smith and close associates, but also by other members for prayers. Wilford Woodruff recorded such an occasion:

> I repaired to the house of the Lord at an early hour in the morning to spend the day in prayer and fasting with the saints in Kirtland, as this was a day set apart for that purpose. Immediately after entering the house in company with several other Elders, I went within the veil and we bowed down before the Lord in the Aronic stand & offerd a morning sacrifice, & the Spirit of God rested upon us with joy to our Souls.[16]

Because a household was rarely without one or two boarders, the temple served as a place where one could pray undisturbed.

*Washings and Anointings.* The curtains also provided privacy for washings and anointings, which were performed in the temple. Washing and anointing constituted part of the endowment of power promised earlier in revelations through Joseph Smith and anticipated by W. W. Phelps, Levi Jackman, and other Saints in Kirtland. That these ceremonies were private with details known only to participants is clear from George A. Smith's description: "He [the Lord]. . . . told us to wash ourselves, and *that* almost made the women mad, and they said, as they were not admitted into the Temple while this washing was being performed, that some mischief was going on, and some of them were right huffy about it."[17]

While these ceremonies of washing and anointing were later extended to women, they were always restricted to men and women who had proven themselves faithful. Wilford Woodruff described how the temple's curtains helped maintain privacy for those participating in the washing ceremonies:

> The veils were closed & each apartment commenced the duties of the day the washing of the feet of the anointed was the first business that was performed. . . . After the washing of feet, the veils were rolled, which brought the congregation into one assembly, the stand of the Priesthood were still covered with the veils the Presidency stood in the lower stand & President Joseph Smith jr arose and addressed the congregation for the term of three hours clothed with the power, spirit, & image of GOD.[18]

*Regular Congregational Meetings.* The lower court was used for weekly worship services; for prayer meetings, held most Thursday evenings; and for monthly fast meetings, which were held the first Thursday of the month. Eliza R. Snow explains how the temple's curtains accommodated these meetings:

> Public meetings were regularly held in the Temple, after its dedication, on Sundays; and on the first Thursday in each month a fast meeting, commencing at or before 10 a.m., and closing at 4 p.m. The Temple was so constructed, that with white canvas curtains, which could be dropped and raised at pleasure, the lower story was, whenever occasion required, divided into four sections or apartments. This was invariably done at those fast meetings. The two sets of pulpits, one on the east and the other on the west end of the building, were intersected by the curtain extending from east to west, so as to leave half their lengths in each apartment, and they were occupied by the presiding officers who directed the services. Thus four separate meetings were in session at the same time, without, in the least, interfering with each other—giving opportunity for four to exercise instead of one. . . .
>
> Father Smith [Joseph Smith Sr.], in the capacity of his calling as President, gave general counsel and instructions on fast day; recommending that the greater portion of the forenoon should be spent in prayer, with testimonies of manifestations of the power of God, and with exhortations to faithfulness. At about 3 p.m. he would order the curtains to be drawn up—bringing the four congregations into one, over which he then presided until the close of the meeting.[19]

These fast meetings provided an open forum for individuals to express their feelings about God. Dividing the room in quarters gave four times as many people an opportunity to participate in the meeting. Sometimes the rooms were divided with men occupying the two sections on one side and women the two sections on the other.[20] In addition, the temple was open on Thursday fast days in the morning, and at least on some occasions, small groups of people would drop the veils and pray before the regular fast-day service.[21]

## Community Center

The temple functioned as a community center as well, with different organizations meeting in the building throughout the week. A decidedly rosy description of Kirtland in the *Messenger and Advocate* entitled "Our Village" catalogues the temple's various uses.

> Nothing can be more gratifying to the saints in this place and their friends and brethren abroad than to contemplate the scene now before them. Every Lords day our house of worship is filled to the overflowing with atten- tiv-hearers, mostly communicants.
>
> In the evening following the singers meet . . . [receiving] instructions in the principles of vocal music.
>
> On monday evening the quorum of high priests meets in the west room of the attic story. . . . On Tuesday evenings the Seventies, meet in the same room occupied by the high priests the preceding night. . . .
>
> On Wednesday evening the rooms are occupied by the quorum of Elders. . . . On Thursday P.M. a prayer meeting is held in the lower part of the house where any and all persons may assemble and pray and praise the Lord. This meeting, though free for all, is conducted more particularly by J. Smith senior, the patriarch of the church.
>
> The members of the high council, and also "the twelve" meet but we believe not statedly in each week as do others, of the different quorums men- tioned.
>
> Dring [sic] the week a school is taught in the attic story of the house, denominated the "Kirtland High School" con[sist]ing of about 135 or 40 stu- dents under the superintendence of H. M. Hawes Esq. professor of the Greek & Latin languages.[22]

The Kirtland Temple served a number of purposes, and the curtain arrange- ment helped to configure the spaces to function effectively (fig. 6-9).

### Notes

[1]"In the afternoon [of March 5, 1836] the board kiln to[ok] fire & the lumber principally con- sumed—this is the 5 or 6 time it has burnt this winter if my memory serves me corectly." Jessee, *Papers of Joseph Smith,* 2:186; see also 2:101.

[2]Jessee, *Papers of Joseph Smith,* 2:189.

[3]Post, Diary, March 27, 1836.

[4]Jessee, *Papers of Joseph Smith,* 2:195–96; see also Doctrine and Covenants 109:4–5.

[5]*History of the Church,* 2:428. This event was present in the minds of members of the Church years afterward; see George A. Smith, in *Journal of Discourses,* 2:214–15, March 18, 1855. Note that Oliver Cowdery gives the number of people present as 316; see Arrington, "Cowdery's 'Sketch Book,'" 426.

[6]Jessee, *Papers of Joseph Smith,* 2:207.

Photo by author.

**6-9.** Pulley carrier above lower court.

[7]Independence Temple drawings, unsigned set.

[8]Ryder, *Voigtländer and I*, 69.

[9]Andrew, *Early Temples of the Mormons*, 50.

[10]*History of the Church*, 1:188

[11]*Willoughby Independent*, September 23, about 1887.

[12]West, *Interesting Facts*, 5.

[13]"The room above was similar in size as to floor space, but lower in height of ceiling. There were no dividing partitions in this room." Ryder, *Voigtländer and I*, 70. The difference in ceiling heights is only a few inches.

[14]For a summary of some of these experiences recorded by participants, see Karl Anderson, *Joseph Smith's Kirtland*, chapter 10.

[15]Jessee, *Papers of Joseph Smith*, 2:209–10; see also Doctrine and Covenants 110:1–4.

[16]Jessee, "Kirtland Diary of Wilford Woodruff," 385.

[17]Smith, in *Journal of Discourses*, 2:215; italics in original. Previous to this quotation, George A. Smith stated:

> We progressed in this way while we were building the Kirtland Temple. The Saints had a great many traditions which they had borrowed from their fathers, and laid the foundations, and built that Temple with great toil and suffering, compared with what we have now to endure. They got that building so far finished as to be dedicated; this was what the Lord wanted, He wished them to provide a place wherein He could reveal to the children of men those principles that will exalt them to eternal glory, and make them Saviors on mount Zion. Four hundred and sixteen Elders, Priests, Teachers, and Deacons met in the Kirtland Temple on the evening of its dedication. I can see faces here that were in that assembly. The Lord poured His Spirit upon us, and gave us some little idea of the law of anointing, and conferred upon us some blessings. He taught us how to shout hosannah, gave Joseph the keys of the gathering together of Israel, and revealed to us, what? Why the fact of it was, He dare not yet trust us with the first key of the Priesthood.

**6-10.** Detail of winding drums set inside a column, upper court.

Courtesy RLDS Church Archives.

[18]Jessee, "Kirtland Diary of Wilford Woodruff," 390. On the ordinance's exclusiveness, Stephen Post recorded:

> The ordinance of the washing of feet this ordinance is administered to none but those who are clear from the blood of the generation in which they live. I did not expect much to receive the ordinance as I had not laboured much in the vineyard [served a proselytizing mission], but I had endeavored to do as well as I could. however when we came together the word of the Lord was that we all should receive the ordinance. O the goodness & condescension of God. (Post, Diary, March 30, 1836)

[19]Snow, Biography and Family Record, 12.

[20]"After I had made some brief remarks upon the subject the congregation took their seats, for the services of the day, in the following order The house being divided into four parts by veils, the females occupied two parts & the males the others. Some of the presidency presided in each apartment. The time was taken up during each day in each apartment in singing, exhortation, & prayer, some had a tongue, others an interpretation, & all was in order. The power of GOD rested upon the people the gifts were poured out upon us some had the administering of angels & the image of GOD say upon the countenances of the Saints. at 4 o'clock PM. the Veils were all rolled up together which brought the whole congregation in full view of each other and while the presence of the LORD filled the house the congregation of the Saints fell upon their knees & all as one man, vocally poured forth rejoicing." Jessee, "Kirtland Diary of Wilford Woodruff," 385.

[21]"I repaired to the house of the Lord at an early hour in the morning to spend the day in prayer and fasting with the saints in Kirtland, as this was a day set apart for that purpose. Immediately after entering the house in company with several other Elders, I went within the veil and we bowed down before the Lord in the Aaronic stand & offered a morning sacrifice, & the Spirit of God rested upon us with joy to our souls." Jessee, "Kirtland Diary of Wilford Woodruff," 385.

[22]"Our Village," 444.

Chapter 7

# Joseph Smith's Departure and Subsequent Temple History, 1837–1890

## Economics and Opposition

Perhaps the most intractable problem facing the Mormon community at Kirtland was finances. Even before the temple walls began to rise, Joseph Smith found himself unable to meet the Church's financial obligations—a situation that worsened as expenses on the building mounted (D&C 104:78–85). In fact, according to family history, a request for one thousand dollars accompanied the call asking Artemus Millett to go work on the temple.[1]

In 1833 responsibility for the finances of the temple construction was turned over to a building committee composed of Hyrum Smith, Reynolds Cahoon, and Jared Carter (see D&C 94). The committee expanded in the winter of 1835–1836 to include Joseph Smith, Oliver Cowdery, and William Smith. The scarcity of funds was a constant strain on these men and caused friction among Church leaders.[2]

The finances of the temple are difficult to separate from other accounts since temple workers drew needed goods from Joseph Smith's store without exchanging currency and, during the initial phases of construction, the United Firm was in place. Ira Ames's complaint that the temple account books were "complete Confusion" when he took them over suggests that the builders of the temple never really knew what it cost either.[3]

Temple construction was financed by small individual donations from the impoverished Saints and also by a few larger donations. Vienna Jaques came to the rescue early on by donating fourteen hundred dollars when a note for the temple lot came due.[4] Far more significant were John Tanner's donation of thirteen thousand dollars to the temple committee and a loan reportedly made to Joseph Smith for thirty thousand dollars. He probably did not receive repayment.[5] Although few members of the Church of the Latter-day Saints had the amounts of money donated by Artemus Millett, John Tanner, and Vienna Jaques, their relative level of sacrifice was similar.

Despite these and other donations, Joseph Smith had to borrow heavily, not only for the temple structure itself, but also to purchase land in Zion that could be settled by incoming converts.[6] With the recent completion of the Ohio Canal, land prices in the area were rapidly increasing, and Joseph Smith—as well as his creditors—expected continuing increases in prices. In this expanding economy, large sums of money were tied up in land, but little capital was available for investment. Joseph and his associates attempted to establish a bank called the Kirtland Safety Society Bank in order to provide a local currency and source of credit. When the state legislature rejected his application for a charter, Joseph opened the Kirtland Safety Society Anti-Banking Company.[7] He apparently felt that the loyalty of his followers would prevent runs on this "bank," runs that might topple the undercapitalized venture. Insufficient sums of "hard money," reports of embezzlement of funds by some of the directors, and the Panic of 1837, which resulted in dropping land values, caused the entire enterprise to collapse.

Opposition to Joseph Smith and his followers had been constant ever since their arrival in the Kirtland area, but once it became obvious that Joseph Smith would never be able to pay his creditors, everyone left holding the worthless Kirtland Bank scrip (signed by Joseph himself) had cause for holding a personal grudge against him—and this group included many Mormons. As most property was purchased on time, creditors often waited until just before payments were due to demand payment on other IOUs (which circulated much like bank notes) signed or cosigned by the debtors. Hepzibah Richards wrote, "They level upon persons who have signed for others just when they can make the most trouble, take their property and sell it for a trifle. The printing office has been attached with all its contents. . . . Last week on Monday the printing office was sold at auction into the hands of dissenters."[8]

As financial failures and foreclosures swept through the community, emotions escalated, and attempts were made to replace Joseph Smith as President. Warren Parrish, one of the Kirtland Bank directors who had been accused of issuing bank notes without authorization, led an opposition group that regularly disrupted meetings in the temple. In one of the more colorful skirmishes, Parrish and his cohorts interrupted a Sunday-morning speaker and then fled, brandishing pistols and bowie knives:[9]

> Many in the congregation, especially women and children, were terribly frightened—some tried to escape from the confusion by jumping out of the windows. Amid screams and shrieks, the policemen, in ejecting the belligerents, knocked down a stovepipe, which fell helter-skelter among the people; but although bowie-knives and pistols were wrested from their owners, and thrown hither and thither to prevent disastrous results, no one was hurt, and after a short, but terrible scene to be enacted in a Temple of God, order was restored, and the services of the day proceeded as usual.[10]

While this commotion was going on inside, other "men jump[ed] out of the windows, them that had chicken[']s hearts."[11] On another occasion, one of Parrish's group rushed the pulpits by running across the tops of the pews but was quickly hustled out of the temple.[12] As the physical manifestation of the Mormon faith, the temple was a natural setting and symbol for conflicts within the group.

Of course, these incidents of violence in the temple should not overshadow the role it continued to play in the religious life of the Saints living there. For example, Mary Fielding Smith writes about a "quiet comfortable waiting upon god in his House," and others reported similar experiences.[13] However, as these attacks became more numerous, prominent Mormon leaders who defended Joseph Smith received threats and were compelled to leave Kirtland.[14] Finally, to avoid harassment from creditors and disgruntled Church members alike, Joseph Smith and his associate Sidney Rigdon left for Missouri by night on January 12, 1838.[15] Far from obtaining safety, however, in the following year they and the other Saints in Missouri suffered violence that exceeded anything experienced in Kirtland. Considering the far-reaching implications of the Church's financial troubles, the sacrifices made to build the temple were hard indeed.

## Departure of the Saints

Kirtland had always been considered only a temporary gathering place, and with the removal of the Prophet to Missouri, many of those who had remained faithful to him decided to leave Kirtland and join him there. Meetings were held in the temple planning a mass migration, and after an attempt by dissenters to burn down the temple on May 22, these efforts were redoubled.[16] On July 6, 1838—coincidentally two days following a cornerstone-laying ceremony for a new temple in Missouri—515 persons left for Far West.[17] Later in the same month, a broadside was printed announcing the establishment of a new school occupying the temple building:

WESTERN RESERVE TEACHER'S SEMINARY AND KIRTLAND INSTITUTE

The Mormons of Kirtland, Geauga County Ohio, having broken up, and nearly all removed to the State of Missouri, it has been thought expedient to establish an institution of learning in the place, and thus occupy buildings which would otherwise remain comparatively useless. For this purpose, the use of their large and commodious Temple, has been secured for five years from the 1st Sept. 1838. In this edifice we have a single room sufficiently large to seat well, two hundred students. . . . NELSON SLATER, Principal. Kirtland, July 25, 1838.[18]

The broadside is not completely accurate, since a substantial number of Mormons did remain in Kirtland although they prudently kept a low profile. Presumably, the promise of income generated by the five-year lease kept creditors at bay, while the school continued the pattern set by the Kirtland High School, which had met earlier in the temple.

With the departure of most of the Saints from Kirtland, it is unclear if weekly worship services in the temple continued and, if they did, who might have officiated at them. Before long, however, opposition to the Saints must have waned, for by May 1839, Church members living in the eastern states were encouraged to settle in Kirtland, and a presiding authority was sent to oversee the group. Over one hundred members of the Church lived in Kirtland in 1840,[19] and the following year, this number swelled to about five hundred, partly due to the arrival of English converts who did not have sufficient money to continue on to Nauvoo, Illinois. The community in Kirtland made plans to publish a newspaper, prepared the temple for a bell, and made capital investments in industrial enterprises.[20] However, in October of that year, Hyrum Smith wrote to the group in Kirtland instructing them to gather with the main body of Saints in Nauvoo. Most of the new arrivals, who had no ties to the area, followed this instruction, but established citizens with economic interests were slower to leave.

## Ownership Issue

In 1844, with the murder of Joseph Smith by an armed mob in Carthage, Illinois, came a crisis in leadership over the Church. Both Sidney Rigdon, once a counselor in the presidency of the Church, and Brigham Young, President of the Quorum of the Twelve Apostles, claimed the right to succeed Joseph Smith. In a dramatic meeting in Nauvoo, each put forth his claim. The majority of the Saints supported Brigham Young.[21] Although this settled the matter for most of the Saints in Nauvoo, such was not the case in Kirtland. While in Kirtland, Brigham Young had staunchly defended Joseph Smith against dissenters,[22] and many still harbored feelings of animosity toward Brigham. Such feelings would have made it difficult for any of them to return to fellowship.

Parallel to the issue of who was going to lead the Church was the issue of who owned the temple. The original title to the temple, along with the titles to most Church property, was in Joseph Smith's name. Determining who rightfully owned such property was no simple matter, with Brigham Young seeking to keep property in the name of the Church and Emma Hale Smith seeking to preserve some financial security for her family. Reuben McBride, who earlier had been given the power of attorney to act in Joseph

Smith's name, continued to oversee Church property in Kirtland and follow-ing Joseph's death reported to Brigham Young. Apparently Brigham Young was anxious about maintaining legal ownership of the temple for the Church, for in July 1845, McBride informed Brigham that "there has been no suit instituted against the Church property nor no prospect of it."[23]

McBride also reported that Sidney Rigdon had been preaching in the temple as part of an attempt to win over former followers of Joseph Smith and gain control of the temple. No large following materialized, and Sidney Rigdon's attempt to lead the Church remained unsuccessful. Ownership of the temple remained uncontested for another couple of months.[24]

The small Mormon community in Kirtland that maintained allegiance to the Twelve finally lost control of the temple in the fall of 1845. Perhaps encouraged by the Council of the Twelve's vote to abandon the United States and move to the Rocky Mountains or by reports of the unchecked burning of Mormon homes in Hancock County, Illinois, Jacob Bump and others wrested the temple away from the group. McBride reported that Bump and his fol-lowers were "the leaders of the rioters; they had broken into the House of the Lord, and taken possession of it, and were trying to take possession of the Church farm."[25] However, absorbed in preparations for the westward trek and still trying to finish the temple in Nauvoo, Church leaders could do little to respond to the take-over in Kirtland.

In April 1846, just prior to the dedication and subsequent abandon-ment of the Nauvoo Temple, Church leaders discussed if it "would not be better to sell the Temple at Nauvoo and also the Temple and church property at Kirtland, Ohio, and with the proceeds assist the Saints to emigrate west-ward."[26] This must have been a most difficult decision, for nearly all the Church leaders had sacrificed heavily to build the Kirtland Temple. Never-theless, the council, under the direction of the pragmatic Brigham Young,

> decided that the trustees might sell the Temples at Nauvoo and Kirtland, Ohio, and all other property of the Church and help the poor saints to move westward. The council considered that the Temple would be of no benefit to the saints, if they could not possess their private dwellings, and when the time should come that they should return and redeem their inheritances they would then redeem the Temple also; that a sale would secure it from unjust claims, mobs, fire and so forth, more effectually than for the Church to retain it in their hands.[27]

The wisdom of this approach was borne out a few years later when the abandoned Nauvoo Temple was torched by an arsonist; the Kirtland Temple has survived its many vicissitudes precisely because someone in Kirtland has always possessed and occupied the structure, be it by squatter's rights or legal entitlement.

On October 7, 1846, Almon Babbitt was instructed to sell Church property in Nauvoo and Kirtland. He apparently spent the fall trying to dispose of properties in Nauvoo and then left for Kirtland in January 1847.[28] He was reported to have sold the temple for $10,000.[29] However, Jacob Bump had taken possession of the keys of the temple in 1845, and his group had merged with William E. McLellin's Church of Christ in 1846. Without the LDS Church having control over the temple, Babbitt could not have concluded the sale. It was likely this attempted sale that prompted the Church to file a title to the temple in the names of several trustees-in-trust (recorded in Painesville, Ohio).[30] But as often happens, possession apparently took precedence and the title had little effect, for the sale was never concluded.

McLellin, a former Apostle who had served under Joseph Smith,[31] directed this group in Kirtland for another two years. Then a group led by James Brewster controlled the temple until 1851, although in 1850 a traveling photographer reported that the temple was empty and unused.[32] Perhaps the small size of these groups made it advantageous for them to meet in private homes instead of in the temple. Finally, a group led by Zadoc Brooks, who claimed succession to Joseph Smith, held services in the temple throughout the late 1850s.[33] This last group eventually dissolved, with many former members joining the Reorganized Church of Jesus Christ of Latter Day Saints. A small RLDS congregation began meeting in the temple in 1860.[34]

## RLDS Ownership

With the establishment of the RLDS congregation, efforts to maintain the temple began in earnest. By 1860 the roof had been in service for thirty-five years and apparently had developed a number of leaks. A new roof was installed that summer, the exterior woodwork was painted, and the small congregation "promise[d] to restore the ancient splendor of the building." To supplement the RLDS resources, the Kirtland community contributed towards the renovation.[35] Their support in part probably reflects the community's use of the structure for occasional public assemblies. Despite this help, full renovation of the interior of the structure was beyond the resources of the small congregation; instead, only the worship space in the lower court was repaired and maintained for Sunday services.[36]

When the Lake County Probate Court liquidated Joseph Smith's properties in 1862 to pay off his old debts, his large land holdings were purchased by a businessman who quickly sold the temple to Russell Huntley for $150.[37] Huntley had joined the Mormon church in the 1840s and had affiliated with Brooks's group in the 1850s, so he was familiar with the building and its historical importance.[38] One hundred fifty dollars was an extremely low price for a building that had just received a new roof and coat of paint, and it may reflect the fact that Huntley was one of the townspeople who had contributed generously for the repairs. In any event, Huntley had little chance of making a profit from the building. He offered the temple for sale for two thousand dollars (the approximate value of the recent repairs), touting it as a potential town hall, but the offer was rejected by the township trustees.[39] Unable to sell the building, Huntley continued to rent it to the local RLDS congregation for use as a meetinghouse. After joining the RLDS Church, Huntley sold the temple to Joseph Smith III and an associate, Mark Forscutt, for $150 in 1873.[40]

Joseph Smith III, who was considered by members of the Reorganization to be the successor to his father, Joseph Smith Jr., hoped to resell the temple to pay off debts acquired in personal business.[41] He came to Kirtland in 1875 to conclude the sale of the temple to the township for use as a school and town hall. But this time the impediment was not balky trustees but the lack of clear title. The deed that Joseph Smith III and Forscutt held to the temple was a quitclaim deed and not a full legal title. The trustees wanted to purchase only with a full legal title in the name of the RLDS Church. When Joseph Smith III tried to obtain such a deed, the financial officer of the RLDS Church refused to issue it, feeling that the temple should belong to members of the church as a whole.[42]

The RLDS Church's subsequent attempts to obtain a clear title resulted in a legal suit against the LDS Church and several individuals. The timing of the suit coincided with the uproar concerning the LDS practice of polygamy and virtually ensured a judgment in favor of the RLDS Church, which repudiated the practice.[43] Even if the RLDS Church had not obtained clear title in the 1880 decision, the passage of the Morrill Anti-Bigamy Act of 1862, which required the LDS Church to forfeit all property in excess of fifty thousand dollars, and the subsequent Edmunds-Tucker Act of 1887, which called on the attorney general to execute the 1862 act, would likely have resulted in the title being transferred to the RLDS Church.[44]

## RLDS Functions in the Temple

With the temple securely in the hands of the RLDS Church, members E. L. and Cassie Kelley moved to Kirtland to direct ecclesiastical affairs and the renovation of the building. One of their challenges was to convince the townspeople of Kirtland that the temple was a religious structure and not just a community center. Especially attractive to the town was the large upper court, which during these years did not contain fixed pews. The room was apparently used for a variety of community events. In 1874 the Grand Army of the Republic staged a memorial service in the lower court, followed by a banquet in the upper court. The large rooms, and even the "curiously

wrought seats once occupied by the great modern false prophet and his apostles," suited their needs.[45]

Even when most civic events were diverted to an adjacent building
owned by the RLDS Church and referred to as "the Hall," the Kelleys had
difficulty accommodating the wishes of the town and retaining the religious
decorum appropriate to the temple. For instance, while her husband was
away on church business, Cassie Kelley was asked for permission to use the
temple grounds for a dance. She related:

> The Captain came . . . and told me how they were making great preparations
> to have a grand time. Every thing would be in the best of style and guards
> would be out on duty to see that no roughs were allowed on the grounds. . . .
> so I let them use the Hall to dance in. I saw it was going to do us more injury
> to refuse under the circumstances.[46]

The primacy of the temple's religious mission at last became evident
when the RLDS Church held important conferences there in 1883, 1887,
1891, 1896, and 1904.[47] During the 1920s and 1930s, week-long camp meetings held on the temple grounds, called temple reunions, became a prominent part of RLDS culture. Although regular Sunday services are no longer
held in the temple, the numerous visitors to the temple attest to its important place in the religious life of members of both the RLDS and LDS
Churches.

## Notes

[1]Joseph Millet wrote:

The Prophet Joseph Smith, Joseph Young, & Brigham Young were standing upon the
ground where the Kirtland Temple was to be built talking about the work. The Prophet
said. "Who can we get to superintend this work."

Joseph Young said; "I know that very man to take charge of it, he is rich too."
"Who is he?" asked the Prophet. Joseph Young said; "It is Bro Artemas Millett but he
dose not belong to the church." The Prophet turned to Brigham and said; "Do you
know this Brother Artemas Millett." Brigham said; "Yes!" "Then," said the Prophet; "I
give you a mission to go and Baptize him and bring him here. Tell him to bring a thousand dollars with him." (Joseph Millet, "Grandfather Artemus Millet")

A similar account is in Joseph Millet, "A Brief History of Artemus Millet, Son of Ebeneazer Millet."

[2]Ames, Autobiography and Journal, 1836. The temple building committee, which also ran
the Church store in Kirtland, was accused of favoritism in handing out scarce goods. See *History
of the Church*, 2:333, 335–37. Later, disagreements ensued over the soliciting of funds to pay for the
temple; see *History of the Church*, 2:374–75.

[3]Ames, Autobiography and Journal, 1836. On the Saints' exchange-based economy, see Watson, *Orson Pratt Journals*, 26.

[4]Launius, *Kirtland Temple*, 38.

[5]John Tanner arrived in Kirtland with $10,000 in "hard money which probably meant silver
or gold. In addition he was carrying $13,000 in merchandise which he signed over to the Temple

Committee. It is doubtful that any of the loans were ever repaid." George Tanner, *John Tanner and His Family*, 75; see also *Scraps of Biography*, 12–13, 16; and Arrington, "John Tanner Family," 46, 48. Note that the $30,000 donation is not recorded in contemporaneous documents, but the liberality of Tanner's other donations makes the story plausible.

Nathan Tanner recorded another dramatic example of donations meeting the Saints' financial obligations. After hearing Joseph Smith ask for a "hard money" donation to make the payment on a farm, Amos Perry, who was not a member of the Church, said:

> Nathan what would you do if you ware in my plase you no I have the hard money Said I, I dont want to advise you, But you no if I had the money I should lay it down Wall I think I will if you will go & introduse me to Joseph & He went to His wagon & puled out a ca[n]vis sack of hard money sholdered it up & packed it into the temple & laid it down on the sacarement table before Joseph & then I introduced them, It seams that Joseph had the power to call money to his ade when He needed to acomplish His Ends at will. (Nathan Tanner, Reminiscences, 1–2)

[6]In 1835, Joseph Smith sent the Quorum of the Twelve on a mission to the East to regulate and organize branches there but also to raise money for the Kirtland Temple and land purchases in Zion. Apparently not understanding the priority of the temple, the Twelve stressed fund raising for establishing Zion. Esplin, "Emergence of Brigham Young," 161, 167.

[7]Adams, "Chartering the Kirtland Bank," 469; Hell, Rooker, and Wemmer, "Kirtland Economy," 433–34.

[8]Richards to Richards, January 22, 1838, 221.

[9]Snow, *Biography and Family History*, 20–21; Oliver Huntington, Journal, 14.

[10]Snow, *Biography and Family History*, 12.

[11]Oliver Huntington, "Journal."

[12]Coolbear, in Vinson Knight Biographical Sketch, 5, writes:

> During the meetings, when Joseph was trying to preside, one of this class of men was standing in the back of t[he] room, became excited and declared that he would put Joe Smith out of the room of the temple. The aisles being full of standing people, he stepped upon the back of a bench and started for the stand, stepping from one bench to another between the heads of the people. Bro. Joseph was equal to the occasion and remained calm. Turning to Vinson, he said, 'Vinson, take this man out.' Quick as a thought, Vinson caught the man by the legs and tossed him, head down over his shoulder and carried him pawing and struggling, out of the building. Brother Knight's children always remembered the occasion.

[13]Fielding to Thompson, in Godfrey, Godfrey, and Derr, *Women's Voices*, 60. For a detailed account of the 1837 strife in Kirtland, see Esplin, "Emergence of Brigham Young," chapter 6.

[14]Oliver Huntington, Journal, 15; Richards to Richards, January 22, 1838.

[15]Joseph Smith and Sidney Rigdon held a farewell conference in the temple on September 17, 1837, and issued an announcement "To the Saints Scattered Abroad" on September 18, 1837. *History of the Church*, 2:513–18. The two departed on September 27, only to return before leaving permanently on January 12, 1838. Fielding to Thompson, October 7, 1837; Joseph Smith Jr., *Elders' Journal*, 27; Launius, *Kirtland Temple*, 88.

[16]Warren Cowdery notes:

> The Methodist Meeting House was burned, and an attempt was also made on the same evening, and probably by the same person or persons, to fire the stone Temple. A small bundle of straw, a few shavings, and a brand or coal inclosed, was found tied up with a string. . . . The bundle was evidently introduced through the window, by breaking a pane of glass, and was found in the morning. . . . A few straws only were burned which came in immediate contact with the brand; but to all appearance the fire never kindled into a blaze, and happily no damage was done. (Warren Cowdery, "Fire!" 2–3)

This article implies that the burning of the smaller Methodist meetinghouse was only a diversion to allow the temple fire to get well underway before discovery, as the rope for the bucket of the well nearest to the Temple was found cut.

[17]See Allen and Leonard, *Story of the Latter-day Saints*, 124–25; and Prusha, *History of Kirtland*, 67.

[18]Kirtland File.

[19]*History of the Church*, 3:345; Jenson, Journal History, April 27, 1840. Bitton, "Waning of Mormon Kirtland," 456.

[20]Jenson, Journal History, October 3, 1841, 2–3; October 19, 1841, 1–2. Bitton, "Waning of Mormon Kirtland," 456.

[21]Esplin, "Joseph, Brigham, and the Twelve," 301–41. During this meeting, many present reported, Brigham Young's voice and face respectively took on the sound and appearance of Joseph Smith's, which they took as a sign that Brigham Young was to lead the Church. For example, see Tracy, Reminiscences and Diary, 31:

> Brigham Young was the man chosen and sustained by unanimous vote to be the mouthpiece of God to the Saints. I can testify that the mantle of Joseph fell upon Brigham that day as that of Elijah did fall upon Elisha, for it seemed that his voice, his gestures, and all were Joseph. It seemed that we had him again with us.

A compilation of these experiences will be forthcoming in Jorgensen, "Mantle of the Prophet Joseph."

[22]Esplin, "Emergence of Brigham Young," 273–307. The "History of Brigham Young," *Deseret News*, says:

> On a certain occasion [February 20, 1837] several of the Twelve, the witnesses to the Book of Mormon, and others of the authorities of the church, held a council in the upper room of the Temple. The question before them was to ascertain how the Prophet Joseph could be deposed, and David Whitmer appointed President of the Church. Father John Smith, bro. Heber C. Kimball and others were present, who were opposed to such measures. I rose up, and in a plain and forcible manner told them that Joseph was a Prophet, and I knew it, and that they might rail and slander him as much as they pleased; they could not destroy the appointment of the Prophet of God, they could only destroy their own authority, cut the thread that bound them to the Prophet and to God, and sink themselves to hell. Many were highly enraged at my decided opposition to their measures, and Jacob Bump (an old pugilist,) was so exasperated that he could not be still. Some of the brethren near him put their hands on him, and requested him to be quiet; but he writhed and twisted his arms and body, saying, "How can I keep my hands off that man?" I told him if he thought it would give him any relief he might lay them on. This meeting was broken up without the apostates being able to unite on any decided measures of opposition. This was a crisis when earth and hell seemed leagued to overthrow the Prophet and church of God.

[23]*History of the Church*, 4:441–42; McBride to Young, 1.

[24]McBride to Young, 1–2.

[25]Jenson, Journal History, October 22, 1845, 1.

[26]Jenson, Journal History, April 26, 1846, 3.

[27]Jenson, Journal History, April 27, 1846, 1. See also Watson, *Orson Pratt Journals*, 343.

[28]Jenson, Journal History, October 7, 1846, 1; January 7, 1847, 7.

[29]J. Tyler to McLellin, in *Ensign of Liberty*, 60. "A. Babbit preaches here to-night, but I shall oppose him. He says he sold the Temple at Kirtland when he was there for $10,000, but I believe him to be a right Rev. liar." In the article, McLellin later commented on the letter, "Babbit's sale of the Temple here was a mere sham, as events since have proved." The sham referred to is that McLellin, who controlled the temple, obviously felt that Babbitt had no right to sell it.

[30]Jenson, Journal History, April 5, 1847, 1; January 12, 1848, 1.

[31]Porter, "Odyssey of William," 341–46.

[32]Ryder, *Voigtländer and I*, 68.

[33]Launius, *Kirtland Temple*, 98–99.

[34]Launius, *Kirtland Temple*, 99, 104.

[35]"Kirtland Affairs," August 30, 1860, 3; November 22, 1860, 3. "We were gratified to learn while in Kirtland, that the citizens are pleased with the thought of repairing the temple, and some

expressed a willingness to assist by contributions when the work is commenced, and take pride in protecting the building after it is restored." Heman Smith, "Kirtland Temple," 424.

[36]"A branch was organized, holding their services in the Temple, which the little band partially reclaimed from vandalism." Edwards, *History of the Reorganized Church*, 4:425.

[37]Launius, *Kirtland Temple*, 104–5. Since Huntley had invested $2,000 in the building renovations and was charging the RLDS congregation rent for use of the structure, it could be that business arrangements had been made prior to the actual transfer of title. However, profit does not seem to be Huntley's motivation, for in all his attempts to sell the temple he only tried to recoup his original investment and not to make a profit.

[38]Launius, *Kirtland Temple*, 104.

[39]*Willoughby Republican*, June 29, 1921, 4.

[40]Launius, *Kirtland Temple*, 106.

[41]Joseph Smith III to Bidamon.

[42]Joseph Smith III to Fyfe.

[43]"That the Church in Utah the defendant of which John Taylor is President has materially and largely departed from the faith, doctrines, laws, ordinances and usages of the original Church of Jesus Christ of Latter Day Saints and has incorporated into its System of faith the doctrine of Celestial Marriage and a plurality of wives." Court Opinion in Kirtland Temple Suit.

[44]Gustive Larson, *"Americanization" of Utah*, 210–11.

[45]"Reunion in Kirtland."

[46]Cassie Kelley to E. L. Kelley, September 1 [and 6], 1885. See also E. L. Kelley to Cassie B. Kelley, August 27, 1885. Note that it took some time for the more secular activities to be removed from the temple, as the issue was discussed in a 1912 general conference of the RLDS Church. See Launius, *Kirtland Temple*, 134–35.

[47]See Heman Smith, "Kirtland Temple," 428.

**8-1.** Exterior view of facade, Kirtland Temple, 1934. The flush boarding in the pediment (gable end) and the tower is still in place. The painted joint lines on the stucco surface have weathered away and numerous patches have been made in the stucco surface.

# Chapter 8

# Changes in the Building Fabric

Ironically, the Kirtland Temple was something of a white elephant for the smaller religious groups that successfully maneuvered and sued to gain control of it. With its thick masonry walls and high ceilings, the temple was difficult to heat and maintain. For example, because the Western Reserve Teacher's Seminary could not adequately heat the structure, they abandoned their lease and moved classes to the Methodist church. During the winter months of the 1880s, difficulty in heating the structure compelled the RLDS Church to move the meetings that were held in the temple other times of the year.[1]

Another difficulty was the fact that the temple was not systematically maintained until the late 1870s. Joseph Smith III, who visited the temple in 1866, remembered it as being extensively vandalized:

> The temple is in tolerable repair, so far as the outside is concerned, but the inside has become the prey of the despoiler. All the ornamentation, moldings, letters, and carved work have been broken up by curiosity hunters, until the two upper rooms are stripped.[2]

Other reminiscences note that doors of pews and benches were stolen, names were cut into the woodwork, and carvings and pulpit railings were carried away.[3] The tops of the pulpits had to be covered by cloths "because of the four letter words gouged in their tops."[4]

Although the interior doubtless suffered a great deal from neglect, it probably was not purposefully damaged to the extent implied by the above statements. The physical building fabric does not indicate any systematic vandalism. Inaccessible woodwork (such as the cornice supporting the elliptical vaults and the ornamentation surrounding the windows) was probably left untouched. Much of the panel work on the pulpits and pews can be identified as original material because of the hand-plane marks visible on its surfaces. The planks in the pews and pulpits are also original, as indicated by their width. During the 1830s, old-growth timbers of considerable girth were readily available, and sawmills commonly produced planks wider than fifteen inches. By the last decade of the nineteenth century, however, scarcity of

**8-2.** Woodcut prepared from an 1846 sketch by Henry Howe. From Howe, *Historical Collections of Ohio.* The chimney, which served the temple's four stoves, is visible just beyond the tower.

large-diameter trees raised the price of such large planks, and most of the later woodwork incorporates boards less than eight inches wide. Rather than having been the "prey of the despoiler," the temple's interior seems to have suffered damage like that undergone by a well-used school desk.

Joseph Smith III's rather gloomy memory of the temple interior was likely influenced by the peeling paint and cracked plaster. The excessive settlement in the foundation and natural deterioration over time were probably as destructive as visitors with penknives. Beginning in the 1870s, careful restoration work of the interior erased many of the effects of vandalism and natural decay. The RLDS Church, which gained legal ownership of the temple in 1880, embarked on a long series of repairs and alterations that continues today.

## Restoration and Repair in the Nineteenth Century

The only major repair work done on the temple before the RLDS Church obtained clear title was replacing the roof and repainting exterior woodwork. This work was done in the summer and fall of 1860, immediately following the establishment of the RLDS congregation in Kirtland.[5] Although not specifically documented, considerable replacement of broken glass must have been done, too, for the windows had "become extensive ventilators from the number of missing panes."[6] These repairs on the exterior were intended to make the building weathertight, thereby preventing further deterioration.[7]

In 1882, two years after obtaining clear title to the temple, a conference of the RLDS Church appointed a committee to continue repairs on the building and ready it for the 1883 conference to be held in Kirtland. That fall, however, the committee reported that the estimates for repair work were "so much more than we believe the conference contemplated that it would take at the time of the appointing of its committee, we did not feel justified in commencing the work until we obtained further counsel from the church." The committee reported that the reroofing in 1860 was done with poor quality shingles, which had to be totally replaced, and that the "steeple will need to be almost wholly restored, especially all of the ground work, save it may be the corner posts."[8] This committee spent about two thousand dollars on repairs, but repairs continued after the conference with the eventual goal of readying the building for the April 1887 conference. These repairs included replacing woodwork in the lower court, leveling the floor, and replacing broken glass. Repairs were made to the foundation walls and the steeple. In addition, the third floor doors, windows, and partitions were extensively restored, while doors and pulpits were restored on the second floor.[9]

*Inscriptions.* The inscription on the east face of the temple has also changed over time, reflecting a change in the name of the Church and the change in ownership of the temple. Henry Howe gives the original inscription as "House of the Lord, built by the Church of the Latter Day Saints, a.d. 1834."[10] This inscription remained even when the Church was renamed as The Church of Jesus Christ of Latter-day Saints in August 1838 (D&C 115:4) and when the temple was back in the control of LDS leaders from 1839–44.[11] Later, in 1860, the small group in control of the temple altered the inscription to read the Church of Christ, the original name of the Church.[12] However, in 1899, as an acknowledgement of the building's new owners, the inscription was again changed to read, "Reorganized Church of Jesus Christ of Latter Day Saints in succession by decision of Court February, 1880."[13] At some later time, the 1834 date was changed to read "1833–36," a more accurate record of the construction dates of the building but an unfortunate alteration of the historical inscription.

**8-3.** Kirtland Temple from the southeast. Photographed by "Faze the Rambling Artist," ca. 1875. The wooden quoins on the tower were painted to match the stone quoins below. The belfry, not yet fitted with a bell, has solid panels in the openings. Painted joint lines are visible where the temple's walls are in shadow, and faint horizontal markings show where one day's plastering ended and another commenced.

In 1986, in preparation for the sesquicentennial of the temple's dedication, the inscription was changed once again to read, "Dedicated March 27, 1836, Reorganized Church of Jesus Christ of Latter Day Saints."

*Stained Glass.* Perhaps the most noticeable change to the temple in the 1880s was the inclusion of colored glass in the arch above the western pulpits,[14] although the work on the plaster and stucco was far more extensive.

*Plaster and Stucco.* In 1887 the repair committee patched the exterior stucco (in a slightly different color than the original)[15] and replaced all of the plaster in the interior except the underlayers of the plaster on the interior of the masonry walls. This surface was pecked to create a good "key" for the new material, and a new putty coat was smoothed on. Since plaster does not normally deteriorate so completely in fifty years' time as to require replacement, graffiti must have been at least part of the problem. Repairing only the cracks due to building settlement would not have required wholesale replacement of the plaster surface.

*Furnace.* Another important addition during this campaign of work over the winter of 1886–87 was the furnace to heat the structure. The original plans for the Independence Temple specified fireplace chimneys in the sidewalls at the aisles between the pews. These chimneys were never built in the Kirtland Temple; instead, stoves were placed near the locations intended for the fireplaces. This change was made either because workers lacked a detailed plan or because Artemus Millett felt that stoves would heat the space more efficiently. The stoves originally used metal flues that ran up through the floors to a central brick chimney (figs. 8-2, 8-3). A cut in the ridge beam shows where this chimney exited the roof, and the access hatch in the ceiling of the attic offices probably corresponds to the location where flue pipes passed through the ceiling to enter the masonry chimney.

Later, two smaller chimneys, centered between the eastern and western stoves, replaced the single chimney. This change was likely made to improve the draft of the flues since the central chimney would have necessitated long horizontal runs in the flues from the east and west ends. This system caught fire in 1883, prompting the rebuilding of the chimneys in 1887 in a slightly smaller size and a more ornate style.[16] Special beams inserted to support these new chimneys are still visible in the roof structure, and cuts in the floors are visible where the stovepipes passed through each level. The 1886 repair committee improved this system by adding a furnace whose fourteen-inch flue ran from the basement up through the floors on the north side of the temple.[17] However, this new furnace did not replace the earlier system using four separate stoves, for figure 6-8 shows one of the earlier stovepipes still in place. The unsightly stove flues running through the building would have been visible only during winter, as the flues and stoves were removed and stored in warm weather.

**8-4.** Kirtland Temple from the south, ca. 1902. By the time this scene was photographed, louvers had replaced the panels in the belfry arches (compare to fig. 8-3).

The various heating systems relying on exposed flues running through the interior were finally replaced in 1936, when the large heating plant across the road began delivering steam to the temple via a tunnel running underneath Route 306 (the tunnel is still extant, though bricked up). Chimneys were removed at this time, drastically reducing the fire hazard in the structure. An oil-burning furnace was installed in 1959.[18] In recent years, to further reduce fire hazard, heating and air-conditioning units have been installed with all flames and compressors located outside the building. Hot and chilled water pipes now run vertically in the remaining space between the stair and the vestibule wall. This piping connects to heat exchangers located in the crawl spaces between the floors, with ducting distributing conditioned air to the rooms.

*Tower.* Although the building committee reported extensive repairs to the steeple in 1883, additional repairs were soon needed. Of course, this is nothing new in the history of American ecclesiastical buildings. In their exposed location, towers and steeples naturally weather quickly, and since towers are relatively inaccessible, such deterioration often goes unnoticed (or is at least easily ignored). Such seems to have been the case in Kirtland.

Compounding the problem with the tower was the decision in 1890 to install a bell in the belfry. A bell had been called for in the Independence Temple plans, and efforts were made in 1835 to purchase one in Kirtland. Even after the departure of most Mormons from Kirtland in 1838, the remaining Saints continued to prepare the tower to receive a bell. While perhaps a wise decision with respect to instilling a sense of pride among the members of the congregation and serving as a focal point for the community by "announcing services . . . fires and funerals,"[19] the swinging bell created dynamic forces that exacerbated problems in the tower.

When the bell was installed, the panels that had closed up the belfry arches were replaced with horizontal louvers that let the sound of the ringing bell project to the surrounding countryside (figs. 8-3, 8-4). Unfortunately, these louvers also permitted rain and snow to enter the belfry and collect on the bell deck, causing the timbers to rot. By 1904 the deterioration of the structure and the action of the heavy bell swinging to and fro caused the weather vane to rock in the wind.[20] Providentially, a bolt of lightning struck the tower on August 13, 1904, badly damaging the belfry and roof, although a bucket brigade saved the temple from fire (a fate which did not escape a barn immediately adjacent to the temple). Since the temple was fully insured, the insurance money must have been what finally financed the needed repairs, which were undertaken in the fall of 1904.[21]

## Twentieth-Century Exterior Repairs

**8-5.** Repairs on the exterior stucco of the Kirtland Temple, northeast corner, unknown date. Vertical cracks between windows, still present today, allowed moisture to enter the wall and contributed to the deterioration of the exterior finish. The context of the photograph indicates that similar repairs were made to the other three elevations of the temple. Note the rubblestone construction and the two prominant "put-log" holes in the masonry where scaffolding timbers were inserted during construction. Note also that workers have painted joint lines on the repairs. These lines are visible in the photograph on the darker repairs and presumably match lines faded from exposure and not visible in the photograph on the lighter original stucco.

While most of the repairs undertaken on the temple in the nineteenth century restored its original appearance, a number of twentieth-century repairs introduced significant changes. Perhaps the most drastic of these was the replacement of the stucco finish on the exterior of the building. The exterior stucco had required significant patching in 1887, and by the 1950s further patching had given the exterior a mottled appearance (figs. 8-1, 8-5). Restorers decided to remove the exterior stucco and put on a new surface. In order to save money, they applied this finish using a pressure grout technique in which a slurry of cement and sand is sprayed on the surface of the wall and then troweled smooth. This technique created two problems. One was that the force of the cement and sand hitting the wall separated free water from the mixture. This water was driven through the walls and loosened the plaster on the interior surface, necessitating the complete removal and replacement of the plaster four years later. Unfortunately, this interior plaster was the only original finishing material left in the building (covered by the 1887 putty coat). Its removal eliminated the possibility of accurately matching new finishes with original ones.

The second, and more visually prominent, problem is that the new surface is significantly thicker than the original. The new finish should have consisted of a three-quarter-inch undercoat and a one-quarter-inch finish coat,[22] but since the finish was sprayed on with a hose, accurate control of its thickness was difficult. As a consequence, the decorative stone elements—the moldings surrounding doors and windows, the quoins at the corners, and the cornice at the roof level—barely protrude from the surface, when originally they projected one to two inches.[23] In addition, the painted joint lines imitating cut-stone masonry were not replaced, so the walls have a flat, almost thin, appearance. Indeed, the quoins at the corners now look more like hinges than solid elements anchoring the walls. Completed in 1955, the new

## Directing Water out of Belfries

Steeples, spires, and towers always present challenges in maintenance, not only because they are exposed to the weather, but also because their height makes access for normal maintenance difficult. The most common site of deterioration in belfries is the floor. Because of the greater wind velocities present above tree level, water regularly enters belfries—no matter how carefully designed the louvers. The difficulty lies in directing water from inside the belfry, past the enclosing walls, and to the exterior. This problem is often solved by leaving a good-sized gap at the bottom of the wall of the belfry so water can flow underneath. However, one cannot interrupt the columns supporting the belfry walls, so some kind of flashing must be provided to channel water around these columns. In its lofty and rarely visited location, flashing leaking around these columns commonly goes undetected for long periods of time.

The pattern of replacement timbers on the Kirtland Temple's belfry shows that water collected and ran down the eight timber columns that form the corners of the octagonal belfry (fig. 3-10). Where these columns rested on interlocking sets of four beams, the water pooled and was drawn up into the columns by capillary action in the wood cells. This saturation of the wood caused the bottoms of the columns and the four interlocking beams to decay. The repair consisted of splicing new sections on the bottoms of the supporting columns and replacing the interlocking beams that supported the belfry (fig. 8-6). These new timbers are differentiated from the 1830s timbers by the circular-saw marks visible on their surfaces. Graffiti on replacement timbers dates from 1904 and after, coinciding with documented repairs in that year.

Photo by author.

**8-6.** Interior of tower showing the repairs to the columns supporting the octagonal belfry above. New sections were spliced into the bottoms of the supporting columns and the interlocking beams were replaced.

cement finish was left a natural gray color for about a decade before it was painted its current brilliant white. This new appearance of the temple reflects the clean, white look of the Modern Movement in architecture, which was in vogue in the 1960s. Unfortunately, this twentieth-century aesthetic is very different from the Georgian–Greek Revival look of the elements in their original, strongly projecting form (compare with fig. 8-3).

This visual change is even more pronounced due to the changes made to the tower between 1941 and 1950.[24] The flushboard siding originally covering the tower and gable ends (fig. 8-2) was replaced with the more common overlapping clapboard siding (fig. 8-7). Not as weathertight, flushboarding was generally used to imitate the smooth surface of masonry construction. Flushboarding was sometimes used on the facade of public buildings, as the absence of horizontal shadow lines gave what was considered to be a more refined or monumental look. With the smooth stucco surface beneath, flushboarding in the temple's gables and tower visually linked the masonry walls and wooden gables, giving a more unified appearance to the structure. The corners of the tower have wooden blocks imitating the stone quoins of the walls below, and originally these, along with other decorative elements, were painted a darker color imitating the stone ornament below (figs. 8-2, 8-3). This paint scheme strongly tied together the lower walls and tower and emphasized the Georgian ornament of the walls below.

Although the siding in the upper sections of the tower and gables has all been replaced, most of the wooden ornament from the original structure was probably reused or closely copied.[25] Of course, the ornament does not stand out as prominently as it did with the original flushboard siding since the thickness of the overlapping clapboards buries the wooden details.

The rebuilt cornice of the tower also integrates old and new elements. This Doric cornice was composed of alternating triglyphs (blocks with three vertical "slots") and metopes (flat spaces between the blocks). The cornice was rebuilt using the original triglyphs, but the plank that originally composed the metope was replaced with a sheet of composition board similar to Masonite (fig. 8-7). Such a substitution for an original material does not meet current preservation standards but does reflect the 1950s American cultural worship of anything "new and improved."

## Twentieth-Century Interior Changes

Many of the changes made to the temple's interior adapted the building to new technologies. A series of interior photographs of the lower court reveals many of these changes. Figure 6-2 shows the eastern end of the lower court sometime between 1887, when the interior plaster was renewed, and 1899, when gas lights were installed in the temple.[26] At the time of this

Photo by author.

**8-7.** Detail of tower, Kirtland Temple, ca. 1992. Originally, the triglyphs of the Doric entablature would have been backed up by thick planking. The planking was replaced with thin composition board, which visibly bows over the window. Also note the overlapping clapboard, which replaced the original flushboard siding.

photograph, the interior of the pew boxes was stained instead of painted white, although the doors were left white. Kerosene lamps hung down from the vault for lighting. (The lamp on the right in fig. 6-2 has been removed from the holder for cleaning.) Hooks for curtains are visible in the vault, and in fact, in the fourth pew from the east in the left-hand center section, some large piece of fabric, perhaps one of the curtains used to divide the space, is barely visible. Fabric covers are placed on the pulpits to cover the graffiti-marred tops, and small benches are placed at the heads of the pulpits to increase seating capacity.[27] The roller blinds visible on the windows probably kept the morning sun from heating up the space (and also kept down the glare, resulting in very fine detail in the photograph).

Figure 8-8 shows the west view of the lower court at nearly the same time as the previous photograph. This photograph shows the same stained wood finish inside the pew boxes, and the fabric pulpit covers and small benches are similar to those seen on the east. A small organ is visible to the right, and a glimpse of the aisle shows the wood floors typical of the period.

Figure 6-1, dated 1912, shows several small changes that occurred in the years following the previous view. The gas lamps installed in 1899 have already been modified for electricity.[28] A darker color of paint accents the window mullions. The small cracks visible in figure 8-8 between the west wall and the vault have now grown very large and unsightly. It was probably during these years that the west wall shifted outward just over an inch due to the foundation settlement discussed in chapter 3. (Later in the 1950s, tie rods, seen in figure 8-9, were run from wall to wall between the floors to prevent the cracked walls from shifting further.) The water damage visible between the keystones also shows that the cracking on the exterior was

**8-8.** Lower court looking west, Kirtland Temple, ca. 1887, possibly photographed by James S. Ryder.

extensive enough to allow water to seep through the wall and damage the interior plaster. Here, the westernmost (front) pew has been removed, leaving only two pews to the west of the second column instead of the three visible in figure 8-8. This alteration was made to allow passage when the sacrament table was swung up for use during Sunday worship services. Finally, the most visible element in the photograph is the large curtain suspended by ropes from the ceiling. As was discussed in chapter 6, the curtain hangs in an unsightly fashion, destroying the architectural effect of the elliptical vault.

Several more small changes are visible in figure 5-2, which was taken in 1934. The electrified gas lamps have now been replaced by what must have been safer electric lighting. A stovepipe collar from one of the early heating systems is visible in the upper left corner. The interior of the pews has been painted, and the cracking and water damage previously visible above the window has been repaired. Attempts to use curtains in the lower court had probably ceased by this time as all the hooks are removed and the

Photo by author.

**8-9.** Southwest corner between the lower court ceiling and upper court floor, Kirtland Temple. The tie rods were installed during the 1950s to restrain the outward movement of the walls.

plaster repaired. Fire rings—decorative plaster rings that contain the smoke and soot and prevent it from spreading over the ceiling—and the hooks used to support a candelabra are still visible in the vault and were probably present in the original ceiling. The tool used to make the plaster rings has a hand-forged lag screw at the pivot (typical of what one would expect to find in the 1830s) but was reinforced later with a piece of sheet metal fastened with small brads of a type that was not available in the 1830s. Apparently, the original tool that molded the fire rings was refurbished and used in later repairs.[29]

Contemporary photographs point out still more changes to the lower court. The hanging lamps were replaced in 1940 with fluorescent tube lighting placed above the cornice of the elliptical vault and supplemented by wall sconces designed by Earl Curry. Sprinklers were installed in 1957, and smoke detectors were installed in the 1980s.[30]

Another change that has occurred in the interior involves the lettering on the pulpits and sacrament tables. Two documents record the original lettering: one an unsigned note in the LDS Church Archives and the other a description written by Henry Howe in 1846.[31] On the west end, starting from the top tier of pulpits, the letters originally read:

> M. P. C.
> P. M. H.
> M. H. P.
> P. E. (on the swing table).

On the east end were the letters:

B. P. A.

P. A. P.

P. T. A.

P. D. (on the swing table).

By 1880 the gilt letters on the pulpits had all been removed, either by vandals or by others seeking to preserve them from vandals. Black paint was used to reletter the pulpits, and red curtain cord to letter the lowest stand on the west end.[32] This stand, which originally contained the "swing table" for the sacrament, had been removed to make room for a rostrum some time before 1878 but apparently was put back in place by the time of the 1880 description.[33] The painted letters were the same as the original, except that additional letters were added to the lowest pulpits, apparently because the swing tables bearing the original letters had been removed. The additional letters were M.P.E. (on the Melchizedek pulpits) and P.A.D. (on the Aaronic pulpits). The modern lettering matches that described by Howe except the new swing tables have double sets of gilt initials and are lettered in a more consistent pattern as follows:

(on the west end, lower court)

P.     E.                    P.     E.

  M.                              M.

(on the east end, lower court)

P.     D.                    P.     D.

A.                          A.

What was meant by each of these initials has been the subject of varied speculations by observers over the years, but in the Independence Temple specifications (unsigned set), the pulpits were designated from top to bottom in this manner: on the west end, "for the president and his council," "for the Bishop and his council," "for the High Priest," and "for the Elders;" and on the east end, "Presidency of Lesser Priesthood," "for the Priests," "for the Teachers," and "for the Deacons."[34]

The upper court has not been as well photographed as the lower court and, as was suggested above, may have suffered more damage from use as a school and community room. John Corrill stated that "the second story was finished similar in form to the first, but was designed, wholly, for instruction, and supplied with tables instead of slips."[35] Just what these tables looked like is unknown, but when a traveling photographer laid a floor on top of them for his photography studio in 1850, he called them pews. By the 1870s, when large banquets were held in the space, the original furniture in the upper court had been mostly removed (fig. 8-10) although the floor still bore marks where the furniture had been positioned. The fixed pews currently located in the center of the upper court were installed by E. A. Stone, who worked on the temple between 1918 and 1931.[36] These pews are similar to those

Courtesy LDS Church Archives.

**8-10.** Upper court looking west, photograph by George Edward Anderson, August 1907. Cracking at the junction between the ceiling and the west wall mirrors that shown in Fig. 6-1 although the cracking is not as extensive. Also note the missing plaster in the ceiling to the left. Chairs were used in the upper court before pew boxes imitating those in the lower court were installed sometime between 1918 and 1931.

installed in the lower court, except they are slightly lower and do not intersect the columns supporting the vault.

The pews give the upper court the appearance of a second worship space. However, the tables originally installed in the room communicated its educational function more directly. The new pews also obscure the upper court's function as a community room in the late nineteenth century. Lighting was not installed in the upper court until 1944, indicating that the room was not in regular use in the early twentieth century.

Despite all the changes to the building fabric in its first 160 years, the Kirtland Temple today retains the essential structure and form present in

1836. Changes to the building fabric are either relatively minor or so obvious that the original form can be deduced. Currently, the most visible changes to the building are the overlapping siding in the gable ends and tower and the new stucco covering without the painted coursing. Hopefully, future maintenance decisions regarding the temple structure will have as their top priority the maintenance of the physical artifact left behind by Joseph Smith, Sidney Rigdon, Frederick G. Williams, Artemus Millett, Jacob Bump, Truman Angell, and all the others who labored on the temple.

## Notes

[1]Prusha, *History of Kirtland*, 81. Even as late as 1886, when stoves heated the temple, an apostle of the RLDS church, Gomer T. Griffiths, purchased a nearby hall previously used for religious and fraternal meetings and deeded it to the church for use in cold weather. Undoubtedly, the large building consumed large quantities of fuel. See Launius, *Kirtland Temple*, 120.

[2]Quoted in Vida Smith, *Young People's History*, 2:129. His specific comment about the two upper rooms having been nearly stripped bare suggests that the lower worship space did not suffer as much damage.

[3]Mather, "Early Days of Mormonism," 209; Gomer Griffiths, "Reminiscences of Kirtland Temple," 723. Also, Mary Griffiths to Lewis, 1, states that the temple

> was so terribly abused and polluted; the cellar was used as a stable for cattle and sheep, and other parts of the Temple used for dancing. The doors of the pews and benches were carried away; railings to the pulpits and carvings taken off anf [sic] carried away. Names cut into the woodwork and all kinds of writing upon the walls; plastering knocked off the walls; all of this leaving the Temple open to destruction and decay.

[4]Hankins, Reminiscences. The initials on the pulpits in 1846 recorded by Henry Howe are the same as those on the pulpits today, although the initials on the sacrament tables are slightly different on both the east and the west ends. Howe records initials of P.D. on the sacrament table at the base of the Aaronic pulpits, instead of the P.D.A. currently in place. Likewise Howe records P.E. for the sacrament table at the base of the Melchizedek pulpits instead of P.E.M. Howe, *Historical Collections of Ohio* (1847), 282.

[5]"Reorganization of the Mormons at Kirtland"; "Kirtland Affairs," August 30, 1860, 3. Accounts do not specify whether all of the woodwork was repainted.

[6]"About Kirtland."

[7]"Kirtland Affairs," November 22, 1860, 3.

[8]Heman Smith, "Kirtland Temple," 424.

[9]William Kelley and Blakeslee, "Report of Committee," 560–61, 563. See William Kelley and Blakeslee, "To the Saints," 351–52; "Kirtland," February 10, 1887, 3; and Heman Smith, "Kirtland Temple," 427.

[10]Howe, *Historical Collections of Ohio* (1847), 35.

[11]Jenson, Journal History, May 4, 1839. "And the inscription upon the front stone is, 'HOUSE OF THE LORD, BUILT BY THE CHURCH OF THE LATTER DAY SAINTS A.D. 1834.'" "Name of the Church," *Ensign of Liberty*, 21.

[12]"Some changes are being made in the Temple, and one is, the old and original inscription high up on its front, to wit 'House of the Lord built by the latter day Saints A.D. 1834,' has been removed and the simple one 'Church of Christ' put on." *Painsville Telegraph*, June 14, 1860, 3.

[13]*General Conference Minutes*, April 11, 1900, 229–30.

[14]"The pulpits against the western end are built up against an outer window, with alternate panes of red and white glass in the arched transom." Mather, "Early Days of Mormonism," 209.

[15]"The winds and storms, the frosts and rains, of half a century nearly, had denuded the walls in many places of its plastering. The plastering has been replaced and the marking, though unfortunately the color of the new plaster is different from the old." "Kirtland," February 10, 1887, 3.

[16]"Sunday night, about 7 o'clock, the Temple was discovered to be on fire in the ceiling of the third story, where the pipe goes into the chimney." "Kirtland," October 4, 1883, 3. Heman Smith, "Kirtland Temple," 427.

Note that 1883 was an eventful year for firefighters in Kirtland as the *Willoughby Independent* reported,

> Kirtland came very near having a first-class fire last Thursday. Mr. Yaxley was engaged in putting a tin roof on the Temple belfry, and the wind being high some coal from his furnace was blown to the roof and cornice, some fifteen and thirty feet below, which was soon ablaze, and being in rather an inaccessible place the danger for a short time was quite imminent; but by cutting a hole from the inside the fire was finally reached and extinguished. Kirtland, May 15, 1883. (From the Kirtland Newspaper Clippings File)

[17]"Kirtland Temple: Recent Architectural Changes," 2.

[18]Yarrington, "Kirtland Temple Is Closed for Repairs"; "Kirtland Temple Repairs Completed."

[19]Independence Temple Drawings, signed set; Gomer Griffiths, "Reminiscences," 723; see also Launius, *Kirtland Temple*, 55; Jenson, Journal History, October 19, 1841, 1; W. W. Phelps to Sally Phelps, January 1836, 577, "History of the Kirtland Temple," 22.

[20]Arthur Allen to Kelly, 2.

[21]*Painesville Telegraph*, August 18, 1904, 2.

[22]Wellington, "Kirtland Temple Gets Face Lifting."

[23]One of the guides at the temple, Elbert Shepard, relates that young boys would climb the quoins quite easily because of their large projection, and if no mothers were around, some would make it nearly to the eaves.

[24]"Kirtland Temple: Recent Architectural Changes," 2.

[25]E. L. Kelley to William Kelley.

[26]Edwards, *History of the Reorganized Church*, 5:472.

[27]These benches were removed in 1952, and similar seats placed along the sidewalls may have been removed at the same time. "Kirtland Temple: Recent Architectural Changes," 1.

[28]The modification likely would have occurred after 1907, when Edison purchased the tungsten filament patent and began production of light bulbs with a long enough service life to make them practical.

[29]The tool is currently on display in a glass case on the third floor.

[30]Ross to Curry; "Kirtland Temple, Recent Architectural Changes," 1; Launius, *Kirtland Temple*, 122. Note that some kind of fire protection was installed twelve years earlier. See "Kirtland Temple: Recent Architectural Changes," 2.

[31]Kirtland Temple Pulpit Lettering; Howe, *Historical Collections of Ohio* (1908), 2:35. Howe's description gives the initials in ascending order while the Kirtland Temple Pulpit Lettering note graphically locates each location, eliminating, however, the letters on the "communion table[s]." See also Petersen, "Kirtland Temple," 406–9.

[32]Mather, "Early Days of Mormonism," 209.

[33]"Report of Elders," 788. Note that the observer could have misunderstood that the lowest tier in the stands never had pulpits like those above, and it is possible that nothing was removed from the lowest tier when the rostum was put in place.

[34]Note that other temples has different lettering systems on the pulpits. See Cowen, "House of the Lord in Kirtland," 114–15.

[35]Corrill, *Brief History of the Church*, 22.

[36]Ryder, *Voigtländer and I*, 70; Mather, "Early Days of Mormonism," 210; Mary Griffiths to Lewis, 1. Lachlan Mackay proposes a different interpretation for the known evidence concerning the pews in the upper court. He suggests that the tables described by Corrill in 1839 were replaced with pews by the Saints between 1839–44, which explains why Ryder mentions them in 1850. Later, he suggests, the town removed the pews in order to have an open room for community functions, explaining why there were no pews in 1860. Lachlan Mackay, personal communication, 1997.

**9-1.** St. George Temple under construction, March 1876.

# Chapter 9

# The Kirtland Temple's Influence on Later Temple Building

The Kirtland Temple stands at the head of a line of temples constructed by followers of Joseph Smith. Each time they moved, the Saints initiated plans for building temples, plans that were not always realized. In each case, the temple was to be the focal point of the larger city plan. For example, Joseph Smith's "Plat of the City of Zion," which accompanied the Independence Temple plans, shows twenty-four temples forming a complex in the center of the city. Just what one would do with twenty-four temples was not specified, but given that the Kirtland Temple was to be a "house of learning . . . [and] a house of order" (D&C 88:119), educational and administrative uses can be understood as part of the temple functions. Furthermore, the dimensions and arrangement given in Doctrine and Covenants 94 for the Kirtland printing house are the same as those given for the Kirtland Temple, and both buildings are called, simply, "houses." These similarities imply that if the printing house had been built as originally envisioned, it would have been considered a temple, also. These various functions may explain part of the need for multiple "temples" at what the Saints hoped would be the eventual headquarters of the Church. Thus Joseph Smith's designation of twenty-four temples may refer to an administrative center not unlike the building complexes that serve in Salt Lake City as the headquarters of the LDS Church and in Independence, Missouri, of the RLDS Church.[1]

## Missouri Temples

After being forced out of Jackson County, Missouri, the intended site of the Independence Temple, the Saints laid and dedicated the cornerstone for a new temple in Far West, Missouri. The Saints also began to raise funds for construction.[2] However, persecution in this area rapidly overtook the Mormon communities, and the plans were never realized.

## The Nauvoo Temple

The next temple built, and the only other temple fully designed under the leadership of Joseph Smith, was the Nauvoo Temple, which was begun in 1841 and completed in 1846. The Nauvoo Temple plans called for a building about 128 feet by 88 feet, approximately a 60 percent increase over the dimensions of the Kirtland Temple. Because of the building's increased size, the interstitial spaces between floors to each side of the arched ceiling were tall enough to hold a series of offices. The Nauvoo Temple was built of cut limestone, not rubble sandstone plastered over to look like cut stone. The general plan established in Kirtland was followed in Nauvoo, with the proportion of length to breadth roughly the same in both temples and as were the two large congregational spaces and sets of double pulpits intended for each space. This time, however, Joseph Smith could capitalize on the skills of a trained architect, William Weeks, who produced several preliminary renderings (fig. 9-2). Owing to the skill of Weeks, the original design of the Nauvoo Temple was not a combination of several architectural styles but was a far more coherent composition in the Greek Revival style.[3]

Specific elements in the Nauvoo Temple design can be attributed directly to Joseph Smith. The sun and moon motifs on the capitals and bases of the pilasters certainly were done under his direction. In addition, the preliminary concept of Gothic arches in the pediment window recalls the specification of "gothic tops" for the windows in Kirtland. Happily, this Gothic detailing was eliminated in final designs, as it does not blend well with the boldly articulated Greek Revival shell. Joseph directed that the pediment be replaced with a full attic story on the facade to provide additional office space (fig. 9-3). Having commissioned the construction of one temple and various schoolhouses, offices, and homes, Joseph began to voice aesthetic opinions as well. Despite the architect's objections, Joseph was determined to include round windows in place of the semicircular ones on the side elevation.[4]

The construction of the Nauvoo Temple was radically different from that of the Kirtland Temple. Weeks's detailed drawings eliminated the errors in design that can result from overlooking structural spaces. Furthermore, the initial construction phases were not marked by scarcity of materials and workers as they were in Kirtland although there were some problems. Truman Angell recalled that the foundations were "much botched" by the committee that began construction.[5] But this problem seems to have resulted from a lack of communication between the committee and the architect and not from a lack of architectural expertise.

The larger Nauvoo Temple was also designed for a more elaborate series of functions. Because baptisms on behalf of the dead had been instituted, the basement was provided with a large baptismal font instead of a dirt crawl space. Like its Solomonic counterpart, this font sat on the backs of twelve oxen.[6]

A key functional difference between the Kirtland and Nauvoo Temples is the provision for the expanded endowment ceremony, which was initiated in Nauvoo. This ceremony portrays the history of the earth from the Creation up to the establishment of God's law on earth. In the endowment, faithful Saints make personal promises to God. Prior to the completion of the Nauvoo Temple, Joseph Smith conducted endowments and sealings with close associates in an upper room of his red brick store. Joseph Smith was murdered before the Nauvoo Temple was completed, and Brigham Young later continued these ceremonies in the temple. The temple endowment marks a point of departure between the LDS and RLDS Churches. The RLDS Church rejects much of the doctrine, including temple ceremonies, that the LDS Church believes Joseph Smith established in Nauvoo.

The endowment ceremony was conducted in the Nauvoo Temple in the long central area of the attic that was flanked by offices.[7] Unlike the roof of the Kirtland Temple, whose king-post trusses divided the attic space into five separate areas, the Nauvoo Temple roof was framed with a queen-post truss, which leaves the central portion of the attic undivided. Curtains organized the large attic space into cubicles sized appropriately for the endowment, eliminating the need to divide up the larger congregational spaces in the rooms below.[8] An unusual access complication was thus created: the basement and attic had precisely defined functions that were not open to public viewing, while the two main congregational spaces (the upper one of which was never finished) were intended for public meetings.

The awkwardness of this division was never realized, however, because the Nauvoo Temple was still incomplete when the Saints were driven out of the city.[9] Most of the Saints left under duress in February 1846, while a skeleton crew of carpenters and joiners under the supervision of Truman Angell finished the structure[10]—the commitment to complete the temple against all odds, originally demonstrated in Kirtland, was fully evident in Nauvoo. The temple was finally dedicated in a secret session on April 30, 1846, and in a public session the following day. It must have been with some emotion that Wilford Woodruff (who later became the fourth president of the LDS Church), Orson Hyde, and Joseph Young, along with Angell and his crew, closed the doors after the dedication ceremonies and essentially abandoned the temple on which they had worked so long and hard. The crew then joined the ten thousand Saints and their leaders who had already settled on the banks of the Missouri River and were making preparations for the trek west.

The Nauvoo Temple survived the following summer but must have sustained substantial superficial damage when the city was attacked by the "Carthage guerrillas" in September and the remaining six hundred Saints

**9-2.** Front elevation of the Nauvoo Temple, preliminary design by William Weeks. Joseph Smith specified the sun and moon motifs for the pilaster capitals and bases.

Drawn by W<sup>m</sup> Weeks Nauvoo

**9-3.** Nauvoo Temple, final design by William Weeks. In contrast to the earlier design, this one, as directed by Joseph Smith, provides for a full attic story rather than a pediment.

were driven across the Mississippi River. The extent of such damage is largely a moot point as an arsonist's fire gutted the structure in November 1848. The blackened walls were leveled by a tornado in May 1850, and in later years, local inhabitants used the site as a quarry.

## The Salt Lake Temple

The next temple employing the Kirtland pattern of two stacked congregational rooms was the Salt Lake Temple, whose site was designated July 28, 1847, only four days after Brigham Young arrived in the Salt Lake Valley. This temple became the first to function as a city's focal point, a function envisioned in 1833 by Joseph Smith in his "Plat of the City of Zion."[11] When William Weeks found conditions in the frontier religious community not to his liking, Truman Angell, who had finished major portions of the temple in Kirtland and supervised the final phase of construction in Nauvoo, became the official architect of the Salt Lake Temple.

Originally designed to follow the basic pattern established in Kirtland, the Salt Lake Temple was to have had two main congregational spaces, each provided with sets of pulpits at each end.[12] Similar to that of the Nauvoo Temple, the plan for the Salt Lake Temple included a baptismal font in the basement and offices in the mezzanine floors beside the arched ceilings of the main spaces. A departure from the pattern was necessary, however, because the roof pitch was not high enough for additional rooms in the attic to be used for temple ceremonies. The original intent seems to have been to use either one of the main rooms or the mezzanine offices for temple ceremonies.

An obvious difference between the Salt Lake Temple and the Kirtland and Nauvoo Temples is the multiple towers at each end representing offices in the Aaronic and Melchizedek Priesthoods. However, the most significant difference from the Kirtland-Nauvoo tradition is the Salt Lake Temple's radical change in style. Rather than employ current architectural fashion (relative to the skills of available craftsmen), the Salt Lake Temple follows a nonacademic design best described as castellated Gothic. The Gothic period is characterized by decorative battlements, or crenellations, on the roof parapet and by squared towers topped by pointed spires. A rather successful design composition, the temple's thick stone walls beautifully communicate its pioneer heritage, while the castellations perhaps reflect an unconscious desire to defend it against the fate that befell the Nauvoo Temple (fig. 9-4).[13]

The temple's unique design is generally attributed to Truman Angell, for he drew the initial designs and plans (fig. 9-5). However, the design's attribution is more complex than is generally conceded. First, the heavy, massive

**9-4.** Exterior view, Salt Lake Temple, by H. H. Thomas, Ogden, Utah, 1893. The decorative battlements on the roof parapet and the squared towers topped by pointed spires are characteristic of the Gothic style. The battlements perhaps reflect an unconscious desire to defend the temple.

wall buttresses are very different from the lighter, more planar ornament used by Angell in the Kirtland Temple. Second, the overall proportions of the Salt Lake Temple are more pleasing than are those of other buildings designed by Truman Angell, for example, Angell's plans for a state capitol in Fillmore, Utah, and for a temple in St. George, Utah. These two structures are awkwardly designed and reflect the work of someone with little training in aesthetic composition. The oversized, stilted dome of the Fillmore capitol and

**9-5.** Salt Lake Temple, south elevation drawing by Truman O. Angell, 1854.

Courtesy LDS Church Archives.

the squat, undersized spire designed (but never built) for the St. George Temple show that Angell's main skill was in working with his hands and not in designing. On the other hand, the Salt Lake Temple design with its sturdy, but well-proportioned, towers bespeaks a sensitive aesthetic eye, although one that was academically untrained. The person who had painted and glazed the Kirtland Temple, who had succeeded Joseph Smith as a prophet and who directly supervised Angell's work—Brigham Young—is surely the one who envisioned the very successful design of the Salt Lake Temple.

One of Angell's assistants, William Ward, described the beginnings of Brigham Young's involvement in the temple's design:

> Brigham Young drew upon a slate in the architect's office a sketch, and said to Truman O. Angell: "There will be three towers on the east, representing the President and his two Counselors; also three similar towers on the west representing the Presiding Bishop and his two Counselors; the towers on the east the Melchisedek priesthood, those on the west the Aaronic preisthood [sic]. The center towers will be higher than those on the sides, and the west towers a little lower than those on the east end. The body of the building will be between these and pillars will be necessary to support the floors." Angell . . . drew the following vertical section according to Brigham's instructions. . . . The second story like the first. The construction of the roof was left to Mr. Angell.[14]

The most immediate source for the Salt Lake Temple's Gothic style would have been the Early English period of architecture. In 1856, Brigham Young sent Angell to England on a mission partly to study architecture. Angell described the purpose of that mission in his diary:

> I am now makeing ready for a visit to Europe my ame [aim] will be to vissit the works of men a preaching as I go at the same time visit [?] the old cathederals &c&c and seek to improve the art of building if the experence can be got more extenelly then at home.[15]

However, this mission to England occurred two years after the initial design of the Salt Lake Temple was published in 1854. Not only was it impossible for this trip to have any effect on the style chosen for the initial design of the Salt Lake Temple, but Angell also remained singularly unimpressed with the architecture he saw. On the other hand, Brigham Young had seen English cathedrals firsthand during his 1840 mission to England fourteen years before the public announcement of the Salt Lake Temple's design.

Ward states that he never heard any discussion of style between Brigham Young and Truman Angell, and he implies that the choice of a Gothic style was Angell's.[16] However, the differences in experience between the President and the architect indicate Brigham Young was certainly the source of the temple's style.[17] Brigham Young would have been primarily responsible for the overall style and composition of the Salt Lake Temple, while Angell would have worked out the details and benefited from Brigham Young's craftsman's eye.

While the choice of the Gothic style certainly reflected the temple's cultural associations with the great cathedrals of Europe, the Salt Lake Temple does not replicate any building from England or anywhere else. Both Brigham Young and Angell sought to create a building that did not copy the buildings of the religious world that had rejected them.[18]

Another major difference between the Kirtland and the Salt Lake Temples was a heightened concern for permanence. During the construction of the Kirtland Temple, Church members optimistically prepared for the establishment of the New Jerusalem and the imminent return of Jesus Christ. While the object of their preparation had not changed, the general perception of its time frame had. The Saints expected the Salt Lake Temple to last not only until a distant Second Coming, but also through the thousand years of the Millennium.[19]

Due to this expectation of longevity and probably due to the observation of settlements and cracks in the Kirtland Temple, particular care was taken with the foundations of the Salt Lake Temple. In 1858 the foundations were covered over to hide them from the approaching Johnston's army, a disciplinary force sent to curb the "rebellion" reported by the territorial governor, who apparently was frustrated by Brigham Young's de facto power.[20]

When the foundations were uncovered several years later, the red sandstone had cracked. As a consequence, the upper sections of the foundation were torn out and replaced with more durable granite blocks. At one point, Brigham Young championed the use of adobe for the structure, arguing that over time it would solidify into a solid rock mass.[21] Fortunately, he was overruled by others, and a hard, durable granite was eventually chosen.

## The St. George Temple

During the construction of the Salt Lake Temple, another temple was built in St. George, Utah. Begun in 1871 and dedicated in 1877, this smaller structure was built rapidly, in contrast to the Salt Lake Temple, whose hewn granite blocks required tremendous amounts of time to prepare. Like the Kirtland Temple, the St. George Temple was built of a rough local stone and then plastered over. Obviously this building technique recalled Artemus Millett's contribution at Kirtland. However, at St. George no lines were painted on the temple's surface to imitate cut stone. Instead, its architect, Truman Angell, leaned heavily on his experience from the Salt Lake Temple design, employing similar stepped wall buttresses, window patterns, and a castellated parapet. The brilliant white stucco covering provides a dramatic contrast with the red cliffs that surround St. George, and the light and shadow of the buttresses handsomely articulates the surface of the temple.

However, as was mentioned previously, the overall proportioning of the building is awkward at best. Angell, who loved to work with his hands, could replicate ornament from pattern books with great skill but could not deal effectively with overall design. The short, stubby spire in the original design (as well as the original cupola (fig. 9-1), which was replaced with a taller, more elegant cupola after being struck by lightning) looks like it was proportioned to fit on the sheet of paper on which the plan was drawn rather than designed to provide an effective accent to the vertical wall buttresses (fig. 9-6).

The interior arrangement of the St. George Temple is virtually identical to that of the previous completed temples, having two large rooms with arched ceilings (fig. 9-7). The St. George Temple's lower roof pitch does not allow for attic rooms. To accommodate the temple ceremonies, a light framework to hold curtains was erected in the center of the large open room.[22] But the St. George Temple was the last to preserve the internal arrangement developed in Kirtland. The Salt Lake Temple interior was modified before completion (as were the interiors of the Logan and Manti Temples) to provide four separate rooms that could be occupied in succession as the endowment ceremony progressed.

FRONT ELEVATION OF THE TEMPLE
ST GEORGE

**9-6.** St. George Temple, elevation drawing by Truman O. Angell. When the temple was built, a squat cupola was substituted for the awkwardly proportioned spire shown in the drawing. Later it was replaced with a taller, more elegant cupola.

**9-7.** St. George Temple, section drawing by Truman O. Angell. The two large rooms with arched ceilings are similar to those of the Kirtland and Nauvoo Temples. The St. George Temple was the last temple where this arrangement was followed.

However, all the nineteenth-century temples (as well as larger twentieth-century ones) continue the Kirtland tradition of an upper court, now called a solemn assembly room. These rooms retain the multiple pulpits placed at each end of the hall. However, no curtains are provided in the solemn assembly rooms, and in several of the temples, the lower ceilings above the side seating areas have been replaced with a balcony to provide additional seating.

As of 1996, approximately sixty temples are built or planned by the LDS Church. The introduction of audiovisual media in the temple ceremony greatly changed the physical requirements of temple plans. As a consequence, temples built after World War II share only formal imagery with the early temples. However, temples continue to be the focal point of Latter-day Saint worship, serving as physical symbols of the Latter-day Saint faith.

## Temples and the RLDS Church

The temple-building tradition of the RLDS Church has been markedly different from that of the LDS Church since the RLDS Church rejects post-Kirtland Temple doctrine.[23] When the RLDS Church established their headquarters in Independence, Missouri, they had to deal with the plot of land dedicated by Joseph Smith for the construction of the Independence Temple. This plot was designated as the point of "gathering of his saints to stand upon Mount Zion. . . . The city New Jerusalem shall be built by the gathering of the saints, beginning at this place, even the place of the temple, which temple shall be reared in this generation" (D&C 84:2, 4). The persecutions in Independence and surrounding counties from 1833 through 1839 had prevented the fulfillment of this command, but by inference, establishing the New Jerusalem required building a temple there.

In 1968, President W. Wallace Smith received a revelation instructing the RLDS Church to build the Independence Temple.[24] The 1968 revelation concerning the temple was not without controversy since the adoption of temples had been one of the outward differences that distinguished the RLDS and LDS Churches from each other. However, one of the provisions added to the revelation flatly states that no "secret ordinances," referring to ceremonies such as those in LDS temples, would be performed in the temple.[25]

Photo by author.

9-8. The Temple, Independence, Missouri, RLDS Church. Designed by Hellmuth, Obata, and Kassabaum, Independence, Mo., 1990–92. The temple's design is a complete break from the Kirtland Temple form.

The architectural plans were unveiled twenty years later. Much like the Kirtland Temple, the twentieth-century RLDS Temple in Independence serves as a general administrative center, educational center, and headquarters for the first presidency. In contrast to the unusual spire and strikingly beautiful sanctuary interior, the office wing attached to the sanctuary directly relates to the function of the attic offices in the Kirtland Temple.

The architectural form of the RLDS Independence Temple reflects the contemporary stance of the church towards its historical past. Designed by the well-known architectural firm of Hellmuth, Obata, and Kassabaum, the temple, with its conchlike spiral above the sanctuary, represents a complete stylistic break from LDS temple architecture and the Kirtland Temple form (fig. 9-8). In spite of the RLDS Church's tendency to divide into traditional and progressive camps—the former wishing to emphasize Joseph Smith Jr.'s role in the history of the Church, the latter desiring to align itself more closely with mainstream Protestantism—the design managed to appeal to all. The mere presence of a temple appeals to the traditionalists, while the unusual design appeals to the progressives. Although the temple's functional role in the RLDS Church is still evolving, it seems clear that the Temple in Independence will not be the first of a series, as in LDS tradition, but rather will remain the sole RLDS temple.

## Notes

[1]Cowan, "History of Latter-day Saint Temples from 1831 to 1990," 4:1451, states that in June 1833, Joseph Smith "drew up a plat for the city of Zion, specifying that twenty-four temples *or sacred buildings* would be built in the heart of the city to serve a *variety of priesthood functions*" (italics added). For information on the multiple functions of temples in the ancient world, see Parry, *Temples of the Ancient World*.

[2]"March 27th [1837] I signed $50. fifty Dollars for the building of the house of the Lord in Zion the subscription list was in the hands of Elder Elisha H. Groves." Jessee, "Kirtland Diary of Wilford Woodruff," 386.

[3]For Andrew, this poses the question of "how did he [Joseph Smith] maintain any pretense of the Lord's having inspired the structure while at the same time employing a professional architect?" Andrew, *Early Temples of the Mormons*, 62. This line of reasoning is confused by calling Weeks in the previous paragraph a "builder rather than an architect." However, choosing to designate those responsible for working out the design of the Kirtland Temple as builders and Weeks as a professional architect does not change the nature of the responsibility for the design. In fact, the Nauvoo commission is quite similar to that in Kirtland. In both cases, Joseph Smith dictated the general pattern while the best available experts worked out the details, including the style. Joseph Smith's "pretense" did not pose a problem for anyone in Nauvoo, nor did it provide grist for the mills of his detractors.

[4]*History of the Church*, 6:196–97. Joseph Smith said, "I have seen in vision the splendid appearance of that building illuminated, and will have it built according to the pattern shown me."

[5]Angell to Taylor and Council, 2.

[6]Proxy baptisms for deceased individuals had been conducted in the Mississippi River for a short period of time but were continued in the font in the still-unfinished Nauvoo Temple. Colvin, "Nauvoo Temple," 3:1001–3. These and other ordinances for deceased persons contributed to the

sense of urgency in completing the temple, since individuals wished to perform what they believed were saving ordinances for departed loved ones.

The building's original font was wooden and was dedicated before the completion of the building so that these ordinances could take place. After Joseph Smith's death, the wooden font was replaced by a more substantial stone font. See Brigham Young, "Epistle of the Twelve," 779.

[7]Lisle Brown, "Sacred Departments," 366–74.

[8]The line of queen posts to each side marks the walls that formed the offices for the Quorum of the Twelve Apostles and the dressing rooms for the participants in the endowment ceremony.

[9]Andrew suggests that public access to the Nauvoo Temple would have had to have been restricted had the Saints not been driven out of the city. See Andrew, *Early Temples of the Mormons*, 85, 89.

[10]Lisle Brown, "Sacred Departments," 374.

[11]In the sense that the streets of Salt Lake were surveyed and numbered starting from the southeast corner of Temple Square, the Salt Lake Temple is the first one to serve as the geographical focal point. Nauvoo was not laid out around the temple as was Salt Lake City, but in other ways the Nauvoo Temple also was a focal point. See Esplin, "Significance of Nauvoo," 71–73.

[12]In "Exterior Symbolism of the Salt Lake Temple," Oman notes that the tiered towers of the Salt Lake Temple reflect the Kirtland Temple's tiered pulpits.

[13] Oman takes the position that the temple's battlements, narrow doorways, walls up to sixteen feet thick, and orientation to the surrounding wall and streets symbolize the guardedness and exclusivity of the temple's teachings and rituals. Oman, "Exterior Symbolism of the Salt Lake Temple."

[14]"Who Designed the Temple?" 578–79.

[15]Angell, Diary, April 11, 1856.

[16]"On several occasions the foundation and thickness of the walls was the subject of conversations. But I do not recollect any talk between Brigham and Angell in regard to the style of the building." "Who Designed the Temple?" 578–79. However, Brigham did say he saw the temple in vision:

> Five years ago last July I . . . saw in the Spirit the Temple not ten feet from where we have laid the Chief Corner Stone. I have not inquired what kind of a Temple we should build. Why? Because it was represented before me. I have never looked upon that ground, but the vision of it was there. I see it as plainly as if it was in reality before me. . . . It will have six towers, to begin with, instead of one. (Brigham Young, in *Journal of Discourses*, 1:133, April 6, 1853)

[17]Brigham Young also supervised the architectural design of the Logan and Manti Temples. Paul Anderson, "William Harrison Folsom," 253.

[18]"Angell's idea and aim was to make it [the Salt Lake Temple] different to any other known building, and I think he succeeded as to the general combination." Ward, "Who Designed the Temple?" 578–79.

Traditional meetinghouse forms were not used as a pattern for the early Utah temples. Nonetheless, this observation does not confirm Andrew's assertion that "none of the temples erected in Utah has any relationship to architecture having religious connotations." Andrew, *Early Temples of the Mormons*, 134. Even if one makes the rather pejorative assessment that the Kirtland and Nauvoo temples are nonreligious buildings (thereby discounting the obvious heritage owed by the Utah temples to these two forerunners), Andrew seems to be unaware of the general connection between Gothic architecture and ecclesiastical buildings, a symbolic relationship already noted in relation to the windows of the Kirtland Temple.

[19]Brigham Young said, "I want to see the Temple built in a manner that it will endure through the Millennium. This is not the only Temple we shall build; There will be hundreds of them built and dedicated to the Lord. This Temple will be known as the first Temple built in the mountains by the Latter-day Saints." Brigham Young, in *Journal of Discourses*, 10:254, October 6, 1863.

[20]Holzapfel, *Every Stone a Sermon*, 20.

[21]"I want to occupy a few moments more, and talk about our contemplated temple. It has been moved, seconded, and carried by this Conference, that we build a temple here of the best material that America affords. If this is done, it will have to be built of platina; and I do not know that there is any of it to be got in this territory. . . . If we cannot get the platina, we must build a temple of pure gold;

that is here, I know. But if the Conference wants us to build a temple of pure gold, they will have to put into the tithing stores something besides old half-dead stinking cows, and old broken-kneed horses; or if they even put in all the good cattle they possess, will it build a temple of gold, of silver, or of brass? No, it will not. . . .

"If you take this clay, which is to be found in abundance on these bottom lands, and mix with it these pebble rocks, and make adobies of the compound, it will petrify in the wall and become a solid rock in five hundred years, so as to be fit to cut into millstones to grind flour, while the other materials I have mentioned will have decomposed, and gone back to their native elements. . . . As for the durability of such a building, the longer it stands the better it becomes; if it stands five thousand years, it increases in its strength until it comes to its highest perfection, before it begins to decay." Brigham Young, in *Journal of Discourses*, 1:218–20, October 9, 1852.

[22]These "curtains and frames for partitions" were mentioned in the dedicatory prayer by Daniel H. Wells. DeMille, *St. George Temple*, 64.

[23]Although the endowment ceremony as practiced by the LDS Church was never accepted by the RLDS Church, Joseph Smith III apparently contemplated performing baptisms for the dead, which would have required some sort of special structure. See Launius, "Ambivalent Rejection."

[24]Book of Doctrine and Covenants, 149:6a.

[25]Launius, "Reorganized Church and the Independence Temple."

# Conclusion

# Visitors to the Temple

The Kirtland Temple is a remarkable structure when viewed in its time and place. Few buildings of this size and scale were built with such meager economic resources and such constant outside opposition. The temple is also unusual because of its construction techniques. The rubblework-and-stucco construction technique imported from Canada and the unusual design of two stacked main rooms with multiple pulpits and curtains set the temple apart from contemporaneous religious structures in the United States. Further-more, the different craftsmen who worked on the building each left his mark. Jacob Bump's older design style, with its deep carving and its reliance on moldings formed with simple circular curves, represents the generation trained at the beginning of the nineteenth century. With Bump's departure, younger artisans such as Truman Angell took over and updated the interior details using newer carpenter's manuals. These stylistic changes in interior de-sign provide a unique opportunity to study in one building the vernacular design practices of several decades.

Those who revere Joseph Smith as a prophet have always looked upon the Kirtland Temple with special reverence. One reason for this reverence is the numerous visitations from heavenly beings that have occurred in the temple. Mary Ann Winters recalls how such visitations made the temple more significant to her as a girl:

> After the close of one of the meetings, mother took me to the stand and showed me the place on the pulpit where the Savior had stood when He appeared to the Prophet, and where afterwards Moses and Elias came and delivered the keys for the gathering of the Saints (Israel), and the redemption of the dead.[1]

This simple action by mother and daughter demonstrates the temple's role as a kind of pilgrimage site in Mormon life, both during the Kirtland period and after. Early Mormon missionaries traveling to the eastern United

States and abroad would often stop in Kirtland to view the temple. Martin Harris led one such group during the time he possessed keys to the temple:

> In answer to our knock there came to the door of the cottage a poorly clad, emaciated little man, on whom the winter of life was weighing heavily. . . . After some time, however, the old man said, "You want to see the Temple, do you?" "Yes, indeed," I exclaimed, "If we may." "Well, I'll get the key." From that moment, Martin Harris, in spite of occasional outbursts, radiated with interest. He led us through the rooms of the Temple and explained how they were used. He pointed out the place of the School of the Prophets. He showed where the temple curtain had at one time hung. He related thrilling experiences in connection with the history of the sacred building.[2]

That the building itself left quite an impression on visitors is clear from this reminiscence: "Well do I remember the feelings of awe and wonder I experienced attending a Mormon service upon the first floor as the great white scrolls rose and fell."[3]

Not all residents of the area viewed these visits with enthusiasm. A rather disdainful area resident in 1842 stated that "many of that misguided people still linger around their former Zion, and look upon their first temple as an object of uncommon sanctity—hence it has become a kind of Mecca—to these miserable fanatics, and if any get in trouble they flee here for a refuge."[4] The attitude behind this statement seems to be a holdover from the controversies which swirled through Kirtland in 1837. The fact that relatively few worshipers and visitors came to the temple in the 1840s seems to have calmed the fears and resentment of area residents, and eventually the temple was accepted as part of the community. Some visitors, however, shared in this disdain for the group that produced the temple. On one occasion a

> man called to see the House of the Lord, in company with another gentleman. On entering the door they were politely invited, by the gentleman who had charge of the house, to take off their hats. One of them replied with the request unhesitatingly, while the other observed that he would not take off his hat nor bow to "Jo Smith," but that he had made "Jo" bow to him at a certain time. He was immediately informed by Elder Morey, the keeper of the house, that his first business was to leave, for when a man insulted Joseph Smith he, Brother Morey, was himself insulted. The man manifested much anger, but left the house.[5]

Other visitors were motivated purely by inquisitiveness and not by rancor. As part of "an equestrian party of eight," Lucia Goldsmith reports attending a service held in the temple while it was still under construction.[6] Many were doubtless anxious to see the prophet who had caused such a stir in the neighborhood. Similarly, James Ryder, who visited the temple in 1850 and set up a photography studio for a brief period, stated, "I visited the temple and explored it with much interest and curiosity."[7]

When the RLDS Church gained ownership of the Kirtland Temple, Bishop E. L. Kelly began giving informal tours. Although visitors were few, his wife Cassie reported that "they pay one usually," a welcome event given the great expense incurred in repairing the structure.[8] By 1888 the uproar over the issue of polygamy in Utah had captured the nation's eye; although the Reorganized Church had nothing to do with polygamy, the *Willoughby Independent* reported that the "Temple is daily receiving a large number of visitors."[9] Such was the popular interest that several businessmen offered the RLDS Church one hundred thousand dollars to purchase the temple, intending to dismantle it and re-erect it at the Columbian Exposition held in Chicago in 1892.[10] When the LDS Church discontinued the practice of polygamy, interest in the temple by the curious waned.

Visitors to the Kirtland Temple increased again when the RLDS Church instituted temple reunions. Later, the development of interstate highways (I-90 is only about three miles north of the temple) facilitated visits by individuals and tour groups on the way to other significant Mormon historical sites in upstate New York and Vermont. This influx eventually led in the 1960s to the establishment of a Visitors' Center and a regular program of guided tours of the temple. With the LDS Church's recent restoration of the Newel K. Whitney Store in Kirtland, the numbers of visitors to the Kirtland Temple will undoubtedly increase.

More than any other factor, the claim of its design's divine origins sets the Kirtland Temple apart from most nineteenth-century American structures, as American Protestantism has generally eschewed such close communication with deity. Although monetary difficulties are normal in building projects, the Saints' degree of economic sacrifice to build the Kirtland Temple, especially when faced with local opposition, seems almost absurd from the vantage point of late-twentieth-century American society. However, this sacrifice underscores the deep commitment the early Saints brought to the project. More than a record of the lives of the early Saints, the Kirtland Temple is a monument to a people's faith and commitment to their God. The Kirtland Temple's physical fabric communicates to us, living in a different century and different societal framework, the challenges, sacrifices, and faith of these early Saints.

*Notes*

[1] "Autobiographical Sketch of Mary Ann Stearns Winters," 3.

[2] Homer, "Passing of Martin Harris," 469.

[3] Tayer, undated newspaper clipping.

[4] La Moody to Postmaster. La Moody's reason for writing was the sighting of Orrin Porter Rockwell.

[5]*History of the Church*, 2:401.
[6]Goldsmith, "Rigdon, the First Mormon Elder."
[7]Ryder, *Voitländer and I*, 69.
[8]Cassie Kelley to E. L. Kelley, September 1 [and 6], 1885.
[9]*Willoughby Independent*, July 1888?.
[10]Launius, *Kirtland Temple*, 129.

# Appendix A

# Documented Chronology of the Kirtland Temple

List of abbreviations used in this chronology:

HC    Joseph Smith Jr. *History of The Church of Jesus Christ of Latter-day Saints*. Edited by B. H. Roberts. 2d ed., rev. 7 vols. Salt Lake City: Deseret Book, 1971.

JD    Brigham Young and others. *Journal of Discourses*. 26 vols. Liverpool: F. D. Richards, 1855–86.

PJS    Dean C. Jessee, ed. *The Papers of Joseph Smith*. 2 vols. Salt Lake City: Deseret Book, 1992.

PWJS    Dean C. Jessee, comp. and ed. *The Personal Writings of Joseph Smith*. Salt Lake City: Deseret Book, 1984.

**December 28, 1832.** Revelation given to Joseph Smith commanding Saints to "establish . . . a house of God."

D&C 88:119.

**January 11, 1833.** "The Lord commanded us in Kirtland to build an house of God."

Joseph Smith Jr. to Phelps, in *PWJS*, 263.

**June 1, 1833.** Temple building committee (Hyrum Smith, Reynolds Cahoon, and Jared Carter) issues a circular asking members to contribute funds. Revelation specifies the dimensions of the temple and the function of the upper and lower courts and chastises the Church members for "not consider[ing]" the commandment to build a temple. Hyrum, "determined to be the first at the work," clears the ground.

HC, 1:349–52. D&C 95. Lucy Mack Smith, "History of Lucy Smith," 189–90.

**June 3–4, 1833.** Conference held in which construction of temple was discussed. Joseph Smith, Sidney Rigdon, and Frederick G. Williams appointed "to obtain a draft or construction of the inner court."

> HC, 1:352.

Joseph Smith, Sidney Rigdon, and Frederick G. Williams see temple plan in vision. Later, leading mechanic John Carl, a carriage builder, wants to arrange seats in the temple contrary to Joseph's proposal. Joseph insists on arranging seating according to the vision.

> Angell, "Journal," 124. Kimball, "Extract of Journal," 771. "History of Brigham Young," *Millennial Star*, 535. Orson Pratt, "Order," in *JD*, 14:273–74. *JD*, 2:31; 13:357; 18:131–32; 19:16. *Ohio (Hudson) Observer*, August 11, 1836. Angell to Taylor and Council. Coe, "Mormonism," 4. Belnap, Autobiography, 11–12.

Plan and site for temple construction are selected.

> Lucy Mack Smith, *History of Joseph Smith*, 230–31.

**June 5–6, 1833.** George A. Smith hauls first load of stone; Hyrum Smith and Reynolds Cahoon dig a trench for the walls. Conference votes that the building committee should immediately start obtaining the stone, brick, and lumber.

> HC, 1:353–54. Lorenzo Young, "Narrative," 42. George Smith, "Memoirs," 10.

**July 23, 1833.** Cornerstones are laid.

> HC, 1:400. Brigham Young, "Temple Corner Stones," 1:133–35. Jenson, Journal History, July 23, 1833, 1–2.

**July–August 1833.** Joel Hills Johnson begins making bricks for the temple.

> Joel Johnson, Autobiography, 5.

**Summer 1833.** Levi W. Hancock donates $50 to temple fund. Works on temple "when ever I could."

> Hancock, Diary, 76.

**1833.** Work on temple continues.

> William Smith, *William Smith on Mormonism*. Cahoon, Autobiography.

**September 4, 1833.** Temple work makes great progress. Joseph Smith hopes to be finished by spring 1834 so "we can have a place to worship where we shall not be molested." Joseph Smith labors with his own hands.

> Joseph Smith Jr. to Jaques, in *PWJS*, 295–96.

**September 1833.** William Burgess is one of the chief carpenters. Walls reach four feet above the ground.

William Burgess, Autobiography, 95–96.

**September 25, 1833.** Members are so poor that "there was not a scraper and hardly a plow that could be found among the Saints" to dig temple foundation.

Benjamin Johnson, *Life's Review*, 16. Joel Johnson, Autobiography, 5.

**October 10, 1833.** Temple construction is discontinued for the winter due to lack of materials. Workers plan to recommence "early in the spring."

Williams to Saints in Missouri, in *HC*, 1:418.

**Fall–Winter 1833–34.** Men stand guard at night to protect temple walls from mob destruction. Walls are still being built.

Hancock, Diary, 77. Joel Johnson, Autobiography, 5. *HC*, 2:2.

**February 20, 1834.** Orson Hyde and Orson Pratt are sent east "to obtain . . . means to redeem the farm on which the house of the Lord stands."

*HC*, 2:35.

**April 1834.** The basement walls, which had been covered the previous autumn, are uncovered. Members covenant at April conference to finish the walls that season.

Draper, Autobiography, 2.

**April 17, 1834.** Sidney Rigdon gives a speech concerning the building of the temple.

Joseph Smith Jr., Ohio Journal, in *PJS*, 2:30.

**May 6, 1834.** Sidney Rigdon, Newel K. Whitney, and Oliver Cowdery state their expectations that Pentecostal experiences will occur in the temple.

Rigdon, Whitney, and Cowdery to Boynton, in Karl Anderson, *Joseph Smith's Kirtland*, 169–70.

**May 7, 1834.** The departure of Zion's Camp leaves "but few men in Kirtland," including "a few working on the Temple." Those who remain in Kirtland are required to work on the temple one day of each week.

*HC*, 2:64. Coe, "Mormonism," 4.

**June 22, 1834.** Zion will not yet be redeemed, but Zion's Camp members are told "the first elders of my church should receive their endowment from on high in my house."

D&C 105:33.

**September 1, 1834.** After Zion's Camp returns, all Church members are working on the temple again. The Stannard and Russell Quarries are used for stone. Joseph Smith acts as foreman in stone quarry and, "when other duties would permit," labors with his own hands. Every Saturday all teams are used to bring stone from quarry for masons to use during the week to come. Men without teams labor in the quarry. Emma Smith supervises cooking and sewing for workers. Women are constantly sewing and doing other work.

> HC, 2:161. Kimball, "Building the Temple," in JD, 10:165–66. Kimball, "Extracts from H. C. Kimball's Journal," 867. Crary, *Pioneer and Personal Reminiscences*, 32–33.

Description given of the completed temple interior.

> Crary, *Pioneer and Personal Reminiscences*, 32–33.

**October 1834.** Walls grow quickly. "Great exertions were made to expedite the work of the Lord's house." Father Fisher falls from scaffolds and becomes "disabled from manual labor." Scant food and clothing are available for workers; still, they are cheerful. Sidney Rigdon walks the temple walls day and night, praying and crying for financial aid to complete the temple.

> William Burgess Jr., Autobiography, 1–2. HC, 2:167. Draper, Autobiography, 1. Daniel Tyler, "Temples," 283. Larson, *Erastus Snow*, 466. Kimball, "Extracts from H. C. Kimball's Journal," 867; "House of God," 147.

**January 21, 1835.** John Tanner arrives in Kirtland on January 20 in answer to Joseph Smith's prayer. The next day, Tanner loans Joseph Smith $2,000 to keep the mortgage from foreclosing and later loans $13,000 to the temple committee.

> E. Pingree Tanner, "John Tanner," 2. Nathan Tanner, Autobiography, 25–27.

**February 1835.** Walls are "up to the square," and the roof is being put on.

> Joseph Young to Harvey, November 16, 1880, 6.

**March 7–8, 1835.** Blessings are given to 121 men who participated in building.

> HC, 2:205–8. Benjamin Johnson, *Life's Review*, 22–23. Joel Johnson, Autobiography, 5.

**Spring 1835.** "Many of the first Elders" in Missouri have been instructed to travel to Kirtland to help with temple construction.

> Jackman, "Short Sketch," 8.

**Spring 1835.** Roof on temple partly completed. Nancy Tracy attends meeting in unfinished temple.

> Tracy, Autobiography, 8.

**May–September 1835.** The Twelve Apostles travel on a mission to the East "for the express purpose of soliciting donations."

HC, 2:239, 252, 375.

**June 18, 1835.** Kirtland members subscribe $950.

HC, 2:234.

**June 25, 1835.** $6,232.50 is subscribed, including large donations from Joseph Smith, Oliver Cowdery, W. W. Phelps, John Whitmer, and Frederick G. Williams.

HC, 2:234.

**July 1835.** Roof is completed. Expected features of the finished building are described.

"House of God," 147.

**July 19–20, 1835.** Work on steeple underway. Meetings are held in the temple.

W. W. Phelps to Sally Phelps, in Van Orden, "Writing to Zion," 555.

**July 26, 1835.** Sabbath meeting held in temple. Sidney Rigdon preaches four hours to one thousand people.

Jackman, "Short Sketch," 17.

**August 1835.** Sarah Leavitt hears Joseph Smith preach in temple, "which proved to be a very good house." She tours upper rooms and sees mummies and papyrus.

Leavitt, "History," 7.

**August 25, 1835.** Truman Coe, not a member of the Church, describes the temple. Women have been instructed "to part with even the necessities of life" for the temple. The Saints expect Christ's return following the completion of the temple. Saints very zealous in building the temple. Coe is full of awe, especially when seeing the "imposing splendor of the pulpits." Estimates $40,000 as total cost.

Coe, "Mormonism," 4.

**September 16, 1835.** Many of the elders from Missouri are at work on the temple. It is being finished slowly.

Phelps to Phelps, in Van Orden, "Writing to Zion," 565.

**September 23, 1835.** Noah Packard loans one thousand dollars for temple construction.

Joseph Smith Jr., Ohio Journal, in *PJS*, 2:39, 41.

**Uncertain date.** Eliza R. Snow donates cash to temple. In exchange, leaders give her "a note of hand for the amount," which they redeem by deeding her a valuable city lot.

Snow, "Sketch of My Life," 7.

**Fall 1835.** Truman O. Angell moves to Kirtland. Sunday meeting is held in temple, on the loose floor, with members seated on work benches; temple is two-thirds filled with people. Roof is supported by four trusses. Angell "had supervision of finishing the second, or middle Hall of the temple, including the stands, etc."

Angell, "Journal," 121, 123.

**October 1835.** Reminder issued to those who have subscribed: they need to pay.

"House of the Lord," 207.

**November 2, 1835.** Exterior stuccoing and hard-finishing work begins.

HC, 2:363.

**November 9, 1835.** Interior plastering begun by Jacob Bump (cost: $1,500) on November 9. Artemus Millett and Lorenzo Young engaged in exterior plastering and finishing (cost: $1,000). They endure extreme cold weather, and Young contracts consumption.

Lorenzo Young, "Narrative," 43.

**November 12, 1835.** Temple must be prepared so that members can experience "the ordinance of washing of feet." Joseph Smith writes about that ordinance.

Joseph Smith Jr., Ohio Journal, in PJS, 2:75–77.

**November 19, 1835.** Finishing coat of plaster is being applied to temple interior.

Joseph Smith Jr., Ohio Journal, in PJS, 2:86–87.

Newspaper article mentions the "Heathen Temple": "a stone building, 58 feet by 78 feet, with dormer windows."

Noah, *New York Evening Star*, in HC, 2:351.

**December 10 and 13, 1835.** The kiln that prepares wood for the temple catches fire on these days; considerable lumber is lost.

Joseph Smith Jr., Ohio Journal, in PJS, 2:101, 104. Phelps to Phelps, in Van Orden, "Writing to Zion," 570.

**December 31, 1835.** Joseph Smith gives directions concerning the temple's upper rooms, especially the translating room.

> Joseph Smith Jr., Ohio Journal, in *PJS*, 2:124.

**January 1836.** Preparation for washings and anointings is underway. Fifty men (carpenters, joiners, masons, mortar masons) at work on temple. The exterior finishing is half complete, and the scaffolds are taken halfway down. Plastering on the lower part of the inner court is nearly complete. Great effort is being made to procure a bell for the temple.

> Phelps to Phelps, in Van Orden, "Writing to Zion," 577.

**January 4, 1836.** Hebrew School held in west upper room for the first time. Room consecrated by Joseph Smith Sr. Parley Pratt describes some of the ordinances performed during priesthood meetings. A meeting is also held in the temple to start a "Singing School."

> Joseph Smith Jr., Ohio Journal, in *PJS*, 2:128–29. Pratt, *Autobiography*, 108. Luke Johnson, Autobiography, 5.

**January 8, 1836.** Work on the temple continues. Exterior plastering and hard-finishing work completed.

> *HC*, 2:363. Caroline Crosby, Memoirs and Diary. Jonathan Crosby, Autobiography.

Artemus Millett and Lorenzo Young complete the exterior plastering and hard-finishing. Young recalls that they finished the work in the early part of December. January date is perhaps an error in *History of the Church* as the paragraph contains another date misattribution.

> *HC*, 2:363. Lorenzo Young, "Narrative," 43. Artemus Millett, Biography, in Karl Anderson, *Joseph Smith's Kirtland*, 163.

Artemus Millett records that old crockery and glass are mixed into the cement he had invented.

> Artemus Millett, Biography, in Karl Anderson, *Joseph Smith's Kirtland*, 163.

**January 14–15, 1836.** Rules and regulations of the temple are drafted by Joseph Smith and accepted by priesthood holders. Temple doorkeepers are selected. Temple keys are assigned to Kirtland High Council presidency and the bishopric of the Aaronic Priesthood. John Corrill is "appointed to take charge" of the temple.

> Joseph Smith Jr., Ohio Journal, in *PJS*, 2:136–43. Kirtland High Council Minutes, January 15, 1836.

**January 18, 1836.** The Elders' School moves into a third-floor room of the temple.

Joseph Smith Jr., Ohio Journal, in *PJS*, 2:149.

**January 21–22, 1836.** The ordinance of anointing is administered in upper (attic) west room. Revelations, ministering of angels, and visions, including one of the face of Christ, occur. Joseph Smith receives a vision of the celestial kingdom (D&C 137).

Joseph Smith Jr., Ohio Journal, in *PJS*, 2:156–60. Partridge, Diaries. Detailed description of these meetings in Arrington, "Cowdery's 'Sketch Book,'" 410–26. *JD*, 19:16, 19, contrasts Kirtland and Nauvoo ordinances.

**January 28, 1836.** Visions are seen during the sealing of anointings.

Joseph Smith Jr., Ohio Journal, in *PJS*, 2:163–64. Harrison Burgess, Autobiography, in Backman, *Heavens Resound*, 292. Kimball, Autobiography, 35. Post, Diary. Record of the First Quorum of Elders, January 25, 28, 1836. High Priest Minutes.

**February 6, 1836.** Priesthood meeting is held in the temple; some participants see visions.

Joseph Smith Jr., Ohio Journal, in *PJS*, 169–71.

**February 22–24, 1836.** Lower room ready for painting. Brigham Young had to leave Hebrew class to "superintend the painting of the lower room until finished." Sisters make veil. Joseph Smith states that "the sisters now are the first to work on the inside of the temple." In meeting of priesthood holders, the Prophet pronounces a blessing upon the sisters "for their liberality in giving their services" in making the veil. Another meeting held in the upper west room determines priesthood ordination for various individuals. Similar meeting is held on March 17, 1836.

HC, 2:399. Joseph Smith Jr., Ohio Journal, in *PJS*, 2:178–79. Watson, *Manuscript History of Brigham Young*, 12.

**February 29, 1836.** Two visitors, not members of the Church, come to see the temple and are asked to remove their hats when entering. Elder Morey is the "keeper of the house."

Joseph Smith Jr., Ohio Journal, in *PJS*, 2:181.

**March 16, 1836.** Choir performs for Joseph Smith in the temple.

Joseph Smith Jr., Ohio Journal, in *PJS*, 2:189.

Exterior and interior are described. "Peculiar" inner court instills viewers, both those who are members of the Church and those who are not, with awe.

Snow, "Kirtland Temple," 56–57. Belnap, Autobiography, 11–12.

The two windows in the gable end of the attic story are intended to give light to the Prophet's room.

Angell, Autobiography.

Temple is described. Total cost of the temple is $40,000. Church is $13,000–14,000 in debt at time of its completion. The second story is entirely for instruction; thus, it contains tables instead of slips.

Corrill, *Brief History*, 21–22.

**March 26, 1836.** Oliver Cowdery, Joseph Smith, Rigdon, W. A. Cowdery, and W. Parrish meet to write the prayer for the temple dedication.

Arrington, "Cowdery's 'Sketch Book,'" 426.

**March 27, 1836.** Temple is dedicated. Ira Ames, who had previously organized the confused financial records for the temple, is the chorister for dedication service. Some members struggle with Joseph Smith's reading the dedication prayer instead of simply pronouncing it. Evening priesthood meeting is held in temple. Several people see visions, prophesy, and speak in tongues. Angels are seen hovering around the temple exterior. A mighty, rushing wind is heard. Some women are "right huffy" about the washings taking place in the temple.

HC, 2:410–28. Joseph Smith Jr., Ohio Journal, in *PJS*, 2:191–203. JD, 2:10, 214–15; 9:376; 11:10; 18:132. Arrington, "Cowdery's 'Sketch Book,'" 426. "Kirtland, Ohio, March 27, 1836," 274–81. Angell, "Journal," 124–25. Partridge, Diaries. Kimball, Autobiography, 66. Hale, Autobiography, 4–5. Tracy, Autobiography, 8–9. Hyde, Autobiography, 7. Elliott, *Reminiscences*, 44. Ames, Autobiography and Journal, 193. Post, Diary. Brown, *Testimonies*, 10–11. Jackman, "Short Sketch," 17. Snow, "Sketch of My Life," 6–7. Snow, "Kirtland Temple," 57–62. Knight, *Scraps of Biography*, 94–95. Hyde, Journal. Caroline Crosby, Memoirs and Diary, 49. Webb, "Autobiography," 289. Joel Johnson, Autobiography, 5. Robinson, "Items of Personal History," 89–90.

Claims about the total cost of the temple range from $40,000 to $250,000.

"Anniversary of the Church," 488. Corrill, *Brief History*, 21. JD, 2:214; 24:15–17.

Later, after becoming alienated from the Church, Winchester claimed that the dedication ended in a drunken revel.

Winchester, "Primitive Mormonism," 2.

**March 29–30, 1836.** All-day, all-night fast meetings are held. Ordinance of washing of feet performed for over three hundred. Some see the Savior; others ministered to by angels.

Joseph Smith Jr., Ohio Journal, in *PJS*, 2:203–7. Partridge, Diaries.

**Spring 1836.** Duncan mentions that he received his washing in the "cellar of the temple."

Duncan, Autobiography, 6–7.

**March 31, 1836.** Another dedicatory ceremony is held for those who, due to space constraints in the temple, were unable to attend the first dedication.

Joseph Smith Jr., Ohio Journal, in *PJS*, 2:207–8. Partridge, Diaries.

Law of common consent practiced in Kirtland Temple. Each quorum stands, in turn, to vote. Then all, including women, stand to vote.

Orson Pratt, Journal, October 5, 1877. *JD*, 19:199–20.

**April 3, 1836.** Appearance of Christ, Moses, Elias, and Elijah restoring keys to Joseph Smith and Oliver Cowdery.

Joseph Smith Jr., Ohio Journal, in *PJS*, 2:209–10.

**April 5–6, 1836.** Priesthood holders gather for ordinance of anointing (April 5) and washing of feet (April 6). They experience speaking in tongues, visions of angels, and the Spirit of the Lord filling the temple.

Draper, Autobiography, 2–3. Hale, Autobiography. Kimball, Autobiography (enlarged), 37.

**April 16, 1836.** Ordinance of washing of feet performed.

Burkett, Diary, 6.

**May 1, 1836.** Ordinances of anointing and washing of feet performed in temple. Some receive gift of prophecy; some see angels.

Robinson, "Items of Personal History," 90–91.

**1836–1837.** Temple overflowing with communicants. Services are held on Sunday morning, afternoon, and occasionally evenings. Choir practice is held on other evenings. Various priesthood quorums assigned weeknights to meet in upper west room. Prayer meeting for all members is held on Thursday evenings. The first Thursday of each month is fast and testimony meeting from ten o'clock in the morning to four o'clock in the afternoon. Beginning in November, Kirtland High School meets in attic story during daytime. Numerous descriptions of Pentecostal experiences.

*HC*, 2:474–75. Ames, Autobiography, 1836. Duncan, Autobiography, 3. Tanner, Autobiography, 1836. Andrus, Autobiography, 5. Joel Johnson, Autobiography, 2. Snow, Autobiography, 7. Fielding to Thompson, in Godfrey, Godfrey, and Derr, *Women's Voices*, 60–61. Snow, "Kirtland Temple," 63–64. Snow, *Biography and Family Record*, 11–13. Benjamin Johnson, *Life's Review*, 23, 28. "Our Village," 444. Luke Johnson, Autobiography, 834–46. "Minutes of a Conference," 51. Pratt, *Autobiography*, 130. Watson, *Manuscript History of Brigham Young*, 12. *JD*, 9:375–76; 14:273; 25:158. Prescindia Huntington, Reminiscences, 207–9. Corrill, *Brief History*, 23.

**Fall 1836.** George Albert Smith attends school in temple for four months.

George Smith, "Sketch," 440.

**October 1836.** Temple policy is established that when the Saints are not using the building it is available, except on Sunday, to preachers of other sects or to other people "of respectability."

"Judge after Hearing," 395–96.

**November 25, 1836.** Wilford Woodruff tours temple and sees papyrus and four mummies in upper rooms.

Jessee, "Kirtland Diary of Wilford Woodruff," 371. Woodruff, *Journal*, 1:106–7.

**November 27, 1836.** Wilford Woodruff attends Sunday services in temple.

Upon this Lords day Elder Smoot & myself accompanied Elder Parrish to the house of the Lord for the first time to behold the Congregation of the Saints assembled Within its Walls for the Purpose of worshiping God. It was truly an interesting scene. It brought a lengthy Catalogue of transactions Contemplations & experience of my youth to my mind & the experiance of this day fulfilled many things of a spiritual nature which I had looked [for] for a number of years which I viewed as Promises of God.

After I entered the house & was seated I cast my eyes upon the Pulpits aranged in order for the High Priest. I beheld the Patriarch Joseph Smith sen. Standing in the upper Pulpet, & President Joseph Smith, jr. & Elder Carter in the Second one & in the third Elders Parley and & Orson Pratt & W Parrish was seated. Soon Elder Carter arose & opened meeting by Prayer & then Preched the gospel unto us & was followed by President Joseph Smith, jr. when meeting was dissmissed & after an intermishion of an hour we again met in the house of the Lord & I was called into the stand in company with Elder Smoot & requested to Preach to the People. I opened by Prayer & read the LVI Chapter of Isaiah & made some brief remarks upon the same & gave a sketch of my travels in the South. I was then followed by Elder Smoot. After he closed I was blessed with the priviledge of communing with a multitude of Saints in the house of the Lord assembled together from the east, west, north & South many with whom I had been intimately acquainted. (Woodruff, *Journal*, 1:108–9)

**December 1, 1836.** Joseph Smith Sr. gives patriarchal blessings in temple. Wilford Woodruff notes:

Repaired to the house of the Lord whare Father Smith met a number of Saints to Pronounce upon them a Patriarchal Blessing. This was the first meeting of the kind that I ever attended & I found it to be highly edefying & interesting as their was great & glorious things pronounced upon their heads by the spirit of Prophesy & Revelation. (Woodruff, Journal, 1:110)

**December 11, 1836.** Wilford Woodruff goes "up to the house of God to worship & O what a meeting. May it be Printed upon my heart as a memorial forever."

Woodruff, *Journal*, 1:111.

**December 18, 1836.** Wilford Woodruff goes to the temple. William Smith delivers a sermon. Joseph Young administers the sacrament. "President Joseph Smith jr. Solumnized the rights of matrimony."

> Woodruff, *Journal*, 1:111.

**December 20, 1836.** Wilford Woodruff meets with the "quorum of the Seventies" in the temple.

> Woodruff, *Journal*, 1:112.

**January 1837.** Parties of pleasure drive to Kirtland to view the temple. One woman, not a member of the Church, is appalled by the temple's extravagance; she could not bear to see the temple adorned and beautiful.

> "Our Village," 444. Brigham Young, "Speech," 956.

**January 3, 1837.** Wilford Woodruff reports, "At early Candle light I repaired to the house of the Lord in company with Elder Milton Holmes for the purpose of meeting with the quorum of the Seventies."

> Woodruff, *Journal*, 1:118.

**March 1837.** Members of other faiths praise the temple. Parley P. Pratt allows them to preach in it.

> Davis, "Kirtland—Mormonism," 490–91.

**March 23, 1837.** Saints attend meetings and experience spiritual gifts in temple.

> I repaired to the house of the Lord at an early hour in the morning to spend the day in prayer and fasting With the saints in Kirtland, as this was a day set apart for that purpose. Immediately after entering the house in company with several other Elders, I went within the veil and we bowed down before the Lord in the Aronic stand & offer'd a morning sacrifice, & the Spirit of God rested upon us with joy to our Souls.
>
> I was Called upon, by the Patriarch JOSEPH to read a Chapter in the book of Mormon. I then read the third Chapter of the Book of Jacob, which contains the parable of the tame olive tree likend unto the house of Israel as was spake by the Prophet Zenos. The same God that touched Isaiah's lips with hallowed fire, gave Zenos great wisdom in setting forth this parable.
>
> After I had made some brief remarks upon the subject the congregation took their seats, for the sevices of the day, in the following order: The house being divided into four parts by veils, the females occupied two parts & the males the others. Some of the Presidency presided in each appartment.
>
> The time was taken up during the day in each appartment in singing, exortation, & prayer. Some had a tongue, others an interpetation, & all was in order. The power of GOD rested upon the people. The gifts were poured

out upon us. Some had the administering of angles & the image of GOD sat upon the countenances of the Saints.

At 4 oclock PM the Veils were all rolled up together which brought the whole Congregation in full view of each other and while the presence of the LORD filled the house the congregation of the Saints fell upon their knees & all as one man, vocally poured forth rejoicing, supplication & Prayer, before the God of Israel which Closed the services of the day, after contributing for the support of the poor. (Woodruff, *Journal*, 1:126–27)

**April 2, 1837.** Wilford Woodruff "attended worship in the Lords house upon this Sabbath day."

Woodruff, *Journal*, 1:127.

**April 6, 1837.** Solemn assembly convenes "for the purpose of washing, anointing, washing of feet, receiving instructions, and the further organization of the ministry." Unliquidated debt on temple is $13,000. Members are encouraged to contribute to discharge the Church's various debts. Joseph Smith conducts a testimony meeting; gifts of tongues, interpretation of tongues, and prophecy are present.

HC, 2:475–80. Jessee, "Kirtland Diary of Wilford Woodruff," 389–92. Warren Cowdery, "Anniversary of the Church," 488.

**April 7, 1837.** Night meeting is held, in which gift of prophecy is present. Holy Ghost "immersed our bodies like a consuming fire."

Jessee, "Kirtland Diary of Wilford Woodruff," 392–93. JD, 13:332–33.

**April 20, 1837.** During temple service, members receive gift of tongues and interpretation of tongues.

Jessee, "Kirtland Diary of Wilford Woodruff," 396.

**May 13, 1837.** Temple rooms and the mummies and papyri in the attic are seen.

Foote, Autobiography, 5–6. Holden, "Recollections," 153.

**June 1837.** Heber C. Kimball prays daily in attic of temple in preparation for his mission to England.

"History of Brigham Young," *Deseret News*, 385.

**Summer 1837.** Many prominent priesthood leaders meet in upper room to discuss replacing Joseph Smith with David Whitmer as President. Other leaders strongly oppose this idea. Meeting ends without agreement.

Watson, *Manuscript History of Brigham Young*, 15–16.

**August–September 1837.** Boynton, Parrish, and others disrupt Sunday service with guns and knives, attempting to seize the temple. Apostates ousted by police and members. Soon after, dissidents begin holding Thursday meetings in the temple for their "pure church."

> Snow, *Biography and Family Record*, 20–21. Oliver Huntington, Diary, 28–29. Lucy Mack Smith, *History of Joseph Smith*, 241, 243.

**September 18, 1837.** Before leaving Kirtland, Joseph Smith and Sidney Rigdon hold a farewell meeting in the temple.

> Fielding to Thompson and Thompson, in Godfrey, Godfrey, and Derr, *Women's Voices*, 68. Joseph Smith Jr., *Elders' Journal*, 28.

**January 16, 1838.** Temple scorched when arsonist sets fire to nearby printing office. Dissidents have temple keys and plan a Sunday meeting in the temple.

> Richards to Willard Richards, in Godfrey, Godfrey, and Derr, *Women's Voices*, 71. Barnes, Journal.

**March 1838.** Vision is seen of steamboat full of people passing over the temple to the West. Saints are encouraged; they feel the Lord has not forgotten them.

> John Pulsipher, Autobiography, 2. Zerah Pulsipher, Autobiography, 9.

Pulsipher prays in attic story for God to deliver Kirtland Saints.

> Zerah Pulsipher, Autobiography, 8–9.

**May 1838.** Attempt is made to burn temple by throwing flaming straw through a window.

> Joseph Smith Jr., *Kirtland Revelations Book*, 222. Zerah Pulsipher, Autobiography, 9–10. Shurtliff, Autobiography, 30–31.

**1838.** Nelson Slater starts a school in the temple—the Western Reserve Teachers' Seminary. He uses temple for a year until thick, damp walls, high ceiling, long flights of stairs, and the difficulty of heating the building make it unsuitable. There is "much complaint of sickness," and one woman's death is blamed on cold caught in the temple.

> Crary, *Pioneer and Personal Reminiscences*, 35.

**Spring 1839.** Crosby visits unoccupied temple. Fixtures, curtains, and seats seen "with astonishment, being so different from anything we had before seen."

> Jesse Crosby, Autobiography, 5–6.

**November 10 and 17, 1839.** Brigham Young, Heber C. Kimball, and John Taylor preach at the temple and administer ordinances of anointing and washing of feet. On the evening of November 17, these ordinances are administered to John Taylor and Theodore Turley in the attic story of the temple.

Watson, *Manuscript History of Brigham Young*, 57–58.

**July 1840.** Joseph Smith hopes that Oliver Granger will be able to free temple from financial "incumbrances."

Joseph Smith Jr. to Granger, in *PWJS*, 490–91.

**January 26, 1841.** Joseph Smith is gratified to hear of Oliver Granger's success in redeeming the temple and securing the keys. Advises him to hold those keys until Joseph himself arrives.

Joseph Smith Jr. to Granger, in *PWJS*, 475.

**May 4, 1841.** Joseph Smith writes concerning the temple mortgage and instructs Oliver Granger to maintain possession of the temple keys.

Joseph Smith Jr. to Granger, in *PWJS*, 494–95.

**October 1841.** Temple prepared for a bell.

Jenson, Journal History, October 19, 1841, 1–2.

**June 9, 1844.** Brigham Young preaches in the temple to unreceptive Saints.

Watson, *Manuscript History of Brigham Young*, 169.

**July 1845.** Sidney Rigdon preaches in the temple, attempting to win over the former followers of Joseph Smith and gain control of the building.

McBride to Young, 1–2.

**September 1845.** Apostates led by Jacob Bump break into temple and take possession of it.

Jenson, *Church Chronology*. Jenson, Journal History, October 22, 1845, 1.

**December 1846.** William E. McLellin's Church of Christ holds services in temple.

*Ensign of Liberty* 1 (1847): 1, 14. Backman, *Heavens Resound*, 443.

**1846–1848.** Brigham Young decides to sell the temple in order to save it from vandalism and attack. Almon Babbitt is unable to carry out this assignment, probably because of Bump's control over the building. A title to the temple is filed in the names of several trustees-in-trust for the Church and recorded in Painesville, Ohio.

Jenson, Journal History, April 27, 1846, 1; October 7, 1846, 1; January 7, 1847, 7; April 5, 1847, 1; January 12, 1848, 1.

**June 1847.** William E. McLellin has keys to temple. Lyman Omer Littlefield goes out on temple roof to see the view.

Littlefield, *Reminiscences of Latter-day Saints*, 192.

**About 1850.** Temple is used as a community hall. Patience Simonds Cowdery attends lectures in it.

Patience Cowdery, Diary.

**Summer 1850.** James Ryder, a traveling photographer, sets up studio in upper court.

Patience Cowdery, Diary.

**1860.** New roof is installed, the exterior woodwork is repainted, and a small RLDS congregation begins meeting in the temple.

"Kirtland Affairs," November 22, 1860, 3. Edwards, *History of the Reorganized Church* 4:425.

**1862.** Russell Huntley buys the temple for $150.

Launius, *Kirtland Temple*, 104–5.

**1866.** By this date, much of the interior woodwork and ornamentation has been broken up and stripped by curiosity hunters.

Vida Smith, *Young People's History*, 2:129.

**1869.** Martin Harris is "daily bearing testimony of the Book of Mormon to many who visited the Temple." Temple keys are held by a Mr. Bond.

Gunnell, "Martin Harris," 273.

**August 1870.** Temple in "dilapidated" condition when Martin Harris, who has been custodian, leaves Kirtland.

Pilkington, "Testimony," 3–4.

**1873.** Huntley sells temple to Joseph Smith III and Mark Forscutt for $150.

Launius, "Joseph Smith III," 112.

**September 1874.** Civic meeting held in the lower court and banquet in the upper court.

"Reunion in Kirtland," 3.

**1875.** Joseph Smith III arrives in Kirtland to sell the temple to the township for use as a school and town hall. He is unable to sell it because there is no clear title.

Launius, "Joseph Smith III," 112.

**1880.** RLDS Church obtains clear title to temple in court action.

Joseph Smith III, Autobiography.

**1880s.** Temple is too cold for winter services; the RLDS Church uses other facilities for its meetings during the winter months.

Prusha, *History of Kirtland*, 81. Launius, *Kirtland Temple*, 120.

**1880s.** Extensive restoration work performed by the RLDS Church.

Heman Smith, "Kirtland Temple," 427. Kelley, "Report of Committee," 560–61, 563; Kelley, "To the Saints," 351–52. "Kirtland," *Painesville Telegraph*, February 10, 1887, 3.

**1899.** Gas lights installed.

Edwards, *History of the Reorganized Church*, 5:472.

**August 13, 1904.** Lightning strikes the temple tower, damaging the belfry and roof.

*Painesville Telegraph*, August 18, 1904, 2.

**1940s.** RLDS Church makes changes to the tower, installs fire protection, and replaces the hanging lamps with fluorescent tube lighting.

"Kirtland Temple: Recent Architectural Changes," 2. Ross to Curry.

**1955.** New cement finish applied to exterior walls.

Wellington, "Kirtland Temple Gets Face Lifting," 687.

**1959.** Oil-burning furnace installed.

Yarrington, "Kirtland Temple Is Closed for Repairs," 194; "Kirtland Temple Repairs Completed," 698.

**1977.** Temple designated a National Historic Landmark by the U.S. Department of the Interior and U.S. Park Service.

Certificate on file at Kirtland Temple Visitor's Center.

# Appendix B

## Blessing of Those Who Assisted in Building the House of the Lord at Kirtland

*March 7* [1835].—This day a meeting of the Church of Latter-day Saints was called for the purpose of blessing, in the name of the Lord, those who have heretofore assisted in building, by their labor and other means, the House of the Lord in this place.

The morning was occupied by President Joseph Smith, Jun., in teaching the Church the propriety and necessity of purifying itself. In the afternoon, the names of those who had assisted to build the house were taken, and further instructions received from President Smith. He said that those who had distinguished themselves thus far by consecrating to the upbuilding of the House of the Lord, as well as laboring thereon, were to be remembered; that those who build it should own it, and have the control of it.

After further remarks, those who performed the labor on the building voted unanimously that they would continue to labor thereon, till the house should be completed.

President Sidney Rigdon was appointed to lay on hands and bestow blessings in the name of the Lord.

The Presidents were blessed; and Reynolds Cahoon, Hyrum Smith, and Jared Carter, the building committee, though the last two were not present, yet their rights in the house were preserved.

The following are the names of those who were blessed in consequence of their labor on the house of the Lord in Kirtland, and those who consecrated to its upbuilding:

| | |
|---|---|
| Sidney Rigdon, | Jared Carter, |
| Joseph Smith, Jun., | Jacob Bump, |
| F. G. Williams, | Artemus Millet, |
| Joseph Smith, Sen., | Alpheus Cutler, |
| Oliver Cowdery, | Asa Lyman, |
| Newel K. Whitney, | Josiah Butterfield, |
| Reynolds Cahoon, | Noah Packard, |
| Hyrum Smith | James Putnam, |

Isaac Hill,
Maleum C. Davis,
Jaman Aldrich,
John Young, Sen.,
Ezra Strong,
Joel McWithy,
Matthew Foy,
James Randall,
John P. Greene,
Aaron E. Lyon,
Thomas Burdick,
Truman Wait,
Edmund Bosley,
William Bosley,
William Perry,
Don Carlos Smith,
Shadrach Roundy,
Joel Johnson,
Edmund Durfee, Sen.,
Edmund Durfee, Jun.,
Gideon Ormsby,
Albert Miner,
Ira Ames,
Salmon Gee,
Peter Shirts,
Isaac Hubbard,
Horace Burgess,
Dexter Stillman,
Amos F. Herrick,
Mayhew Hillman,
William Carter,
William Burgess,
Giles Cook,
Almon Sherman,
Warren Smith,
Moses Bailey,
Sebe Ives,
Andrew H. Aldrich,
Ebenezar Jennings,
Oliver Granger,
Orson Johnson,
James Lake,
William Redfield,

Cyrus Lake,
Harvey Smith,
Isaac Cleveland,
William Barker,
Samuel S. Brannan,
John Wheeler,
Henry Baker,
William Fisk,
Henry Wilcox,
George Gee,
Lorenzo D. Young,
David Clough,
James Durfee,
Joseph Coe,
Thomas Gates,
Loren Babbitt,
Blake Baldwin,
Oliver Higley
Evan M. Greene,
Levi Osgood,
Alpheus Harmon,
Joseph C. Kingsbury,
Ira Bond,
Z. H. Brewster,
Samuel Thomson,
John Ormsby,
Luman Carter,
John Smith,
Samuel H. Smith,
Thomas Fisher,
Starry Fisk,
Amos R. Orton,
Gad Yale,
John Johnson,
John Tanner,
Henry G. Sherwood,
Sidney Tanner,
Joseph Tippits,
Robert Quigley,
Erastus Babbitt,
Samuel Canfield,
Phineas H. Young,
Samuel Rolfe,

Calvin W. Stoddard,

Josiah Fuller,

Erastus Rudd,

Isaac G. Bishop,

Roswell Murray,

Benjamin Wells,

Nehemiah Harman,

Oliver Wetherby,

Thomas Hancock,

Josuah Grant,

William Draper,

Ransom Van Leuven,

Tunis Rappellee,

John Reed,

Samuel Wilcox,

Benjamin Johnson,

Joseph B. Bosworth.

The blessings and ordinations of particular individuals of the foregoing were as follows:—Reynolds Cahoon, Jacob Bump, and Artemus Millet, were blessed with the blessings of heaven and a right in the house of the Lord in Kirtland, agreeable to the labor they had performed thereon, and the means they had contributed.

Alpheus Cutler, Asa Lyman, Josiah Butterfield, Noah Packard, Jonas Putnam, and Isaac Hill received the same blessing. The blessing referred to was according to each man's labor or donation.

*History of the Church, 2:205–7*

# Appendix C

# Kirtland Temple Dedication Services

This composite text is from the report in *Messenger and Advocate* 2 (March 1836): 274–81, and from the Ohio journal of Joseph Smith printed in Jessee, *Papers of Joseph Smith*, 2:191–203. Being longer and more detailed, the *Messenger and Advocate* account was the primary source. Additional details and the dedicatory prayer were supplied from Joseph's journal (see also D&C 109).

27 March 1836 • Sunday

The congregation began to assemble at the chapel at about 7 oclock one hour earlier than the doors were to be opened many brethren had come in from the region's round about to witness the dedication of the Lords House and share in his blessings and such was the anxiety on this occasion that some hundreds, (probably five or six,) assembled before the doors were opened—

The presidency entered with the door ke[e]pers and aranged them at the inner and outer doors also placed our stewards to receiv[e] donations from those who should feel disposed to contribute something to defray the expenses of building the House of the Lord—<we also dedicated the pulpits and consecrated them to the Lord> The doors were then opened President Rigdon President Cowdery and myself seated the congregation as they came in, and according to the best calculation we could make we received between 900 and 1000 which is as many as can be comfortably situated we then informed the door keepers that we could rec[e]ive no more, and a multitude were deprived of the benefits of the meeting on account of the house not being sufficiently capacious to receive them, and President Smith felt to regret that any of my brethren and sisters should be deprived of the meeting, and he recommended them to repair to the School-house and hold a meeting which they did and filled that house also and yet many were left out—

The assembly were then organized in the following manner.—viz.
West end of the. house—

Presdt. F G. Williams Presdt. Joseph Smith, Sen and Presdt. W W. Phelps occupied the 1st pulpit for the Melchisedic priesthood—Presdt. S. Rigdon myself and Presdt Hyrum Smith in the 2nd—Presdt. D. Whitmer Presdt. O. Cowdery and Presdt. J. Whitmer in the 3d—The 4th was occupied by the president of the high-priests and his counsellors, and 2 choiresters— The 12. Apostles on the right in the 3 highest seats—The presdt of the Eld[e]rs his clerk & counsellors in the seat immediatly below the 12—The high council of Kirtland consisting of 12, on the left in the 3, first seats—the 4th seat below them was occupied by Eldr's W A. Cowdery and W. Parrish who served as scribes.—The pulpits in the east end of the house for the Aaronic priesthood were occupied as follows.—The Bishop of Kirtland and his coun- sellors in the 1st pulpit.—The Bishop of Zion and his counsellors in the 2nd—The presdt. of the priests and his counsellors in the 3d—The presdt. of the Teachers and his counsellors and one choirister in the 4th—The high council of Zion consisting of 12 counsellors on the right—The presdt of the Deacons and his counsillors in the seat below them—The 7 presdts of the Seventies on the left—The choir of singers were seated in the 4 corners of the room in seats prepared for that purpose—

9 oclock A. M the services of the day were opened by Presdt S. Rigdon by reading 1st the 96 Psalm secondly the 24th Psalm—the choir then sung hymn on the 29th page of Latter day Saints collection of hymn's:

TUNE—*Sterling*.

Ere long the vail will rend in twain,
The King descend with all his train;
The earth shall shake with awful fright,
And all creation feel his might.

The trump of God, it long shall sound,
And raise the nations under ground;
Throughout the vast domain of heav'n
The voice echoes, the sound is given.

Lift up your heads ye saints in peace,
The Savior comes for your release;
The day of the redeem'd has come,
The saints shall all be welcom'd home.

Behold the church, it soars on high,
To meet the saints amid the sky;
To hail the King in clouds of fire,
And strike and tune th' immortal lyre.

Hosanna now the trump shall sound,
Proclaim the joys of heav'n around,
When all the saints together join,
In songs of love, and all divine.

With Enoch here we all shall meet,
And worship at Messiah's feet,
Unite our hands and hearts in love,
And reign on thrones with Christ above.

The city that was seen of old
Whose walls were jasper, and streets gold
We'll now inherit thron'd in might;
The Father and the Son's delight.

Celestial crowns we shall receive,
And glories great our God shall give,
While loud hosannas we'll proclaim,
And sound aloud the Saviors name.

Our hearts and tongues all joined in one,
A loud hosanna to proclaim,
While all the heav'ns shall shout again,
And all creation say, Amen.

A prayer was given by Presdt Rigdon and the choir then sung the hymn on
14th page:


TUNE—*Weymouth.*

O happy souls who pray
        Where God appoints to hear?
O happy saints who pay
        Their constant service there!
                We praise him still;
                And happy we;
                We love the way
                To Zion's hill.

No burning heats by day,
        Nor blasts of evening air,

Shall take our health away,
    If God be with us there:
        He is our sun,
        And he our shade,
        To guard the head
        By night or noon.

God is the only Lord,
    Our shield and our defence;
With gifts his hand is stor'd:
    We draw our blessings thence.
        He will bestow
        On Jacobs race,
        Pecular grace,
        And glory too-

Presdt Rigdon then read the 18, 19, and 20, verses of the 8th Chapter of Mathew and preached more particularly from the 20th verse.—his prayer and address were very forcible and sublime, and well adapted to the occasion. He spoke two hours and a half in his usual, forcible and logical manner. At one time in the course of his remarks he was rather pathetic, than otherwise, which drew tears from many eyes. He was then taking a retrospective view of the toils, privations and anxieties of those who had labored upon the walls of the house to erect them. And added, there were those who had wet them with their tears, in the silent shades of night, while they were praying to the God of Heaven, to protect them, and stay the unhallowed hands of ruthless spoilers, who had uttered a prophecy when the foundation was laid, that the walls would never be reared. This was only a short digression from the main thread of his discourse, which he soon resumed.

The speaker assumed as a postulate, what we presume no one was disposed to deny, (viz:) that in the days of the Savior there were Synagogues, where the Jews worshipped God, and in addition to them, the splendid Temple at Jerusalem. Yet, when on a certain occasion, one proposed to follow him whithersoever he went, He though heir of all things cried out like one in the bitterness of his soul in abject poverty, The Foxes have holes, and etc.— This, said the speaker, was evidence to his mind, that the Most High did not put his name there, and that he did not accept the worship of those who payed their vows and adorations there. This was evident from the fact that they would not receive him, but thrust him from them, saying, away with him, crucify him! crucify him! It was therefore abundantly evident that his spirit did not dwell in them. They were the degenerate sons of noble sires:

but they had long since slain the Prophets and Seers through whom the Lord revealed himself to the children of men. They were not led by revelation, *This*, said the speaker, was the grand difficulty among them. Their unbelief in present revelation. He further remarked, that, their unbelief in present revelation was the means of dividing that generation into the various sects and parties that existed. They were sincere worshipers, but their worship was not required of them, nor was it acceptable to God.—The Redeemer himself who knew the hearts of all men, called them a generation of vipers. It was proof positive to his mind, that there being Pharisees, Sadducees, Herodians and Essens, and all differing from each other, that they were led by the precepts and commandments of men. Each had something peculiar to himself, but all agreed in one point, (viz:) to oppose the Redeemer. So that we discover he could with the utmost propriety, exclaim, notwithstanding their synagogue and Temple worship. The foxes have holes, the birds of the air have nests, but the Son of man hath not where to lay his head. He took occasion here to remark that such diversity of sentiment ever had, and ever would obtain when people were not led by present revelation. This brought him to the inevitable conclusion that the various sects of the present day, from their manifesting the same spirit, rested under the same condemnation with those who were coeval with the Savior. He admitted there were many houses: many sufficiently great, built for the worship of God, but not one except this, on the face of the whole earth, that was built by divine revelation, and were it not for this, the dear Redeemer might in this day of science, this day of intelligence, this day of religion, say to those who would follow him, The foxes have holes, the birds of the air have nests, but the Son of man hath not where to lay his head.

Here his whole soul appeared to be fired with his subject. Arguments, strong and conclusive seemed almost to vie with each other for utterance. Indeed, there was no sophistry in his reasoning, no plausible hypothesis on which the whole rested, but on the contrary plain scripture facts. Therefore his deductions and inferences were logical and conclusive.

The comparison drawn between the different religious sects of ancient and modern times, was perfectly natural, and simple yet it was done in that confident, masterly manner, accompanied with those incontrovertable proofs of his position, that was directly calculated to cheer and gladden the hearts of the Saints, but to draw down the indignation of the sectarian world upon him and we have no doubt, had our speaker uttered the same sentiments, with the same proof of their correctness, had there been those present that we might name, his voice would doubtless have been drowned as was that of the ancient apostle in the Athenian Temple, when his auditors cried incessantly for about two hours "Great is Diana of the Ephesians."

But to conclude, we can truly say no one unacquainted with the manner of delivery and style of our speaker can, from reading form any adequate idea of the powerful effect he is capable of producing in the minds of his hearers: And to say on this occasion he showed himself master of his subject and did well, would be doing him injustice; to say he acquitted himself with honor or did very well, would be detracting from his real merit; and to say that he did *exceeding* well; would be only halting praise.

After President Rigdon closed his sermon, he called upon the several quorums commenceing with the presidency, to manifest by rising up, their willingness to acknowledge President Smith as a prophet and seer and uphold him as such by their p[r]ayers of faith, all the quorums in their turn, cheerfully complyed with this request he then called upon all the congregation of Saints, also to give their assent by rising on their feet which they did unanimously. The following hymn was then sung:

TUNE—*Hosanna.*

Now let us rejoice in the day of salvation,
No longer as strangers on earth need we roam,—
Good tidings are sounding to us and each nation,
And shortly the hour of redemption will come;

When all that was promis'd the saints will be given,
And none will molest them from morn until even,
And earth will appear as the garden of Eden,
And Jesus will say to all Israel: Come home!

We'll love one another and never dissemble,
But cease to do evil and ever be one;
And while the ungodly are fearing and tremble.
We'll watch for the day when the Savior shall come:

When all that was promis'd the saints will be given,
And none will molest them from morn until even,
And earth will appear as the garden of Eden,
And Jesus will say to all Israel: Come home!

In faith we'll rely on the arm of Jehovah,
To guide through these last days of trouble and gloom:
And after the scourges and harvest are over,
We'll rise with the just, when the Savior doth come:

Then all that was promis'd the saints will be given,
And they will be crown'd as the angel of heaven:
And earth will appear as the garden of Eden,
And Christ and his people will ever be one.
Services closed for the forenoon.

Intermission was about 15 minutes during which none left their seats except a few females, who from having left their infants with their friends, were compelled to do so to take care of them. The P. M. services commenced by singing Adam ondi ahman.
TUNE—*Adam-ondi-Ahman.*

This earth was once a garden place,
  With all her glories common;
And men did live a holy race,
And worship Jesus face to face,
    In Adam-ondi-Ahman.

We read that Enoch walk'd with God,
  Above the power of Mammon:
While Zion spread herself abroad,
And saints and angels sung aloud,
    In Adam ondi-Ahman.

Her land was good and greatly blest,
  Beyond old Israel's Canaan:
Her fame was known from east to west:
Her peace was great, and pure the rest
    Of Adam-ondi-Ahman.

Hosanna to such days to come
  The Savior's second comin'—
When all the earth in glorious bloom,
Affords the saints a holy home
    Like Adam-ondi-Ahman.

President Smith then made a short address and called upon the several quorums, and all the congregation of saints to acknowledge the Presidency as Prophets and Seers, and uphold them by their prayers, they all covenanted to do so by rising; He then called upon the quorums and congregation of saints to acknowledge the 12 Apostles who were present as Prophets and Seers and special witnesses to all the nations of the earth, holding the keys of the kingdom, to unlock it or cause it to be done among them; and uphold them by their prayers, which they assented to by rising. He then acknowledged the Presidents of the seventy's and called upon the quorums and congregation of saints to acknowledge the high council of Kirtland in all the authorities of the Melchisedec priesthood and uphold them by their prayers which they assented to by rising. He then called upon the quorums and congregation of saints to acknowledge and uphold by their prayer's the Bishops of Kirtland and Zion and their counsellors, in all the authority of the Aaronic priesthood, which they did by rising. He then called upon the quorums and congregation of saints to acknowledge the high-council of Zion, and uphold them by their prayers in all the authority of the high priesthood which they did by rising. He next called upon the quorums and congregation of saints to acknowledge the Presidents of the seventys who act as their represent[at]ives as Apostles and special witnesses to the nations to assist the 12 in opening the gospel kingdom, among all people and to uphold them by their prayer's which they did by rising—He then called upon the quorums and all the saints to acknowledge [the] president of the Elders and his counsellors and uphold them by their prayers which they did by rising—The quorums and congregation of saints were then called upon to acknowledge and uphold by their prayers the Presidents of the Priests, Teachers, and Deacons and their counsellors, which they did by rising.

At or about the close of his remarks, President Smith prophesied to all, that inasmuch as they would uphold these men in their several stations, alluding to the different quorums in the church, the Lord would bless them; yea, in the name of Christ, the blessings of Heaven shall be yours. And when the Lord's anointed go forth to proclaim the word, bearing testimony to this generation, if they receive it, they shall be blessed, but if not, the judgments of God will follow close upon them, until *that* city of *that* house, that rejects them, shall be left desolate. The following hymn was then sung:

TUNE—*Dalston.*

How pleasd and blest was I,
To hear the people cry,
"Come, let us seek our God to-day!"
Yes, with a cheerful zeal,
We'll haste to Zion's hill,
And there our vows and honors pay.

Zion thrice happy place,
Adorn'd with wondrous grace,

And walls of strength embrace thee 'round!
 In thee our tribes appear,
 To pray, and praise, and hear
The sacred gospel's joyful sound.

 There David's greater Son
 Has fix'd his royal throne:
He sits for grace and judgment there:
 He bids the saint be glad,
 He makes the sinner sad,
And humble souls rejoice with fear.
 May peace attend thy gate,
 And joy within thee wait,
To bless the soul of every guest:
 The man that seeks thy peace,
 And wishes thine increase,
A thousand blessings on him rest!

 My tongue repeats her vows,
 "Peace to this sacred house!
For here my friends and kindred dwells?"
 And since my glorious God
 Makes thee his blest abode,
My soul shall ever love thee well.

After the hymn on the hundred and 14 page was sung, President Smith offered to God the following dedication prayer.

Prayer,

At the dedication of the Lord's House in Kirtland Ohio March 27, 1836.—by Joseph Smith, jr. President of the Church of the Latter Day Saints.

Thanks be to thy name, O Lord God of Israel, who keepest covenant and shewest mercy unto thy servants, who walk uprightly before thee with all their hearts; thou who hast commanded thy servants to build an house to thy name in this place. (Kirtland.) And now thou beholdest, O Lord, that so thy servants have done, according to thy commandment. And now we ask the[e], holy Father, in the name of Jesus Christ, the Son of thy bosom, in whose name alone salvation can be administered to the children of men: we ask the[e], O Lord, to accept of this house, the workmanship of the hands of us, thy servants, which thou didst command us to build; for thou knowest that we have done this work through great tribulation: and out of our poverty we have given of our substance to build a house to thy name, that the Son of Man might have a place to manifest himself to his people.

And as thou hast said, in a revelation given unto us, calling us thy friends, saying—"Call your solemn assembly, as I have commanded you; and as all have not faith, seek ye diligently and teach one another words of wisdom; yea, seek ye out of the best books words of wisdom: Seek learning; even by study, and also by faith,

"Organize yourselves; prepare every ~~thing~~ needful thing, and establish a house, even a house of prayer, a house [of] fasting, a house of faith, a house of learning a house of glory, a house of order, a house of God: that your incomings may be in the name of the Lord, that your outgoings may be in the name of the Lord: that all your salutations may be in the name of the Lord, with uplifted hands to the Most High."

And now, Holy Father, we ask thee to assist us, thy people with thy grace in calling our solemn assembly, that it may be done to thy honor, and to thy divine acceptance, and in a manner that we may be found worthy in thy sight, to secure a fulfilment of the promises which thou hast made unto us thy people, in the revelatio[n]s given unto us: that thy glory may rest down upon thy people, and upon this thy house, which we now dedicate to thee; that it may be sanctified and consecrated to be holy, and that thy holy presence may be continually in this house; and that all people who shall enter upon the threshold of the Lord's house may feel thy power and be constrained to acknowledge that thou hast sanctified it, and that it is thy house, a place of thy holiness.

And do thou grant, holy Father, that all those who shall worship in this house, may be taught words of wisdom out of the best books, and that they may seek learning, even by study, and also by faith, as thou hast said; and that they may grow up in thee and receive a fulness of the Holy Ghost, and be organized according to thy laws, and be prepared to obtain every needful thing and that this house may be a house of prayer, a house of fasting, a house of faith, a house of glory, and of God, even thy house: that all the incomings of thy people, into this house, may be in the name of the Lord; that all their outgoings, from this house, may be in the name of the Lord; that all their salutations may be in the name of [the] Lord, with holy hands uplifted to the Most High; and that no unclean thing shall be permitted to come into thy house to pollute it.

And when thy people transgress, any of them, they may speedily repent and return unto thee, and find favour in thy sight, and be restored to the blessings which thou hast ordained, to be poured out upon those who shall reverance thee in this thy house.

And we ask, holy Father, that thy servants may go forth from this house, armed with thy power, and that thy name may be upon them and thy glory be round about them, and thine angels have charge over them, and from this place they may bear exceeding great and glorious tidings, in truth, unto the ends of the earth, that they may know that this is thy work, and that thou hast put forth thy hand, to fulfil that which thou hast spoken by the mouths of thy prophets concerning the last days.

We ask the[e], holy Father, to establish the people that shall worship and honorably hold a name and standing in this thy house, to all generations, and for eternity that no weapon formed against them shall prosper; that he who diggeth a pit for them shall fall into the same himself; that no combination of wickedness shall have power to rise up and prevail over thy people, upon whom thy name shall be put in this house: and if any people shall rise against this people, that thine anger be kindled against them: and if they shall smite this people, thou wilt smite them—thou wilt fight for thy people as thou didst in the day of battle, that they may be delivered from the hands of all their enimies.

We ask thee, holy Father, to confound, and astonish and bring to shame, and confusion, all those who have spread lying reports abroad over the world against thy servant or servants, if they will not repent when the everlasting gospel shall be proclaimed in their ears, and that all their works may be brought to nought, and be swept away by the hail, and by the judgments, which thou wilt send upon them in thine anger, that their may be an end to lyings and slanders against thy people: for thou knowest, O Lord, that thy servants have been innocent before thee in bearing record of thy name for which they have suffered these things, therefore we plead before thee for a full and complete deliverance from under this yoke. Break it off O Lord: break it off from the necks of thy servants, by thy power, that we may rise up in the midst of this generation and do thy work!

O Jehovah, have mercy upon this people, and as all men sin, forgive the transgressions of thy people, and let them be blotted out forever. Let the anointing of thy ministers be sealed upon them with power from on high: let it be fulfilled upon them as upon those on the day of Pentacost: let the gift of tongues be poured out upon thy people, even cloven tongues as of fire, and the interpretation thereof. And let thy house be filled, as with a rushing mighty wind, with thy glory.

Put upon thy servants the testimony of the covenant that where they go out and proclaim thy word, they may seal up the law, and prepare the hearts of thy saints for all those judgements thou art about to send, in thy wrath, upon the inhabitants of the earth because of their transgressions, that thy people may not faint in the day of trouble.

And whatever city thy servants shall enter, and the people of that city receive the testimony let thy peace and thy salvation be upon that city, that they may gather out from that city the righteous, that they may come forth to Zion, or to her stakes, the places of thine appointment, with songs of everlasting joy,—and until this be acomplished let not thy judgements fall upon that city.

And whatever city thy servants shall enter, and the people of that city receive not the testimony of thy servants, and thy servants warn them to save themselves from this untoward generation let it be upon that city according to that which thou hast spoken, by the mouths of thy prophets; but deliver thou, O Jehovah, we beseech thee, thy servants from their hands, and cleanse them from their blood. O Lord, we delight not in the destruction of our fellow men: their souls are precious before thee; but thy word must be fulfilled:—help thy servants to say, with thy grace assisting them, thy will be done, O Lord, and not ours.

We know that thou hast spoken by the mouth of thy prophets, terrible things concerning the wicked in the last days, that thou wilt pour out thy judgements, without measure; therefore, O Lord, deliver thy people from the calamity of the wicked, enable thy servants to seal up the law and bind up the testimony, that they may be prepared against the day of burning.

We ask thee, holy Father, to remember those who have been driven by the inhabitants of Jackson county Missouri, from the lands of their inheritance, and break off, O Lord, this yoke of affliction that has been put upon them. Thou knowest, O Lord, that they have been greatly oppressed and afflicted, by wicked men, and our hearts flow out in sorrow because of their grevious burdens. O Lord, how long wilt thou suffer this people to bear this affliction, and the cries of the innocent ones to ascend up in thine ears, and their blood to come up in testimony before thee and not make a display of thy power in their behalf?

Have mercy, O Lord, upon that wicked mob, who have driven thy people, that they may cease to spoil, that they may repent of their sins, if repentance is to be found; but if they will not, make bare thine arm, O Lord, and redeem that which thou didst appoint a Zion unto thy people,

And if it cannot be otherwise, that the cause of thy people may not fail before thee, may thine anger be kindled and thine indignation fall upon them that they may be wasted away, both root and branch from under heaven; but inasmuch as they will repent, thou art gracious and merciful, and will turn away thy wrath, when thou lookest upon the face of thine anointed.

Have mercy, O Lord, upon all the nations of the earth: have mercy upon the rulers of our land may those principles which were so honorably and nobly defended: viz, the constitution of our land, by our fathers, be established forever. Remember the kings, the princes, the nobles, and the great ones of the earth, and all people; and the churches: all the poor, the needy and the afflicted ones of the earth, that their hearts may be softened when thy servants shall go out from thy house, O Jehovah, to bear testimony of thy name, that their prejudices may give way before the truth, and thy people may obtain favour in the sight of all, that all the ends of the earth may know that we thy servants have heard thy voice, and that thou hast sent us, that from among all these thy servants, the sons of Jacob, may gather out the righteous to build a holy city to thy name, as thou hast commanded them.

We ask thee to appoint unto Zion other stakes besides this one, which thou hast appointed, that the gathering of thy people may roll on in great power and majesty, that thy work may be cut short in righteousness.

Now these words, O Lord, we have spoken before thee, concerning the revelations and commandments which thou hast given unto us, who are i[de]ntified with the Gentiles;—But thou knowest that we have a great love for the children of Jacob who have been scattered upon the mountains; for a long time in a cloudy and dark day.

We therefore ask thee to have mercy upon the children of Jacob, that Jerusalem, from this hour, may begin to be redeemed; and the yoke of bondage may begin to be broken off from the house of David, and the children of Judah may begin to return to the lands which thou didst give to Abraham, their father, and cause that the remnants of Jacob, who have been cursed and smitten, because of their transgression, to be converted from their wild and savage condition, to the fulness of the everlasting gospel, that they may lay down their weapons of bloodshed and cease their rebellions. And may all the scattered remnants of Israel, who have been driven to the ends of the earth, come to a knowledge of the truth, believe in the Messiah, and be redeemed from oppression, and rejoice before thee.

O Lord, remember thy servant Joseph Smith jr. and all his afflictions and persecutions, how he has covenanted with Jehovah and vowed to thee O mighty God of Jacob, and the commandments which thou hast given unto him, and that he hath sincerely strove to do thy will.—Have mercy, O Lord, upon his wife and children, that they may be exalted in thy presence, and preserved by thy fostering hand.—Have mercy upon all their immediate connexions, that their prejudices may be broken up, and swept away as with a flood, that they may be converted and redeemed with Israel and know that thou art God.

Remember, O Lord, the presidents, even all the presidents of thy church, that thy right hand may exalt them with all their families, and their immediate connexions, that their names may be perpetuated and had in everlasting remembrance from generation to generation.

Remember all thy church, O Lord, with all their families, and all their immediate connexions, with all their sick and afflicted ones, with all the poor and meek of the earth, that the kingdom which thou hast set up without hands, may become a great mountain and fill the whole earth, that thy church may come forth out of the wilderness of darkness, and shine forth fair as the moon, clear as the sun, and terrible as an army with banners, and be adorned as a bride for that day when thou shalt unveil the heavens, and cause the mountains to flow down at thy presence, and the valleys to be exalted, the rough places made smooth, that thy glory may fill the earth. That when the trump shall sound for the dead, we shall be caught up in the cloud to meet thee, that we may ever be with the Lord, that our garments may be pure, that we may be clothed upon with robes of righteousness, with palms in our hands, and crowns of glory upon our heads, and reap eternal joy for all our sufferings.

O Lord, God Almighty, hear us in these our petitions, and answer us from heaven, thy holy habitation, where thou sittest enthroned, with glory, honour, power majesty, might, dominion, truth, justice judgement, mercy and an infinity of fulness, from everlasting to everlasting.

O hear, O hear, O hear us, O Lord, and answer these petitions, and accept the dedication of this house, unto thee, the work of our hands, which we have built unto thy name; and also this church to put upon it thy name. And help us by the power of thy spirit, that we may mingle our voices with those bright shining seruphs, around thy throne with acclamations of praise, singing hosanna to God and the Lamb: and let these thine anointed ones be clothed with salvation, and thy saints shout aloud for joy. Amen and Amen.

Sung Hosanah to God and the Lamb

TUNE—*Hosanna.*

The Spirit of God like a fire is burning;
    The latter day glory begins to come forth;
The visions and blessings of old are returning;
    The angels are coming to visit the earth.
We'll sing and we'll shout with the armies of heaven:
    Hosanna, hosanna to God and the Lamb!
Let glory to them in the highest be given,
    Henceforth and forever: amen and amen!

The Lord is extending the saints' understanding—
    Restoring their judges and all as at first;
The knowledge and power of God are expanding:
    The vail o'er the earth is beginning to burst.
We'll sing and we'll shout and etc.
We call in our solemn assemblies, in spirit,
    To spread forth the kingdom of heaven abroad,
That we through our faith may begin to inherit
    The visions, and blessings, and glories of God.
We'll sing and we'll shout and etc.

We'll wash, and be wash'd, and with oil be anointed
    Withal not omitting the washing of feet:
For he that receiveth his PENNY appointed,
    Must surely be clean at the harvest of wheat.
We'll sing and we'll shout and etc.

Old Israel that fled from the world for his freedom,
    Must come with the cloud and the pillar, amain:
A Moses, and Aaron, and Joshua lead him,
    And feed him on manna from heaven again.
We'll sing and we'll shout and etc.


How blessed the day when the lamb and the lion
    Shall lie down together without any ire;
And Ephraim be crown'd with his blessing in Zion,
    As Jesus descends with his chariots of fire!
We'll sing and we'll shout with *His* armies of heaven:
    Hosanna, hosanna to God and the Lamb!
Let glory to them in the highest be given,
    Henceforth and forever: amen and amen.


President Smith then asked the several quorums separately and then the congregation, if they accepted the prayer. The vote was, in every instance, unanimous in the affirmative.

The Lords supper, the Eucharist, was administered—D. C. Smith blessed the bread and wine and they were distributed by several Elders present, to the church.

President J. Smith jr. then arose and bore record of his mission and testified of the administering of angels. D. C. Smith bore record of the truth of the work of the Lord in which we are engaged.

President O. Cowdery spoke and testified of the truth of the book of Mormon, and of the work of the Lord in these last days.

Presdt Williams also arose and testified that while Presdt Rigdon was making his first prayer an Holy Angel of God entered the window and took his seat between J. Smith sen., and himself, and remained their while the house was being dedicated. Presdt David Whitmer also saw angels in the house.

President Hyrum Smith, (one of the building committee) made some appropriate remarks concerning the house, congratulating those who had endured so many toils and privations to erect it, That it was the Lord's house built by his commandment and he would bless them.

President S. Rigdon then made a few appropriate closing remarks; and a short prayer which was ended with loud acclamations of Hosanna! Hosanna! Hosanna to God and the Lamb, Amen. Amen and Amen! Three times. Elder B. Young, one of the Twelve, gave a short address in tongues; Elder D. W. Patten interpreted and gave a short exhortation in tongues himself; after which, President J. Smith jr. blessed the congregation in the name of the Lord, and at a little past four P. M. the whole exercise closed and the congregation dispersed. We requested all the official members to meet again in the evening we retired—met in the evening and instructed the quorums respecting the ordinance of washing of feet which we were to attend to on wednesday following.

We further add that we should do violence to our own feelings and injustice to the real merit of our brethren and friends who attended the meeting, were we here to withhold a meed of praise, which we think is their just due; not only for their quiet demeanor during the whole exercise, which lasted more than eight hours, but for their great liberality in contributing of their earthly substance for the relief of the building committee, who were yet somewhat involved. As this was to be a day of sacrifice, as well as of fasting,—There was a man placed at each door in the morning to receive the voluntary donations of those who entered. On counting the collection it amounted to nine hundred and sixty three dollars.

# Appendix D

# Historical Descriptions of the Kirtland Temple

From John Corrill, *A Brief History of the Church of Christ of Latter Day Saints*, *(Commonly Called Mormons;) Including an Account of Their Doctrine and Discipline; with the Reasons of the Author for Leaving the Church* (St. Louis: By the author, 1839), 21–22.

John Corrill was an early member of the Church of Christ of Latter-day Saints who later left the group and became a prominent politician in Missouri. He published this statement concerning his past, apparently to defuse concerns about the character of one who had at one time espoused Mormonism. This account is especially important because Corrill acted in a supervisory position in the construction of the temple and wrote this account only three years after its completion.

> The church also kept gathering at Kirtland. They laid out a town, appointed certain lots for various purposes, one of which was to build the house of the Lord upon, for the building of which they had received a revelation. This building they commenced, if I recollect rightly, in '33, in poverty, and without means to do it. In 1834 they completed the work, and in '35 and 6 they nearly finished it. The cost was nearly $40,000. A committee was appointed to gather donations. They traveled among the churches and collected a considerable amount, but not sufficient, so that in the end they found themselves 13 or $14,000 in debt. This house was 80 feet by 60; and 57 [*sic*] feet high to the top of the wall. It was divided into two stories, each twenty-two feet high, and arched overhead. Ten feet was cut off from the front end by a partition and used as an entrance, and it also contained the stairs. This left the main room 55 by 65 feet in the clear, both below and above. In each of these rooms were built two pulpits, one in each end. Each pulpit consisted of four different apartments; the fourth standing on a platform raised a suitable height above the floor; the third stood directly behind and elevated a little above the fourth; the second in rear of and elevated above the third; and so was the first above the second. Each of these apartments was just large enough, and rightly calculated to receive three persons, and the breast-work in front of each of these three last mentioned, was

constituted of three semi-circles, joining each other, and finished in good style. The fourth, or lower one, was straight in front, and had a table-leaf attached to it, that could be raised at pleasure, for the convenience of administering the sacrament, &c. These pulpits were alike in each end of the house, and one was for the use of the Malchisedec [sic], or high priesthood, and the other for the Aaronic, or lesser priesthood. The first, or higher apartment, was occupied by the first presidency over all the church; the second apartment, by the President of the high priests, and his two counsellors; the third by three of the High Priests; and the fourth by the President of the Elders, and his two counsellors. The highest apartment of the other pulpit was occupied by the Bishop of the church and his two counsellors; the next by the President of the priests and his two counsellors; the third by the President of the teachers and his two counselors; and the fourth by the President of the deacons and his two counsellors. Each of these apartments had curtains hanging from the ceiling, over head, down to the top of the pulpit, which could be rolled up or dropped down at pleasure; and, when dropped down, would completely exclude those within the apartment from the sight of all others. The room itself was finished with slips and seats, so calculated that, by slipping the seats a little, the congregation could change their faces towards either pulpit they choose, for in some cases the high priesthood would administer, and in other cases the lesser would. The room was also divided into four apartments, by means of curtains hanging from the ceiling, over head, down to the floor, which could be rolled up at pleasure, so that the room could be used all in one, or divided into four rooms, and used for different purposes. Thus the house was constructed to suit and accommodate the different orders of priesthood and worship peculiar to the church. The first story, or lower room, was dedicated for divine worship alone. The second story was finished similar in form to the first, but was designed, wholly, for instruction, and supplied with tables instead of slips. In the roof were finished five rooms for the convenience of schools, and for the different quorums of the church to meet in, &c.

From Henry Howe, *Historical Collections of Ohio* (Cincinnati: Derby and Bradley, 1847), 282–83.

This account was written in 1846 and appears to be based at least in part on interviews with a former Saint who was currently a follower of James Strang, as can be discerned by the following note: "The Mormons still use the temple at Kirtland. This sect is now divided into three factions, viz.: the Rigdonites, the Twelveites, and the Strangites. The Rigdonites are the followers of Sidney Rigdon, and are but a few in number. The Twelveites—so named after their twelve apostles—are very fanatical, and hold to the spiritual wife system and the plurality of Gods. The Strangites maintain the original doctrines of Mormonism, and are located at this place and Voree" (284).

The temple, the main point of attraction, is 60 by 80 feet, and measures from its base to the top of the spire, 142 feet. It is of rough stone, plastered over, colored blue, and marked to imitate regular courses of masonry. It cost about $40,000. In front, over the large window, is a tablet, bearing the inscription: "House of the Lord, built by the church of the Latter Day Saints, A.D. 1834." The first and second stories are divided into two "grand rooms" for public worship. The attic is partitioned off into about a dozen [five] small apartments. The lower grand room is fitted up with seats as an ordinary church, with canvas curtains hanging from the ceiling, which, on the occasion of prayer meetings, are let down to the tops of the slips, dividing the room into several different apartments, for the use of the separate collections of worshippers. At each end of the room is a set of pulpits, four in number, rising behind each other. Each pulpit is calculated for three persons, so that when they are full, twelve persons occupy each set, or twenty-four persons the two sets. These pulpits were for the officers of the priesthood. The set at the farther end of the room, are for the Melchisedek priesthood, or those who minister in spiritual concerns. The set opposite, near the entrance to the room, are for the Aaronic priesthood, whose duty it is to simply attend to the temporal affairs of the society. These pulpits all bear initials, signifying the rank of their occupants.

On the Melchisedek side, are the initials P.E., *i.e.* President of the Elders; M.P.H., President of the High Priests; P.M.H., Pres. of the High Council, and M.P.C., Pres. of the Full Church. On the Aaronic pulpits, are the initials P.D., *i.e.* President of Deacons; P.T.A., President of the Teachers; P.A.P., Pres. of the Aaronic Priesthood, and B.P.A., Bishop of the Aaronic Priesthood. The Aaronic priesthood were rarely allowed to preach, that being the especial duty of the higher order, the Melchisedek.

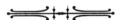

From James F. Ryder, *Voigtländer and I: In Pursuit of Shadow Catching* (Cleveland: Imperial Press, 1902), 69–70.

Ryder, a traveling photographer, set up a studio in the temple during the summer of 1850.

Next morning I visited the temple and explored it with much interest and curiosity. On entering upon the main floor, that which would be in usual churches the auditorium, from the entrance doors of which—there was one on each side—were aisles running back to the altar. On either side of the aisles were broad pews, separated into compartments by partitions of canvas, heavily painted with white upon both sides. These partitions or curtains were heavy as sails to a ship. The were fastened at bottom to large rollers and rigged with ropes and pulleys at top like curtains in theaters, for raising and lowering. Each curtain, with its heavy roller, dropped into the space immediately behind the pew backs and well in front of sitters in the pews, so they could be entirely secluded from occupants of other pews—separated as

completely as though stowed in pigeon-holes. Or, if desired, the partition curtains could be raised and the congregation seen as a whole. Why these partitions, or for what purpose, was one of the things I could never learn. There
were a good many Mormons left in Kirtland, but none who would talk of the
rites or ceremonies practiced in the temple. The room above was similar in
size as to floor space, but lower in height of ceiling. There were no dividing
partitions in this room. It was filled with pews, and at either end with curious
pulpits; as many as six pulpits. This I fancied had been a section or department for the lesser saints, or possibly for Sunday-school. In this room, which
had broad and high north windows, I determined to locate my studio. I built
a floor over the tops of the pew-backs, using them as joists; constructed a
flight of steps with hand-rail, by which to ascend and descend from the floor
proper. With my background, my sidescreen a little table and Voigtländer set
up upon my studio floor, I was ready for business. Here permit me to claim the
unique distinction of being the only photographer extant who ever had a
Mormon temple for a studio—a distinction of which I am proud.

From Frederic G. Mather, "The Early Days of Mormonism," *Lippincott's Magazine* 26 (August 1880): 208–11.

Unlike the previous accounts, Mather's article is a somewhat disdainful discussion of what he considered an odd chapter in Ohio history. While occasionally this attitude does get in the way of the facts (note his designation of
the lowest tier of Aaronic pulpits as being for the "Presiding Aaronic Doorkeeper"), he does record details of the building not written down elsewhere.

By far the most important and enduring monument left by the Mormons in
Kirtland is their Temple. The advent of several hundred strangers into the
midst of the insignificant hamlet was an event of considerable importance,
but when they selected a most commanding site, of easy access to the public
highway, and commenced the building of a church, all Northern Ohio looked
on in wonder. A structure of such pretensions would be a tax upon a goodly-
sized town of this generation, but the several hundred Mormons who built it
gave cheerfully each one his tenth in labor, materials or money for the four
years from 1832 [sic] to 1836, the entire cost being estimated at forty thousand dollars. The visitor, come from whatever direction he may, has the
Temple constantly in view as a reminder of the quainter style of "meeting-
houses" in New England. Its architectural superiority over the meeting-houses
is probably due to the fact that Smith had a "revelation" which gave him the
exact measurements and proportions. The size upon the ground is eighty feet
by sixty, and the eastern gable runs up into a square tower, surmounted by a
domed belfry, to the height of one hundred and twenty-five feet. Two lofty
stories above a low basement are covered by a shingled roof pierced with
dormer windows. Large Gothic windows of the Henry VIII. shape are filled
with seven-by-nine glass, and afford relief to the solid walls of stone and
stucco that have so well survived the ravages of nearly half a century, though

the iron rust streaking the exterior, the moss-grown shingles, and wasps' nests under the eaves, and the two immense chimneys already tottering to their fall, give evidence of approaching ruin.

As much as this even the careless passer-by cannot well avoid seeing. The more patient and accurate visitor may readily repeat my own experience as I went in search of the key on a bleak day in December. "The people ought to fix it up," said one informant: "it is a good thing for Kirtland;" the force of which remark I did not realize till I called upon an old Mormon woman who was said to have the keys. Inquiry at her little cabin resulted in my being directed to "go to Electy Stratton's." The latter personage, my cicerone, stated that her parents were Mormons—that her father had spent several hundred dollars in the cause; and so "it was thought best that their family should have the keys for a while now." The small fee for visiting the Temple was the "good thing for Kirtland," and the custody of the keys was not to remain long in one family. Opening a rickety gate, we entered the church-yard. High aloft, just under the pediment, I could read this inscription in golden letters upon a white tablet: "House of the Lord, built by the Church of Christ, 1834." Instead of the words "of Christ" the original inscription read "of the Latter-Day Saints." The Temple faces the east. Solid green doors, with oval panels, open into a vestibule extending across the entire front, and terminating on either hand in a semi-circular stairway. The ceiling is cut away from the front wall to allow a flood of light to enter from a huge square window above, and the open space is railed off like a steamer's cabin. At the right, under the stairway, is the "Temple Register Room," containing a record of visitors. On the left is the "Library," with a curious collection of whale-oil chandeliers. On the left of the wall, parallel with the front, is the "Gentle-men's Entrance:" on the right is the "Ladies' Entrance." Between these doors are the inscriptions: "Laus Deo," "Crux mihi anchora," "Magna veritas, et prevalebit." The auditorium occupies all the rest of the first story, but one could wish that the wall which divided it from the vestibule need not have spoiled one of the beautiful windows at either end, thus leaving an ungainly half window in the auditorium. A row of wooden pillars on either side gives the effect of galleries as the room is entered, but a closer view shows that the space between the rows is arched toward the centre of the ceiling. One of the pillars contains a windlass, which in former times controlled the heavy canvas curtains from above. The larger curtain fell into grooves between the high-back pews in such a manner as to separate the men from the women: the smaller curtains, at right angles to the other, divided both the men and the women into separate classrooms. Thus the audience was quartered or halved at pleasure, and the whole audience was enabled to face either west-ward or eastward by simply changing the movable benches from one side of the pews to the other. Clusters of richly-carved pulpits, rising by threes, in three tiers, fill up either end of the room. The eastern cluster is devoted to the Aaronic Priesthood, which also includes the Levitical Priesthood, and administered the temporal affairs of the Church. Each of the three pulpits in the upper tier has upon the front the letters "B.P.A.," meaning Bishop Presid-ing over Aaronic Priesthood; the middle tier has the letters "P.A.P.," Pre-siding Aaronic Priest; the lower tier has the letters "P.A.T.," Presiding Aaronic Teacher; a smaller pulpit below is labelled "P.A.D.," Presid-ing Aaronic Doorkeeper. The pulpits against the western end are built up against an outer window, with alternate panes of red and white glass in the arched transom. These pulpits were occupied by the spiritual leaders, or the Melchisedec Priesthood, Joe Smith's seat being in the highest tier. This tier of pulpits is marked "M.P.C.," Melchisedec President of Counsellors; the middle tier is marked "P.M.H.," Melchisedec Presiding High Priest; the lower tier is "M.H.P.," Melchisedec High Priest. Curtains from above were arranged to come down between the different tiers of the priesthood, but so arranged that while those of one degree might shut themselves away from the audience "for consultation," they could not hide themselves from their superiors in ecclesiastical rank. Strings and nails in the ceiling are the only remnants of these remarkable partitions. A simple desk below the Melchisedec pulpit bears the title "M.P.E.," Melchisedec Presiding Elder. The letters are in red curtain-cord, and the desk itself, like all the pulpits above, is covered with green calico. In the days of the Temple's glory rich velvet upholstery set off all the carved work of the pulpits, and golden letters shone from spots which are now simply marked by black paint. The gilt mouldings which formerly set off the plain white finish of the woodwork were first despoiled by the vandals, and then entirely removed by the faithful to prevent further destruction. These mottoes still remain upon the walls: "No cross, no crown;" "The Lord reigneth, let His people rejoice;" and "Great is our Lord, and of great power." Over the arched window behind the ten Melchisedec pulpits, and just beneath the vertical modillion which forms the keystone of the ornamental wooden arch, is the text, "Holiness unto the Lord."

Such is the auditorium to-day—a room which will comfortably hold six hundred people, but which was often packed so full that relays of worshippers came and went during a single service. . . .

Over the auditorium is a similar room with lower ceilings and plainer pulpits, each marked with initials which it would be tiresome to explain. The hall was used as a school of the prophets where Latin and Hebrew were taught. Marks of the desks remain, but the desks themselves have long since been carried away. . . .

The space under the roof is utilized by a series of school-rooms, each with falling plastering and "ratty" floors. Here the young Mormons were taught to ascend the Hill of Science by trudging up some scores of steps several times a day. Strange and dark cubbyholes stare at the visitor from all sides. In one of these was kept the body of Joseph, the son of Jacob, known by a roll of papyrus which was found in his hand. Joe Smith translated the characters on the roll, being favored with a "special revelation" whenever any of the characters were missing by reason of the mutilation of the roll.

Still up the stairway within a small square tower, now without a bell, I thrust my way until a little trap-door allowed an egress. But the railing had gone, and I clung to the belfry-blinds while I surveyed the cold waters of Lake Erie on the north, the rise of Little Mountain on the south, and, between them the broad tract of rolling country divided by the Chagrin River. I descended through labyrinthine passages, and came again to the ground and to the outer air with a sense of relief after my two hours' sojourn within the Mormon Temple.

# Glossary of Architectural Terms

**Architrave**

The lowest of the three parts of an architectural entablature. It sits directly on a column or pilaster. *Architrave* can also refer to ornamental moldings framing a door or window.

**Bay**

A repeating structural unit of a building, usually distinguished by its supporting columns or piers.

**Bead and lozenge**

A molding pattern used in classical architecture and composed of a linear arrangement of a lozenge-shaped element followed by two or more spherical beads. These moldings are generally found in Ionic or Corinthian entablatures.

**Beam**

A slender structural element, usually oriented horizontally, that carries loadings while bridging a gap between supports. There are several types: A simply supported beam bridges a single span. A continuous beam supports loads over multiple spans, has no joints at the supports, and can safely carry higher loads than an equivalent series of simply supported beams. A cantilever beam is supported only at one end, as in an overhang or balcony. Most cantilever beams are continuous extensions of a simply supported or continuous beam.

**Bending moment**

An internal rotational force that produces curvature in a structural member. In the case of a simply supported beam that is evenly loaded, the maximum bending moment will occur at midspan. For continuous beams, the maximum bending moment occurs at the interior columns.

## Capital

The transitional block above a column or pier. In early American building, most capitals were based on the Greek capitals of the Doric, Ionic, or Corinthian orders.

## Castellations

A notched parapet imitating the parapets of castles, where higher parapet walls alternate with open ports for firing.

## Column shaft

The cylindrical body of a column usually supported by a decorative base and always topped by a decorative capital that serves as a transition to the architrave above.

## Compression

An axial pushing force that tends to squeeze or shorten a structural member.

## Concrete

Artificial stone composed of cement, water, and aggregates such as crushed stone and sand.

## Cornice

The uppermost horizontal member of an entablature. See also dentiled cornice.

## Course

A row of stone blocks. Coursed masonry is composed of rows of regularly shaped blocks.

## Crenelations

See castellations.

## Dead weight

The self-weight of a structure.

## Dentiled cornice

A cornice supported by a row of small blocks called dentils (from the Latin word for teeth).

## Egg and dart

A molding pattern used in classical architecture composed of a linear arrangement of egg-shaped protrusions alternating with downward-pointing darts or elongated arrowhead shapes. These moldings are generally found in Ionic or Corinthian entablatures.

## Elliptical barrel vault

The linear extrusion of an arch of an elliptical profile. An elliptical barrel vault looks like half a cylinder that has been flattened out at the crown.

## Engaged column

A partial round column attached to, or engaged with, a wall surface. It is generally topped by an entablature or arch. *See also* pilaster.

## Entablature

A decorative element of Greek architecture running horizontally below the eaves of the roof or below the springing of an arch. It is composed of three parts: the architrave, frieze, and cornice.

## Flashing

Sheet metal that joins roofs and vertical elements such as walls or chimneys, preventing water from entering the gap in between. It was traditionally made of lead or copper, though most modern flashings are made of aluminum.

## Flute

A vertical channel cut in a column or pilaster, usually semicircular when seen in section.

## Fluted pilaster

A pilaster with vertical channels cut in the shaft.

## Footing

The projecting base of a pier or wall that connects with and spreads loads over the subsoil.

## Foundation wall

The wall that connects the footing underground with the structure above. Since it is both above and below grade, a foundation wall is built of materials that will not rot or be damaged by insects. Stone and brick are the most common materials.

## Frame

A skeletal load-bearing structure.

## Fret

A molding composed of ornamental networks of straight bars joining at right angles.

## Gable

The triangular wall bounded by the sloping ends of a ridged roof.

## Girder

A major beam supporting other joists or beams.

## Guilloche

*See* running guilloche.

## Interstitial

In between spaces, especially those between floors or walls.

## Joist

A lightweight beam supporting floor boards. Joists are usually closely spaced at about 16–18 inches on center, with shorter intervals for floors with heavier loadings and wider intervals where lighter loads are expected.

## Joist hangers

U-shaped metal saddles that connect joists to beams without requiring notching. Notching can weaken the joist. Joist hangers are usually made of galvanized sheet metal and nailed into the girder and joist.

## King-post vs. queen-post truss

A king-post truss is a common roof truss consisting of a triangulated arrangement of struts and ties with two diagonal struts connected at the head and joined at the toe by a horizontal tie. The vertical tie in the center is called the king post. These trusses often have additional diagonals inserted to help support loads on the upper chord. In contrast, a queen-post truss is a common roof truss with two vertical ties called queenposts. The queen-post truss can be viewed as a king-post truss with an added bay in the center.

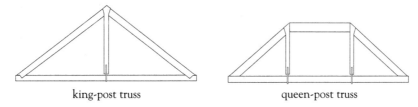

king-post truss                                queen-post truss

## Knee brace

An angled brace between a column and beam. A knee brace can shorten the clear span of a beam, and/or it can stiffen the connection and prevent the beam from rotating.

## Metopes

The portion of a Doric entablature that sits between the triglyphs. Metopes can be plain or ornamented.

## Molding plane

A hand tool used to cut decorative moldings. A complicated molding might require the use of several molding planes to create the curves, fillets, and projections that make up the molding.

## Mortise

A pocket cut into a beam to accept a tenon.

## Mullion

Within a window, a thin upright division that holds the glass panes in place.

## Mutule

A projecting and supporting block under a Doric cornice.

## Nave

The main portion or central aisle of a church.

## Overburden

The soil whose dead weight prevents uplift of the soil immediately adjacent to a loaded footing.

## Palladian window

A tripartite window with an arched top in the center and smaller rectangular sections to each side. In the nineteenth century it was sometimes called a Venetian window.

## Pediment

The triangular gable end bounded by a horizontal and two raking cornices.

## Pier

A structural member mainly supporting vertical loads. Similar to a column in function, it denotes a more massive or heavy element often composed of masonry.

## Pilaster

A flattened, engaged column that is attached to a wall. It is generally topped by an entablature or arch. *See also* fluted pilaster.

## Plain band

An undecorated length on a molding.

## Plaster

A mixture of lime, sand, and water for coating walls and ceilings. Plaster was traditionally applied in multiple coats, which were hard when dry, with underlayers roughened or "scratched" to provide a key for subsequent layers. A binder, such as horsehair, was often added for additional strength. The finish coat usually contained no sand and was applied in a thin layer, sometimes referred to as a putty coat.

## Pressure bulb

The pattern of decreasing stresses as force is applied at a point in a body and it spreads out through the medium.

## Pressure grout

A slurry of Portland cement and sand that is pumped through a hose and sprayed on a surface.

## Purlin

A beam that supports the roof and is oriented parallel to the slope of the roof.

## Quoin

Ornamental blocks located at the corner of a building.

## Rafter

An inclined beam that supports the roof and is oriented perpendicular to the slope of the roof. Principal rafters are larger in cross section and usually coincide with structural bays. Secondary rafters are smaller and are usually located between the supports of structural bays.

## Reed

A projecting molding, usually semicircular in section, used in place of fluting.

## Rubblework

Masonry of irregular-shaped stones of differing sizes that may be roughly squared.

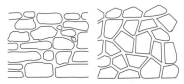

## Running guilloche

A molding composed of intertwining circles. Used in classical architecture.

## Sash

A frame that holds the glass panes of a window. A sash window is opened by sliding sashes vertically behind one another.

## Scantling

The depth and breadth of framing timbers.

## Shear

Sliding forces within or between two elements.

## Shimned

Leveled or spaced by thin wedges, or shims.

## Shouldered tenon

A tenon with a deeper section cut to enter the mortise, allowing for a greater portion of the member to be supported by the mortised member. See fig. 4-5, attic floor, where the mortise is cut so that a small ledge supports the entire depth of the joist.

**Sidelight**

Window panes placed to the side of doors.

**Spiral frets**

Frets formed into squared, spiral patterns.

**Springing**

The point at which an arch is supported.

**Stiffness**

A measure of a structure's resistance to deformation.

**Strength**

The level of stress that causes a material to fail.

**Stress**

A measure of the local intensity of internal forces within a structure, expressed in units of force/area.

**Stucco**

A plaster applied to walls, usually with an aggregate added to give a texture to the wall.

**Template**

A pattern used to establish profiles. Templates can be small-scale for use in drawing, or large-scale for use in creating full-size architectural elements.

**Tenon**

On a wooden member, a projection cut to fit into a mortise, thereby forming a joint.

**Tension**

An axial stretching force tending to elongate a structural member.

**Tie beam**

A main horizontal member of a truss designed to act in tension to prevent the ends of the truss from spreading. In a roof truss, the tie beam prevents the loads carried by the rafters from pushing the walls outward.

## Triglyphs

Ornaments having two vertical grooves separating three raised elements and placed on the architrave of a Doric entablature.

## Truss

A triangle-shaped assembly of tension and compression members that bridges a gap too large, or carries a load too heavy, for a single beam. *See also* king-post vs. queen-post truss.

## Vestibule

An entry or foyer.

## Vitruvian scroll

A classical ornament consisting of a series of stylized waves, sometimes called a running dog. Normally the scrolls face the same direction, but the illustration shows a variant used in the Kirtland Temple with opposed scrolls.

# Bibliography

List of abbreviations used in this bibliography:

| | |
|---|---|
| BYU Archives | Special Collections and Manuscripts, Harold B. Lee Library, Brigham Young University, Provo, Utah. |
| *HC* | Joseph Smith Jr. *History of The Church of Jesus Christ of Latter-day Saints.* Edited by B. H. Roberts. 2d ed., rev. 7 vols. Salt Lake City: Deseret Book, 1971. |
| *LDS CD* | *LDS Historical Library CD-ROM.* 2d ed. Provo, Utah: Infobases, 1993. |
| LDS Church Archives | Archives Division, Historical Department, The Church of Jesus Christ of Latter-day Saints, Salt Lake City. |
| RLDS Library-Archives | Library-Archives, The Auditorium, Reorganized Church of Jesus Christ of Latter Day Saints, Independence, Mo. |
| *PJS* | Dean C. Jessee, ed. *The Papers of Joseph Smith.* 2 vols. Salt Lake City: Deseret Book, 1992. |
| *PWJS* | Dean C. Jessee, comp. and ed. *The Personal Writings of Joseph Smith.* Salt Lake City: Deseret Book, 1984. |

"About Kirtland." *Painesville Telegraph,* January 20, 1859, 3.

Adams, Dale W. "Chartering the Kirtland Bank." *BYU Studies* 23 (fall 1983): 467–82.

Allen, Arthur, to E. L. Kelly, October 4, 1904. In "Kirtland: Renting Out Temple, Lightning Rod, Hotel [1895–1917]." Presiding Bishopric Papers. RLDS Library-Archives.

Allen, James B., and Glen Leonard. *The Story of the Latter-day Saints.* Salt Lake City: Deseret Book, 1976.

Ames, Ira. Autobiography and Journal, 1858. Microfilm. LDS Church Archives.

Anderson, Karl Ricks. *Joseph Smith's Kirtland: Eyewitness Accounts*. Salt Lake City: Deseret Book, 1989.

Anderson, Paul L. "William Harrison Folsom: Pioneer Architect." *Utah Historical Quarterly* 43 (summer 1975): 240–59.

Andrew, David S., and Laurel B. Blank. "The Four Mormon Temples in Utah." *Journal of the Society of Architectural Historians* 30 (1971): 51–65.

Andrew, Laurel B. *The Early Temples of the Mormons*. Albany: State University of New York Press, 1978.

Andrus, Milo. Autobiography, 1875. Typescript. LDS Church Archives.

Angell, Truman O. Autobiography, 1884. Microfilm. LDS Church Archives.

———. Diary, 1851–1868. Typescript. LDS Church Archives.

———. "Journal." In *141 Years of Mormon Heritage*, by Archie Leon Brown and Charlene L. Hathaway, edited by Charlene L. Hathaway, 119–35. Oakland, Calif.: By the author, 1973.

———. Journal, 1851–1856. Holograph. LDS Church Archives.

———, to John Taylor and Council, March 11, 1885. Holograph. John Taylor Presidential Papers. LDS Church Archives.

"Anniversary of the Church." *Messenger and Advocate* 3 (April 1837): 486–89.

Arrington, Leonard J. *Brigham Young: American Moses*. New York: Knopf, 1985.

———. "The John Tanner Family." *Ensign* 9 (March 1979): 46–51.

———. "Oliver Cowdery's Kirtland, Ohio, 'Sketch Book.'" *BYU Studies* 12 (summer 1972): 410–26.

"An Autobiographical Sketch of the Life of the Late Mary Ann Stearns Winters, Daughter of Mary Ann Stearns Pratt." Typescript. LDS Church Archives.

Backman, Milton V., Jr. *The Heavens Resound: A History of the Latter-day Saints in Ohio, 1830–1838*. Salt Lake City: Deseret Book, 1983.

———, Susan Easton [Black], and Keith Perkins, compilors. *A Profile of Latter-day Saints in Kirtland, Ohio, and Members of Zion's Camp, 1830–39*. Provo, Utah: Religious Studies Center, 1982.

Barnes, Lorenzo. Journal. Holograph. LDS Church Archives.

Belnap, Gilbert. Autobiography. Typescript. BYU Archives. In *LDS CD*.

Benjamin, Asher. *The American Builder's Companion; or, A New System of Architecture: Particularly Adapted to the Present Style of Building in the United States of America*. Boston: Etheridge and Bliss, 1806.

———. *The Country Builder's Assistant*. Greenfield, Mass.: Thomas Dickman, 1797.

———. *The Practical House Carpenter*. Boston: R. P. & C. Williams and Annin & Smith, 1830.

Bitton, Davis. "The Waning of Mormon Kirtland." *BYU Studies* 12, no. 4 (1972): 455–64.

Black, Harry. *The Kirtland Temple*. Independence, Mo.: n.p., n.d.

Book of Doctrine and Covenants. Independence, Mo.: Herald Publishing House [Reorganized Church of Jesus Christ of Latter Day Saints], 1989.

Brown, Archie Leon, and Charlene L. Hathaway. *141 Years of Mormon Heritage: Rawsons, Browns, Angells—Pioneers*. Edited by Charlene L. Hathaway. Oakland, Calif.: By the author, 1973.

Brown, Benjamin. *Testimonies for the Truth*. Liverpool, England: n.p., 1853.

Brown, Lisle G. "The Sacred Departments for Temple Work in Nauvoo: The Assembly Room and the Council Chamber." *BYU Studies* 19 (spring 1979): 361–74.

Burgess, Harrison. Autobiography. Photocopy of holograph. LDS Church Archives. In *The Heavens Resound: A History of the Latter-day Saints in Ohio, 1830–1838*, by Milton V. Backman Jr., 284–309. Salt Lake City: Deseret Book, 1983.

Burgess, William. Autobiography. In *Windows: A Mormon Family*, edited and compiled by Kenneth Glyn Hales, 91–110. Tucson, Ariz.: Skyline, 1985. In *LDS CD*.

Burgess, William, Jr. Autobiography. Microfilm of typescript. BYU Archives.

Burkett, George. Diary. Typescript. LDS Church Archives.

Cahoon, William Farrington. Autobiography, 1813–1978. Microfilm of holograph. LDS Church Archives.

Chambers, William. *A Treatise on the Decorative Part of Civil Architecture*. London: Joseph Smeeton, 1791. Reprint, New York: Benjamin Blom, 1968.

Coe, Truman. "Mormonism." *Cincinnati Journal and Western Luminary*, August 25, 1835, 4. In *LDS CD*.

Colvin, Don F. "Nauvoo Temple." In *Encyclopedia of Mormonism*, edited by Daniel H. Ludlow, 3:1001–3. 5 vols. New York: Macmillan, 1992.

Cook, Lyndon W. *The Revelations of the Prophet Joseph Smith*. Salt Lake City: Deseret Book, 1985.

Coolbear, Lola Almira Belnap. Vinson Knight Biographical Sketch. Photocopy of typescript. LDS Church Archives.

Corrill, John. *A Brief History of the Church of Christ of Latter Day Saints (Commonly Called Mormons); Including an Account of Their Doctrine and Discipline; with the Reasons of the Author for Leaving the Church*. St. Louis: By the author, 1839.

Court Opinion in Kirtland Temple Suit, February 23, 1880. In *The Kirtland Temple: A Historical Narrative*, by Roger D. Launius, 195–98. Independence, Mo.: Herald House, 1986.

Cowan, Richard O. "History of Latter-day Saint Temples from 1831 to 1990." In *Encyclopedia of Mormonism*, edited by Daniel H. Ludlow, 4:1450–55. 5 vols. New York: Macmillan, 1992.

———. "The House of the Lord in Kirtland: A 'Preliminary' Temple." In *Regional Studies in Latter-day Saint Church History: Ohio*, edited by Milton V. Backman Jr., 105–22. Provo, Utah: Department of Church History and Doctrine, Brigham Young University, 1990.

Cowdery, Patience Simonds. Diary, 1849–1851. Holograph. LDS Church Archives.

Cowdery, Warren. "Anniversary of the Church." *Messenger and Advocate* 3 (April 1847): 488.

———. "Fire!" *Painesville Telegraph*, May 31, 1838, 2–3.

Crary, Christopher. *Pioneer and Personal Reminiscences*. Marshalltown, Iowa: Marshall Printing, 1893.

Crosby, Caroline Barnes. Memoirs and Diary, 1851–1882. Microfilm of holograph. BYU Archives.

Crosby, Jesse Wentworth. Autobiography. Typescript of holograph. BYU Archives.

Crosby, Jonathan. "A Biographical Sketch of the Life of Jonathan Crosby Writen [*sic*] by Himself." Jonathan Crosby Papers, [ca. 1871–1875]. Microfilm of holograph. LDS Church Archives.

D&C. *See* Doctrine and Covenants.

Davis, S. A. "Kirtland—Mormonism." *Messenger and Advocate* 3 (April 1837): 490–91.

DeMille, Janice Force. *The St. George Temple: First 100 Years*. Hurricane, Utah: Homestead Publishers, 1977.

The Doctrine and Covenants of The Church of Jesus Christ of Latter-day Saints. Salt Lake City: The Church of Jesus Christ of Latter-day Saints, 1981. Cited as D&C.

Draper, William. Autobiography. Typescript. BYU Archives. In *LDS CD*.

Duncan, Chapman. Autobiography. Typescript. BYU Archives. In *LDS CD*.

"Early History of Hanover and Biographical Sketches of Early Settlers—Resumed." *Fredonia Censor*, September 24, 1884, 1.

Edwards, F. Henry. *The History of the Reorganized Church of Jesus Christ of Latter Day Saints*. Independence, Mo.: Herald Publishing House, 1969.

Elliott, Orson Hyde. *Reminiscences, in the Life of Orson Hyde Elliott*. San Francisco: n.p., 1899.

*Ensign of Liberty, of the Church of Christ* 1 (1847): 1–2, 14.

Esplin, Ronald K. "The Emergence of Brigham Young and the Twelve to Mormon Leadership, 1830–1841." Ph.D. diss., Brigham Young University, 1981.

———. "Joseph, Brigham and the Twelve: A Succession of Continuity." *BYU Studies* 21 (summer 1981): 301–41.

———. "Significance of Nauvoo for Latter-day Saints," *Journal of Mormon History* 16 (1990): 71–86.

Fielding, Mary, to Mercy and Robert Thompson. October 7, 1837. In *Women's Voices: An Untold History of the Latter-day Saints, 1830–1900*, by Kenneth W. Godfrey, Audrey M. Godfrey, and Jill Mulvay Derr, 68. Salt Lake City: Deseret Book, 1982.

———, to Mercy R. Thompson, July 8, 1837. LDS Church Archives. In *Women's Voices: An Untold History of the Latter-day Saints, 1830–1900*, by Kenneth W. Godfrey, Audrey M. Godfrey, and Jill Mulvay Derr, 60–61. Salt Lake City: Deseret Book, 1982.

Fields, Clarence L. "History of the Kirtland Temple." Master's thesis, Brigham Young University, 1963.

Foote, Warren. Autobiography. Typescript. BYU Archives. In *LDS CD*.

Frary, I. T. *Early American Doorways*. Richmond, Va.: Garrett and Massey, 1937.

Gee, Lysander, to Joseph Millet, Tooele City, July 18, 1885. In Joseph Millet Record Book [ca. 1850–1947], by Joseph Millet. Holograph. LDS Church Archives.

*General Conference Minutes, Supplement to the* Saints' Herald. Microfiche.

Godfrey, Kenneth W., Audrey M. Godfrey, and Jill Mulvay Derr. *Women's Voices: An Untold History of the Latter-day Saints, 1830–1900*. Salt Lake City: Deseret Book, 1982.

Goldsmith, Lucia A. "Rigdon, the First Mormon Elder." Typescript of photocopy. Kirtland Temple Historic Center.

Griffiths, Gomer T. "Reminiscences of Kirtland Temple." *Saint's Herald* 82 (June 4, 1935): 715–16, 723–24, 734.

Griffiths, Mary, to Sister Lewis, n.d. RLDS Library-Archives.

Gunnell, Wayne Cutler. "Martin Harris—Witness and Benefactor to the Book of Mormon." Masters thesis, Brigham Young University, 1955.

Hale, Aroet L. Autobiography. Holograph. LDS Church Archives.

———. Reminiscences. Microfilm of holograph. LDS Church Archives.

Hales, Kenneth Glyn, ed. and comp. *Windows: A Mormon Family*. Tucson, Ariz.: Skyline Printing, 1985.

Hancock, Levi W. Diary. Typescript. BYU Archives.

Hankins, Wade. Reminiscences [1967–1972]. Typescript of interview conducted by Lachlan Mackay. Kirtland Temple Visitor's Center Archives.

Heywood, Joseph L., to Brigham Young, January 12, 1848. In Journal History of The Church of Jesus Christ of Latter-day Saints, by Andrew Jenson, January 12, 1848, 1. LDS Church Archives.

High Priest Minutes. Spanish Fork North Branch, Utah Stake, 1866–1898. Holograph. LDS Church Archives.

Hill, Marvin S. "Brodie Revisited: A Reappraisal of *No Man Knows My History* by Fawn M. Brodie," *Dialogue* 7 (winter 1972): 72–84.

Hill, Marvin S., C. Keith Rooker, and Larry T. Wimmer. "The Kirtland Economy Revisited: A Market Critique of Sectarian Economics," *BYU Studies* 17 (summer 1977): 391–475.

"History of Brigham Young." *Deseret News*, February 10, 1858, 385–86.

"History of Brigham Young." *Millennial Star* 26 (August 20, 1864): 535–36; 26 (December 31, 1864): 834–36; 27 (January 7, 1865): 5–8; 27 (July 15, 1865): 438–41.

*History of the Church. See* Smith, Joseph, Jr. *The History of the Church* . . .

*The History of the Reorganized Church of Jesus Christ of Latter Day Saints.* Vols. 4 and 5. Independence, Mo.: Herald House, 1967, 1969.

Holden, Edwin. "Recollections." *Juvenile Instructor* 27 (1892): 151–53.

Holzapfel, Richard Neitzel. *Every Stone a Sermon.* Salt Lake City: Bookcraft, 1992.

Holzapfel, Richard Neitzel, and T. Jeffery Cottle. *Old Mormon Kirtland and Missouri: Historic Photographs and Guide.* Santa Ana, Calif.: Fieldbrook, 1991.

Homer, William Harrison. "The Passing of Martin Harris." *Improvement Era* 29 (March 1926): 468–72.

"The House of God." *Messenger and Advocate* 1 (July 1835): 147–48.

"The House of the Lord." *Messenger and Advocate* 2 (October 1835): 207.

Howe, Henry. *Historical Collections of Ohio: Containing a Collection of the Most Interesting Facts, Traditions, Biographical Sketches, Anecdotes, Etc., Relating to Its General and Local History: With Descriptions of Its Counties, Principal Towns and Villages.* Cincinnati: Derby and Bradley, 1847.

———. *Historical Collections of Ohio in Two Volumes: An Encyclopedia of the State: History Both General and Local, Geography with Descriptions of Its Counties, Cities, and Villages, Its Agricultural Manufacturing, Mining, and Business Development, Sketches of Eminent and Interesting Characters, Etc., with Notes of a Tour over It in 1886.* 2 vols. Cincinnati: State of Ohio, 1908.

Huntington, Oliver Boardman. Diary. Utah State Historical Library, Salt Lake City.

———. Journal, 1845–1846. Oliver Boardman Huntington Collection. BYU Archives.

Huntington, Prescindia Lathrop. Reminiscences. In *The Women of Mormondom,* by Edward W. Tullidge, 207–9. New York: Tullidge and Crandall, 1877.

Huntington, William. Reminiscences and Journal, April 1841–August 1846. Typescript. LDS Church Archives.

Hyde, William. Autobiography. Typescript. LDS Church Archives.

———. Journal, 1868–1873. Holograph. LDS Church Archives.

Independence Temple drawings, set signed by F. G. Williams. "Plan of the House of the Lord for the Presidency, 1833." Holograph. LDS Church Archives.

Independence Temple drawings, unsigned set. Holograph. LDS Church Archives.

Jackman, Levi. "A Short Sketch of the Life of Levi Jackman: 1797–1876."
 Typescript. BYU Archives.

———, to Beloved Wife and Family, Kirtland, February 26, 1836. Levi
 Jackman [1797–1876] Papers, 1835–1846. LDS Church Archives.

Jacobs, Stephen W. *Wayne County, the Aesthetic Heritage of a Rural Area:
 A Catalog for the Environment.* [Lyons, N.Y.]: Wayne County Historical
 Society, 1979.

Jacobson, Cecil B. "Our First Temple in the Eyes of the Architectural Historian." *Deseret News,* June 10, 1933, 6, 8.

Jenson, Andrew. Journal History of The Church of Jesus Christ of Latter-day
 Saints. LDS Church Archives.

———. *Latter-day Saint Biographical Encyclopedia: A Compilation of Biographical Sketches of Prominent Men and Women in The Church of Jesus Christ
 of Latter-day Saints.* 4 vols. Salt Lake City: Andrew Jenson History,
 1901–36.

———, comp. *Church Chronology.* 2d ed., rev. and enl. Salt Lake City:
 Deseret News, 1914. In *LDS CD.*

Jessee, Dean C. "The Kirtland Diary of Wilford Woodruff." *BYU Studies* 12
 (summer 1972): 365–99.

———, ed. *The Papers of Joseph Smith.* 2 vols. Salt Lake City: Deseret
 Book, 1992.

———, comp. and ed. *The Personal Writings of Joseph Smith.* Salt Lake City:
 Deseret Book, 1984.

Johnson, Benjamin F. *A Life Review.* Microfilm of holograph. Benjamin
 Franklin Johnson Collection [1852–1911]. LDS Church Archives.

Johnson, George W. Autobiography. Typescript. BYU Archives.

Johnson, Joel H. Autobiography. Typescript. BYU Archives.

———. "A Journal or Sketch of the Life of Joel H. Johnson." Microfilm of
 typescript. LDS Church Archives.

Johnson, Luke. Autobiography. *Millennial Star* 26 (December 31, 1864):
 834–36; 27 (January 7, 1865): 5–7.

Jorgensen, Lynne Watkins. "The Mantle of the Prophet Joseph Passes to
 Brother Brigham: A Collective Spiritual Witness." *BYU Studies* 36, no.
 4 (1997).

*Journal of Discourses.* 26 vols. Liverpool: F. D. Richards, 1855–86. Brigham
 Young, 1:131–37, April 6, 1853; Brigham Young, 1:209–20, October 9,
 1852; George A. Smith, 2:211–20, March 18, 1855; Heber C. Kimball,
 10:163–69, April 6, 1863; Brigham Young, 10:251–56, October 6,
 1863; Orson Pratt, 14:271–76, April 9, 1871.

"Judge after Hearing." *Messenger and Advocate* 3 (October 1836): 395–96.

*Juvenile Instructor* 14 (December 15, 1879): 283; 27 (March 1, 1892): 153.

Kelley, Cassie B., to E. L. Kelley, September 1 [and 6], 1885. Cassie B. Kelley
 Papers. RLDS Library-Archives.

————, to E. L. Kelley, November 10, 1889. Cassie B. Kelley Papers. RLDS Library-Archives.

Kelley, E. L., to Cassie B. Kelley, August 27, 1885. Cassie B. Kelley Papers. RLDS Library-Archives.

————, to William H. Kelley, May 16, 1883. William H. Kelley Papers. RLDS Library-Archives.

Kelley, William H., and G. A. Blakeslee. "Report of Committee on Kirtland Temple." *Saints' Herald* 30 (September 1, 1883): 560–63.

————. "To the Saints." *Saints' Herald* 33 (June 5, 1886): 351–52.

Kimball, Heber C. Autobiography. Holograph. LDS Church Archives.

————. "Extracts from H. C. Kimball's Journal." *Times and Seasons* 6 (April 15, 1845): 866–69.

————. "Extract of Journal of Elder Heber C. Kimball." *Times and Seasons* 6 (January 15, 1845): 770–73.

————. "Speech Delivered by Heber C. Kimball." *Times and Seasons* 6 (July 15, 1845): 970–73.

"Kirtland." *Painesville Telegraph*, October 4, 1883, 3; February 10, 1887, 3.

"Kirtland—Mormonism, and etc." *Messenger and Advocate* 3 (April 1837): 490–91.

"Kirtland, Ohio, March 27, 1836." *Messenger and Advocate* 2 (March 1836): 274–81.

"Kirtland Affairs." *Painesville Telegraph*, August 30, 1860, 3; November 22, 1860, 3.

Kirtland File. Lake County Historical Society, Lake County, Ohio.

Kirtland High Council Minutes. January 15, 1836. LDS Church Archives.

Kirtland Newspaper Clippings File. Kirtland History Room, Kirtland Public Library.

"The Kirtland Temple." *Journal of History* 2, no. 4 (1909): 410–28.

*Kirtland Temple*. N.p.: Kirtland Temple Historic Center [Reorganized Church of Jesus Christ of Latter Day Saints], n.d. [Brochure distributed at the Kirtland Temple Historic Center in the 1980s.]

"Kirtland Temple: Recent Architectural Changes." Typescript. RLDS Library-Archives.

Kirtland Temple Pulpit Lettering. LDS Church Archives.

"Kirtland Temple Repairs Completed." *Saints' Herald* 106 (July 27, 1959): 698.

Knight, Newel. *Scraps of Biography*. Salt Lake City: Juvenile Instructor, 1883.

La Moody, P. M., to Postmaster of St. Louis, Mo. [Samuel B. Churchill], September 26, 1842. Selected papers pertaining to Mormonism, 1831–1859, Missouri State Historical Society. Microfilm copy. LDS Church Archives.

Langley, Batty. *The City and Country Builder's and Workman's Treasury of Designs*. London: S. Harding, 1750. Reprint, New York: Benjamin Blom, 1967.

Larson, Andrew. *Erastus Snow*. Salt Lake City: University of Utah Press, 1971.

Larson, Gustive O. *The "Americanization" of Utah for Statehood*. San Marino, Calif.: Huntington Library, 1971.

Launius, Roger D. "An Ambivalent Rejection: Baptism for the Dead and the Reorganized Church Experience." *Dialogue: A Journal of Mormon Thought* 23 (summer 1990): 61–84.

———. "Joseph Smith III and the Kirtland Temple Suit." *BYU Studies* 25, no. 3 (1985): 112.

———. *The Kirtland Temple: A Historical Narrative*. Independence, Mo.: Herald House, 1986.

———. "The Reorganized Church and the Independence Temple: Confession of a Skeptic." Unpublished manuscript. In possession of the author.

Leavitt, Sarah. "History of Sarah Studevant Leavitt." Edited by Juanita L. Pulsipher. N.p., 1919. In *LDS CD*.

Littlefield, Lyman Omer. *Reminiscences of Latter-day Saints*. Logan, Utah: Utah Journal, 1888. In *LDS CD*.

Luce, W. Ray. "Building the Kingdom of God: Mormon Architecture before 1847." *BYU Studies* 30 (spring 1990): 33–45.

Lumbard, Elizabeth T. "A Family Chronicle." Typescript. LDS Church Archives.

Mace, Wandle. Autobiography. Typescript. BYU Archives. In *LDS CD*.

Mather, Frederic G. "The Early Days of Mormonism." *Lippincott's Magazine* 26 (August 1880): 198–211.

McBride, Reuben, to Brigham Young, July 28, 1845. Holograph. Brigham Young Papers, 1832–1878. LDS Church Archives.

Millett, Artemus. Reminiscences [ca. 1855]. Holograph. LDS Church Archives.

Millet, Joseph. "A Brief History of Artemus Millet, Son of Ebeneazer Millet," In "J. Millet on C[ape] B[reton] Island 1927," by Joseph Millet. Microfilm of holograph. LDS Church Archives.

———. "Grandfather Artemus Millet and the Kirtland Temple. Copied from My Fathers Papers or Records by Mary J. Cox, Hurricane, Utah." Holograph. LDS Church Archives.

———. "J. Millet on C[ape] B[reton] Island 1927." Microfilm of holograph. LDS Church Archives.

———. Record book [ca. 1850–1947]. Holograph. LDS Church Archives.

"Minutes of a Conference." *Millennial Star* 26 (January 23, 1864): 49–54.

"Mormonism." *Millennial Star* 26 (September 10, 1864): 585–87.

"Mormonism." *Painesville Telegraph*, March 13, 1832, 3.

"The Name of the Church." *Ensign of Liberty, of the Church of Christ* 1 (April 1847): 20–24.

"Name of the Church." *True Latter Day Saints' Herald* 1 (February 1860): 39–43.

Newell, Linda King, and Valeen Tippetts Avery. "Sweet Counsel and Seas of Tribulation: The Religious Life of the Women of Kirtland." *BYU Studies* 20 (winter 1980): 151–62.

Newspaper Clippings File. Kirtland History Room, Kirtland Public Library.

Noah, M. M. *New York Evening Star*. In HC, 2:351.

*Ohio (Hudson) Observer*, August 11, 1836.

Oman, Richard G. "Exterior Symbolism of the Salt Lake Temple: Reflecting the Faith That Called the Place into Being." *BYU Studies* 36, no. 4 (1997).

"Our Village." *Messenger and Advocate* 3 (January 1837): 444.

*Painesville Telegraph*, May 1, 1832, 3; July 5, 1832, 3; December 7, 1832, 4; October 25, 1833, 3; November 15, 1833, 4; February 20, 1835, 3; August 18, 1904, 2.

Parry, Donald W., ed. *Temples of the Ancient World: Ritual and Symbolism*. Salt Lake City: Deseret Book; Provo, Utah: FARMS, 1994.

Partridge, Edward. Diaries, 1818, 1835–1836. Holograph. LDS Church Archives.

The Pearl of Great Price. Salt Lake City: The Church of Jesus Christ of Latter-day Saints, 1981.

Perkins, Keith W. "Kirtland Temple." In *Encyclopedia of Mormonism*, edited by Daniel H. Ludlow, 2:798–99. 5 vols. New York: Macmillan, 1992.

Perkins and Osburns Bill against Joseph Smith, May 20, 1837. Accounts Payable, 1835–1844. Joseph Smith Collection, 1827–1844. Microfilm. LDS Church Archives.

Petersen, Lauritz G. "The Kirtland Temple." *BYU Studies* 12 (summer 1972): 400–409.

Petraus, Joseph W., and J. Fred Triggs. "Report of Subsurface Investigation: Kirtland Temple Historical Center, Kirtland, Ohio." August 5, 1976. Triggs and Associates, Consulting Geotechnical Engineers. A copy of the report was kindly provided by the Restoration Trail Foundation.

Phelps, W. W., to Sally Phelps at Liberty, Clay County, Mo., December 18, 1835. In Journal History of The Church of Jesus Christ of Latter-day Saints, by Andrew Jenson, December 18, 1835, 4–5. LDS Church Archives.

*Philadelphia Times*, January 9, 1882.

Pilkington, William. "Testimony Sworn before Joseph W. Peterson, April 3, 1934." BYU Archives. In *LDS CD*.

Porter, Larry C. "The Odyssey of William Earl McLellin: Man of Diversity, 1806–83." In *The Journals of William E. McLellin, 1831–1836*, edited by Jan Shipps and John W. Welch, 291–378. Provo, Utah: BYU Studies; Urbana: University of Illinois Press, 1994.

Post, Stephen. Diary [July 1835–March 1839]. Steven Post Papers. LDS Church Archives.

Pratt, Orson. Journal. Holograph. LDS Church Archives.

Pratt, Parley P., Jr., ed. *The Autobiography of Parley P. Pratt.* 4th ed. Salt Lake City: Deseret Book, 1985.

"The President's Message." *Ohio Star* 6 (January 15, 1835): 4.

Prusha, Anne B. *A History of Kirtland, Ohio.* Mentor, Ohio: Lakeland Community College Press, 1982.

Pulsipher, John. Autobiography. Typescript. BYU Archives. In *LDS CD.*

Pulsipher, Zerah. Autobiography. Typescript. BYU Archives. In *LDS CD.*

Record of the First Quorum of Elders Belonging to the Church of Christ in Kirtland, Geauga County, Ohio, 1836–1870. RLDS Library-Archives.

"Reorganization of the Mormons at Kirtland." *Painesville Telegraph,* June 14, 1860, 3.

"Report of Elders Orson Pratt and Joseph F. Smith." *Millennial Star* 40 (December 16, 1878): 785–89.

"Reunion in Kirtland." *Painesville Telegraph,* September, 17, 1874, 3.

Richards, Hepzibah, to Willard Richards. January 18, 1838. In *Women's Voices: An Untold History of the Latter-day Saints, 1830–1900,* by Kenneth W. Godfrey, Audrey M. Godfrey, and Jill Mulvay Derr, 71. Salt Lake City: Deseret Book, 1982.

———, to William Richards, January 22, 1838. Richards Family Letters, 1801–1883. Typescript. LDS Church Archives.

Rigdon, Sidney, Newel K. Whitney, and Oliver Cowdery to John A. Boynton, May 6, 1834. In *Joseph Smith's Kirtland: Eyewitness Accounts,* by Karl Ricks Anderson, 169–70. Salt Lake City: Deseret Book, 1989.

Roberts, B. H. *A Comprehensive History of The Church of Jesus Christ of Latter-day Saints, Century One.* 6 vols. Provo, Utah: Corporation of the President, The Church of Jesus Christ of Latter-day Saints, 1965.

Robinson, Ebenezer. "Items of Personal History of the Editor." *The Return* 1 (June 1889): 88–91.

Ross, D. R., to Earl R. Curry, January 17, 1940. RLDS Library-Archives.

Ryder, James F. *Voigtländer and I: In Pursuit of Shadow Catching.* Cleveland: Imperial Press, 1902.

*Scraps of Biography; Designed for the Instruction and Encouragement of Young Latter-day Saints.* Salt Lake City: Juvenile Instructor Office, 1883.

Shurtliff, Luman Andros. Autobiography. Typescript of holograph. BYU Archives. In *LDS CD.*

Smith, George A. "Memoirs of George A. Smith." Diary and Correspondence, 1834–1853. Typescript. BYU Archives.

———. "Sketch of the Autobiography of George Albert Smith." *Millennial Star* 27 (July 15, 1865): 438–41.

Smith, Henry C. "An Architectural Appreciation of the Kirtland Temple." *Autumn Leaves* 40 (April 1927): 185–86.

Smith, Joseph, Jr. *Elders' Journal of the Church of Latter Day Saints* 1 (August 1838): 52; 1 (November 1837): 27–29. In *LDS CD*.

———. *History of The Church of Jesus Christ of Latter-day Saints*. Edited by B. H. Roberts. 2d ed., rev. 7 vols. Salt Lake City: Deseret Book, 1971. Cited as *History of the Church* or *HC*.

———. *Joseph Smith's Kirtland Revelations Book*. Salt Lake City: Modern Microfilm, 1979.

———. Joseph Smith's Ohio Journal. In *PJS*, 2:1–210.

———, to Oliver Granger, July 1840. Joseph Smith's Letterbook 2, 159–61. Joseph Smith Papers. LDS Church Archives. In *PWJS*, 490–91.

———, to Oliver Granger, January 26, 1841. Huntington Library, San Marino, Calif. In *PWJS*, 475.

———, to Oliver Granger, May 4, 1841. Joseph Smith Papers. LDS Church Archives. In *PWJS*, 494–95.

———, to Vienna Jacques, September 4, 1833. Joseph Smith Papers. LDS Church Archives. In *PWJS*, 293–96.

———, to William W. Phelps, January 11, 1833. Joseph Smith's Letterbook 1, 18–20. Joseph Smith Papers. LDS Church Archives. In *PWJS*, 258–68.

Smith, Joseph, III. Autobiography, 1832–1910. Microfilm of typescript. BYU Archives.

———, to Alexander Fyfe, July 9, 1881. Joseph Smith III Letterbook, no. 3. BYU Archives. In Roger D. Launius, *The Kirtland Temple: A Historical Narrative*, 109. Independence, Mo.: Herald House, 1986.

———, to Emma Bidamon, March 8, 1872. In Roger D. Launius, *The Kirtland Temple: A Historical Narrative*, 100–116. Independence, Mo.: Herald House, 1986.

Smith, Lucy Mack. *History of Joseph Smith by His Mother*. Edited by Preston Nibley. Bookcraft: Salt Lake City, 1901. Reprint, 1979.

———. "The History of Lucy Smith ca. 1845." Photocopy of manuscript. LDS Church Archives.

Smith, Vida E. *Young People's History of the Church of Jesus Christ of Latter Day Saints*. 2 vols. Lamoni, Iowa: Herald Publishing House, 1914–18.

Smith, William. *William Smith on Mormonism*. . . . Lamoni, Iowa: Herald House Steam Book and Job Office, 1883.

Snow, Eliza R. Autobiography. Microfilm of holograph. BYU Archives.

———. *Biography and Family Record of Lorenzo Snow, One of the Twelve Apostles of The Church of Jesus Christ of Latter-day Saints*. Salt Lake City: Deseret News, 1884.

———. *Eliza R. Snow, An Immortal: Selected Writings of Eliza R. Snow*. Salt Lake City: Nicholas G. Morgan Sr. Foundation, 1957. Includes "Sketch of My Life," 1–53, and "The Kirtland Temple," 54–65.

Sorensen, Steven R. "Schools of the Prophets." In *Encyclopedia of Mormonism*, edited by Daniel H. Ludlow, 3:1269. 5 vols. New York: Macmillan, 1992.

Tanner, E. Pingree. "John Tanner and the Kirtland Temple." *Deseret News*, February 23, 1935, 2.

Tanner, George S. *John Tanner and His Family: A History-Biography of John Tanner of Lake George, New York, Born August 15, 1778, Hopkinton, Rhode Island, Died April 13, 1850, at South Cottonwood, Utah.* Salt Lake City: John Tanner Family Association, 1974.

Tanner, Nathan. Autobiography. Photocopy of holograph. BYU Archives.

———. Reminiscences [n.d.]. Holograph. LDS Church Archives.

Tayer, Mrs. H. Ferry. Undated newspaper clipping. Newspaper Clipping File. Kirtland History Room, Kirtland Public Library.

*Times and Seasons* 5 (January 1, 1845): 752–67.

"Tolls Reduced." *Painesville Telegraph*, March 29, 1833, 3.

Tracy, Nancy Naomi Alexander. Autobiography. Holograph. Bancroft Library, University of California at Berkeley. In *LDS CD.*

———. Reminiscences and Diary, 1896–1899. Typescript. LDS Church Archives.

Tullidge, Edward W. *The Women of Mormondom.* New York: Tullidge and Crandall, 1877.

Tyler, Daniel. "Temples." *Juvenile Instructor* 14 (December 15, 1879): 283.

Tyler, J., to W. E. McLellin, February 1847. In *Ensign of Liberty, of the Church of Christ* 1 (January 1848): 60.

Upton, Harriet Taylor. *History of the Western Reserve.* Vol. 1. Chicago: Lewis Publishing, 1910.

Van Orden, Bruce A., ed. "Writing to Zion: The William W. Phelps Kirtland Letters, 1835–1836." *BYU Studies* 33, no. 3 (1993): 542–93.

Wallis, Frank E. *Old Colonial Architecture and Furniture.* Boston: G. H. Polley, 1887.

Ward, William. "Who Designed the Temple?" *Deseret Weekly*, April 23, 1892, 578–79.

Watson, Elden Jay, ed. *Manuscript History of Brigham Young, 1801–1844.* Salt Lake City: Smith Secretarial Service, 1968.

———, comp. *The Orson Pratt Journals.* Salt Lake City: Elden Jay Watson, 1975.

Webb, Sylvia Cutler. "The Autobiography of Sylvia C. Webb." *Saints' Herald* 62 (March 24, 1915): 289–93.

Wellington, Paul A. "Kirtland Temple Gets Face Lifting." *Saints' Herald* 102 (July 18, 1955): 687.

West, William S. *A Few Interesting Facts Respecting the Rise, Progress and Pretensions of the Mormons.* N.p., 1837.

"Who Designed the Temple?" *Deseret Weekly*, April 23, 1892, 578–79.

Williams, Frederick G., to Saints in Missouri, October 10, 1833. In *HC*, 1:418.

*Willoughby Independent*. September 23, circa 1887; May 15, 1883; July, circa 1888. In Kirtland Newspaper Clipping File. Kirtland History Room, Kirtland Public Library.

*Willoughby Republican*, June 29, 1921, 4.

Winchester, Benjamin. "Primitive Mormonism." *Salt Lake Tribune*, September 22, 1889, 2.

Winter, Robert. "Architecture on the Frontier: The Mormon Experiment." *Pacific Historical Review* 43 (February 1974): 52–60.

Woodruff, Wilford. *Wilford Woodruff's Journal, 1833–1898, Typescript*. Edited by Scott G. Kenney. 9 vols. Midvale, Utah: Signature Books, 1983–84.

Wright, Livingston. "The First Shrine of Mormonism." *Ohio Magazine* 1, no. 2 (August 1906): 164–66.

Yarrington, Roger. "Kirtland Temple Is Closed for Repairs." *Saints' Herald* 106 (March 2, 1959): 194.

Young, Brigham. "An Epistle of the Twelve, to The Church of Jesus Christ of Latter-day Saints in All the World." *Times and Seasons* 6 (January 15, 1845): 779–80.

———. "Speech." *Times and Seasons* 6 (July 1, 1845): 953–57.

Young, Joseph, to Lewis Harvey, November 16, 1880, continued on November 18, 1880. Holograph. LDS Church Archives.

Young, Lorenzo Dow. "Lorenzo Dow Young's Narrative." *Fragments of Experience: Sixth Book of the Faith-Promoting Series*. 42–43. Salt Lake City: Juvenile Instructor Office, 1882.

Young, Mary Ann Angell, to Brigham Young, August 31, 1835. Holograph. LDS Church Archives.

Young, Richard W. "In the Wake of the Church." *Contributor* 4 (December 1882): 105–8.

# Index

Page numbers in **bold** denote illustrations.